Second Language Acquisition Research

Second Language Acquisition Research: Theory-Construction and Testing

Edited by

Fethi Mansouri

Cambridge Scholars Publishing

Second Language Acquisition Research: Theory-Construction and Testing, Edited by Fethi Mansouri

This book first published 2007. The present binding first published 2008.

Cambridge Scholars Publishing

12 Back Chapman Street, Newcastle upon Tyne, NE6 2XX, UK

British Library Cataloguing in Publication Data
A catalogue record for this book is available from the British Library

ISBN (10): 1-4438-0044-9, ISBN (13): 978-1-4438-0044-0

Table of Contents

ACKNOWLEDGEMENTS

This book is based on the proceedings of the fifth international symposium on 'processability theory, second language acquisition and bilingualism' that was held at Deakin University, Australia in September 2005. Turning the conference papers into a thematic book is a challenging task. Indeed, this volume owes a lot to the support and collaboration of the speakers at the symposium who made their papers available for this volume. I gratefully acknowledge their collegiality and assistance in getting this book ready for publication. In particular I would like to thank all of those who took part in the refereeing process which resulted in significant improvements not only for the individual chapters but also for the book as a whole. The symposium was made possible thanks to the financial and logistical support of the Deakin University' Institute for Citizenship and Globalisation. Finally I would like to acknowledge the expert input of Kazumi Jushi from the Institute in the final formatting, preparation and type-setting of this manuscript.

Fethi Mansouri
Melbourne
June 2007

CHAPTER 1

SECOND LANGUAGE ACQUISITION RESEARCH: FROM THEORY FORMATION TO THEORY APPLICATION

Fethi Mansouri

This book[1] deals with second language acquisition research as a field of inquiry concerned with the processes underlying the development of second languages among non-native learners. The book's main focus is on the theoretical attempts at accounting for second language acquisition (SLA) where the focus is more on the mental, cognitive and psychological processes underpinning the learning process. Of course the linguistic structures being acquired will also constitute an integral part of any analyses of SLA as their structural and functional features tend to correlate with certain developmental outcomes. In fact, the key theoretical paradigm employed by most of the chapters in this book, namely Processability Theory (Pienemann, 1998) argues that the learners can produce only those target language linguistic forms, which their language processor (i.e. the learner language) can handle at a given point in time. In other words, the target language structures with their specific level of (grammatical) information marking and exchange are acquired – or in PT's language developmentally emerge- in an order that reflects their processing complexity. Thus, we increasingly see the interconnectedness of linguistic features and processing capacity among learners. It is because this interconnectedness is so fundamental to explaining SLA that learning theories are more and more inclined to employ formal theories of grammar to describe the target language structures. This is the case with PT which uses Lexical Functional Grammar (LFG) as a linguistic analytical framework.

Historical trends and developments in SLA research[2]

The scope and diversity of research into second language acquisition is so broad that it is well beyond the reach of this thematically defined volume. This breadth and depth of SLA research touches both theory construction and theory testing or application (Doughty & Long, 2003). The theoretical dimension of SLA research was not always restricted to the developmental and cognitive aspect of the analysis. In fact, SLA theories and models have historically drawn from and relied upon linguistic and grammatical theories, such as Chomsky's Universal Grammar (cf. Ellis, 1994), and the many approaches to functional linguistics most notably Givon's (1979a) model and the subsequent research that combined SLA theories with functional linguistic models. The fact that independent linguistic theories could potentially be implemented into a theory of second language acquisition to explain the process of learning meant that the resulting predictions were significantly better formalised and thus easier to test and validate

Before discussing this book's key themes and objectives, it would be useful to outline very briefly the type of SLA research that has dominated the filed for the past decades. In this context, it is necessary to review two strands of second language acquisition approaches that have greatly influenced the past two decades namely morpheme order studies and developmental studies.

Within the broad terms of morpheme order studies, second language learning was predicted to consist of the acquisition of the rules and structures of the target language in a gradual process over an extended period of time. Research carried out within this tradition attempted to describe the order of acquisition of certain morphemes and structures with the view to establishing a continuum of acquisition which can account for and predict the acquisition order of grammatical morphemes. Researchers within this tradition (e.g., Dulay et al., 1982) claim that learners acquire certain structures almost immediately as is the case with word order, whereas other structures such as grammatical agreement are invariably acquired later. Many studies of this kind were more interested in attempting to determine the order in which learners acquire the target language structures rather than the processes that allow learners to achieve such an acquisition order. The significance of this type of research, however, came to prominence when researchers in the context of first language acquisition (e.g., Brown, 1973; deVilliers & deVilliers, 1973) demonstrated that first language learners of English acquired a number of morphemes invariably in the same order. This suggested that first language acquisition is guided by a universal cognitive mechanism which must be responsible for the invariance of the order of morpheme acquisition as produced by various learners.

The question that followed from the above suggestions was whether there is a common universal order of acquisition for second language structures. Early research within morpheme order studies (Hakuta 1974; Larsen-Freeman 1975, Dulay & Burt 1973) focused on one major hypothesis stating that there is a kind of 'built-in-syllabus' in second language learners similar to that observed in the context of first language acquisition. The findings of these early studies supported this hypothesis and argued for the possibility of the existence of a universal or natural order of acquisition of syntactic and morphological structures irrespective of the learners' first language background. Thus, the idea that first language acquisition follows the same path as second language acquisition was strongly put forward as the [L1 = L2] hypothesis (c.f., Ellis 1994). Of course, in light of recent advances in SLA research as exemplified with the developmentally moderated transfer hypothesis in Processability Theory, this hypothesis is longer universally accepted as an empirical certainty.

From a purely pedagogic perspective, however, and as Burt & Dulay (1980: 266) argued "the acquisition order studies could also provide practical guidance in the development of the curricula, materials and assessment instruments". Therefore, and by extension if a universal order is observed then it could potentially be used as the basis upon which curricula and course materials ought to be designed, since the universal order of acquisition reflects at least in part psychological reality. This approach was further developed in what became known as the 'natural' approach to second language teaching based on the natural order of the acquisition hierarchy obtained through a number of morpheme order studies such as those carried out by Krashen (1983). The major claim of these studies is the existence of a fixed order of morpheme acquisition that takes place regardless of the variables investigated (e.g., formal vs. informal learning; different L1 backgrounds; written vs. oral data; age). In other words, learners appear to follow a pre-determined universal order of acquisition of grammatical morphemes.

From a theoretical viewpoint, a serious criticism of morpheme order studies is their inadequacy to capture the developmental regularities in second language learners' output. Wode (1978) points out that morpheme order studies miss important phenomena in SLA such as learners' learning strategies. Such strategies can include avoidance of difficult L2 structures and forms as well as the influence of the learner's L1. Because morpheme order studies focus on the learners' production of target-like forms, they are unable to capture developmental aspects which are an essential part of the process of language acquisition.

Another problem with morpheme order studies was the fact that they are based on cross-sectional data rather than longitudinal data which meant that it was impossible to answer questions about how second languages are actually acquired or how individual variation among learners can be accounted for. This is especially crucial as Andersen (1991) puts it since "attention to individual variation is the key to understanding the process of second language acquisition" (Andersen, 1991:02).

Attempting to prove the inadequacy of morpheme order studies, Huebner (1979) argued that to discover developmental features and sequences of second language acquisition, one must look not only to occurrence of morphemes and forms in an obligatory context, but more importantly in contexts where these morphemes and forms would not be critical for successful communication. Language learning is systematic but also dynamic and undergoes continual and constant change. Variation in the learner language is the main indicator of change and progress from one developmental stage to another. In this regard, Huebner (1979) indicated that grammatical forms are produced by second language learners in one linguistic context, then in other linguistic contexts as these learners test and revise their own hypotheses about the target language. The interpretation of language acquisition as a linear process does not illustrate the roles assigned to different factors such as the formalised linguistic factor and the psychological factor. This task was more prominent in SLA studies carried out under the developmental umbrella.

Developmental studies differed from morpheme order studies in that they focused on the learning process and the learner's strategies rather than simply on the order of certain morphemes. The view taken by researchers working within the developmental approach is that while still learning the grammar of the target language, second language learners use forms which do not belong to either the second language or the native language. These forms were known as 'transformational forms' (Dulay et al., 1982). A number of other researchers employed the term 'developmental sequences' to refer to these same transitional constructions and the order in which they occur (Wode 1977, Meisel et al 1981).

The term 'developmental sequences' implies that language learners go through a number of implicational steps before moving to higher developmental stages on the acquisition hierarchy. These steps, more importantly, are not random but rather systematic. The changes, or variations, in the learner language are the result of a number of operations such as modification and generalisation which learners apply to linguistic structures as they gradually move forward along the developmental path.

A number of researchers (e.g., Hatch 1978a) found that errors observed in the transitional constructions produced by L2 learners do not always bear any relation to their L1. These errors can be intra-lingual in nature resulting from a developing system, rather than inter-lingual resulting from the learner's L1 interference. In other words, the learner's language should be analysed as a linguistic system in its own right rather than a distorted version of the target language system (c.f., Larsen-Freemen & Long 1991). Along the lines of the developmental approach, a number of researchers in the field of SLA research conducted investigations on the acquisition of morpho-syntax in a number of different target languages. Processability Theory, described succinctly by

Pienemann in chapter 2 in this book is such a theory that reflects recent insights into the process of second language learning.

Recent developments in SLA research

There is now a growing interest in second language acquisition (SLA) research that is driven as much by new interdisciplinary approaches to the field as it is by the practical needs of understanding language learning and performance in an increasingly inter-connected world. Intellectually, second language acquisition research is now a recognised independent field of academic inquiry that is concerned with cognitive, psychological, social and pragmatic aspects of second language development. Therefore, SLA research tends to be highly theoretical and experimental and as such lends itself well to the rigour of scientific research. It is in this context that the use of explicit and well articulated theories and concepts is increasingly seen as an essential research and 'thinking' tool for understanding and conducting SLA research.

The chapters included in this book report on the various technical and theoretical aspects of experimental SLA research across a number of typologically different languages. The book includes a detailed introduction and a general chapter outlining the key theoretical claims and methodological requirements underpinning this kind of SLA research. It will also relate Processability theory-related studies to the wider field of Sla research. Though the emphasis is on cross-linguistic experimental research undertaken within the parameters of Processability Theory, the boll will nevertheless shed light on the nexus between bilingualism and theory-driven second language acquisition research.

Processability Theory (Pienemann 1998) is one such a theory that has been applied across a number of second languages. It is based on a universal hierarchy of processing procedures derived from the general architecture of the language processor. Processability theory has been tested against an array of data from the target languages English, Swedish, German, Chinese, Arabic and Japanese. As this book shows, the first step in any cross-linguistic testing is to relate a set of linguistic structures of the target language to the general hierarchy of processability and more specifically to the exchange of grammatical information involved in producing these structures. This exercise should yield a set of language-specific predictions for the sequence in which these structures will emerge in the learner language. In a second step this hypothesised sequence can be tested against empirical data from the acquisition of the chosen language.

The logic underlying processability theory is the following: at any stage of development the learner can produce and comprehend only those target language linguistic forms which the current state of the language processor (i.e.

the learner language) can handle. It is therefore crucial to understand the architecture of the language processor and the way in which it handles a second language. This enables one to predict the course of development of the target language linguistic forms in language production and comprehension across different languages.

The book's key themes and structure

The book's key objective is to present a snapshot of empirical studies in the second language acquisition research where both theory formation and theory application are integral elements. This has not always been a straightforward task as it is rather difficult to construct testable research methodologies for application for example in teaching intervention studies.

The book is still focussed on theory formation which is certainly important. The chapter by Pienemann in particular is a good case in point. However, and as the application of SLA research and its key theories becomes more appealing, it would be naïve to dismiss application studies as non-relevant within a book focussed on SLA research. The fact that SLA researchers have tended to be rather defensive about the potential of their research formulations and findings to teaching should not mean that there is no potential in SLA theory application. We can see advantages of PT-based optimal input that is developmentally ordered. Given these two interconnected agendas, this book is organised around two general sections: (a) theory construction and testing and (b) theoretical research on speech processing and bilingualism.

Theory construction and testing

Despite the emergence of clear theoretical paradigms in SLA research, as Pienemann argues in chapter two, we are still a long away from having a coherent comprehensive theory of SLA. This is despite the many attempts that are being made to tackle various aspects of such a theory. Pienemann's point is that to articulate a comprehensive theory of SLA is an enormously complex task that is beyond individual researchers. It was for this reason that Pienemann's processability theory was designed as a modular approach aimed specifically at explaining developmental schedules. In his chapter, Pienemann shows how processability theory can interface with other modules that are jointly capable of explaining a wider array of phenomena in SLA. Pienemann's chapter explores second language development within an LFG framework that exhibits psychological and typological plausibility. As with the his seminal 1998 book, Pienmann's aim is to demonstrate that the interplay between constraints on processability, the re-ranking of Optimality Theory constraints that have to be assumed for SLA and the L2 initial state cause some of the attested L1-L2 differences.

Along similar theoretical lines, Kawaguchi's chapter aims to explain the development of argument-function mapping at the interface of discourse-syntax in learning a second language, based on the Unmarked Alignment Hypothesis and the Lexical Mapping Hypothesis. These hypotheses are posited in the current extension of Processability Theory [3]. The Unmarked Alignment Hypothesis is based on the most harmonious mapping between thematic role, grammatical function and syntactic position. The Lexical Mapping Hypothesis is based on non-default mapping of thematic argument roles onto grammatical structure. Kawaguchi argues that the learning of new lexical features is necessary in order to perform higher-stage language-specific operations which are morpho-lexical in nature. As Kawaguchi shows, such this allows the speaker to make choices with respect to which argument will receive which degree of prominence in production. The successful performance of such morpho-lexical operations contributes to the characterization of the higher stages of learners' development. Kawaguchi's chapter reports on empirical research where these two hypotheses are applied to Japanese L2, and the structural outcomes at different developmental stages are predicted with LFG formalism. The analysis of a three-year longitudinal study shows that the results validate these hypotheses.

Theory construction as outlined above in particular by Pienemann in chapter two is often followed by theory-testing research that in some cases it contributes to the advancement of the theoretical approach being tested. Håkansson and Norrby's study reported in chapter four is such a case as they apply PT to written and oral Swedish L2 data. Håkansson and Norrby's hypothesis is that the hierarchy of processability predicted by PT guides both written and spoken learner production. The results reported in this book show that both learner groups developed the target structures as predicted by PT though some structures occurred more frequently in writing than in speaking. In Håkansson and Norrby's view, the results demonstrate that the planning time that is used in writing does not influence grammatical processability, though the lack of contexts for certain structures in speech suggests that time has an influence on language complexity.

Mansouri's study described in chapter five discusses the feasibility of accounting for intra-stage developmental sequences in second language development and their conceptual potential as additional explanatory tools in second language acquisition research. Mansouri discusses this phenomenon in the context of Arabic as a second language (ASL), focussing on the phenomenon of zero (null) and reduced making of definiteness within noun-phrase agreement structures. Based on the analysis and findings reported in this study, it is argued that zero and reduced marking can be accounted for in terms of processing requirements and typological features (form-function mappings). Using PT as a conceptual framework, the study proposes a conceptual basis for extending Hypothesis Space as an additional explanatory module. This extension could useful for dealing with intra-stage sequences where multiple structures with differing patterns of processing complexity and form-function mappings exist.

Still within the broad PT paradigm, Zhang's research on the acquisition of Chinese syntax incorporates discourse-pragmatic principles into the developmental approach to second language acquisition research. This has led to the formulation of the Topic Hypothesis which predicts the successive acquisition of L2 syntactic structures from a canonical order to a non-canonical. The key feature here is that the latter order deviates from the linearity principle of mapping between argument, functional and constituent structures. Zhang's findings support the Topic Hypothesis, showing an orderly developmental sequence as predicted by the hypothesis.

Dealing with a more applied matter within the PT paradigm, Keßler's chapter reports on a feasibility study of *Rapid Profile* as a tool for online-assessment of EFL learner language development. The study was motivated by the claim that *Rapid Profile* provides a valid and quick means of diagnosing EFL-development in formal settings. Keßler's study reveals an inter-rater-reliability of 85.7 per cent, and thus proves *Rapid Profile* to be both a valid and a feasible diagnostic tool for online-assessment. Additionally, the results imply important SLA-based implications for the EFL classroom.

The significance of studies such as Keßler's is that it shows that it practically feasible to turn findings from second language acquisition research into a basis for language teaching and assessment. This is a theme that is bound to become more prominent within SLA circles as the pressure to link research to practice mounts on theorists and applied researchers alike. The following section of this chapter deals with two aspects of second language acquisition that are not too dissimilar from the chapters described thus far but nevertheless focus on two interconnected notions: bilingualism and speech processing.

Bilingualism and speech processing

Itani-Adams' chapter investigates the relationship between the development of lexicon and grammar in Japanese and English in a bilingual child (age 1;11 to 4;10). The research focuses on the relationship between verbs and the suffixation of morphemes, and the relationship between verbs and the semantic function of the arguments of the two languages. Itani-Adams' study found that regardless of the different input languages, the noun bootstrapped the bilingual child into both languages. Overall, the findings from this study support the prediction of Processability Theory that the initial word order used by a language leaner is the canonical order of the language. The results suggest that, for this bilingual child, Japanese and English each developed in a separate but a parallel manner.

Staying within bilingual research, Suarez and Goh's study investigated codification in short-term memory in bilinguals with different levels of English/Chinese dominance. The experiments manipulated phonological and visual features of words and examined their influence on the degree of semantic proactive interference (PI) in a short-term cued recall task. The results suggest that bilinguals process their two languages according to their language dominance. Particularly, Mixed and English dominant bilinguals showed evidence of phonological influence on PI, implicating phonological codification. There was also evidence of visual influences on PI for English dominant bilinguals, implicating visual codification. Chinese dominant bilinguals did not show any evidence of phonological and visual influences on semantic PI, which may suggest that they have a very integrated phonological, visual and semantic memory system.

Leaving bilingualism and ESL issues aside, Van den Noort, Bosch and Hugdahl's chapter discuss the processing of relative clauses in L1 research where subject relatives are reported to be easier to comprehend than object relatives. In this study, Van den Noort, Bosch and Hugdah test the hypothesis that object relatives cause a greater working memory load on twenty multilinguals, who were all native Dutch speakers (L1) and fluent in German (L2). Ten subjects started their free acquisition of Norwegian (L3) in the last 6 months, whereas ten others started their acquisition of Norwegian more than 3 years ago. Participants conducted a relative clause task in all languages, a reading span task in Norwegian (L3), and a number ordering task. The results show that differences in subject- and object relatives can only be found for participants, who are in an advanced stage of third language acquisition. Moreover, no significant correlations were found between the number ordering task, the reading span task (in L3), and the total comprehension score on the relative clause task in Dutch, German, and Norwegian. Van den Noort, Bosch and Hugdah's findings are in line with the SSIR theory of (foreign) language comprehension.

Dealing with speech processing and procedural features within an integrated theoretical framework, Kim and Kwon's study is inspired by three L2 developmental modules in procedural development, syntactic development, and morphological development. By integrating three separate modules into one, Kim and Kwon's study proposes a model called the Parallel Developmental Sequence (PDS) Model. The three modules from which the PDS Model is derived are the English Developmental Sequence (Pienemann and Johnston, 1987), the Minimal Tree Hypothesis (Vainikka and Young-Scholten, 1998), and the PT (Pienemann, 1988). In essence, the PDS Model proposes that L2 development follows a series of parallel developmental stages sequentially. Each of these stages incorporates three different dimensions of sequential development: the procedural developmental sequence, the syntactic developmental sequence, and the unificational (morphological) developmental sequence. Each stage is operative through parallel activation, parallel connection, parallel strength, and synchronization by the logic of 'parallel connection' of the Parallel Distributed Processing Model. Therefore, the assumption of the PDS is that an L2 learner at a stage will activate the parallel mechanism and synchronize the three parallel systems to process rules in order to understand and produce language in that stage. The question then is whether or not the theoretically built sequence of parallel developmental stages does reflect the actual developmental stages of the L2 learner.

Conclusion

While this book has deliberately focussed on the process of language learning in its right, there is little doubt now that a more direct interaction with language teaching and assessment can pursued more confidently. In fact, as is shown by the Pieneman's teachability hypothesis, the establishment of referential developmental points can have real purchase for grammar instruction and potentially language testing. This book coincides with a gradual shift in language teaching towards employing second language acquisition research as a relevant knowledge source for teaching practice and curriculum design (Lightbown, 1985, 2000; Long & Robinson, 1998). This is clearly evident in the growing number of empirical studies that attempt to test the educational benefits of specific design features in the curriculum, or certain teaching strategies inspired by and based on theoretical claims articulated within second language acquisition research (Mitchell, 2000; Macroy, 2000; Doughty & Williams, 1998). There is also a growing interaction between theoretical research in SLA and other relevant areas of academic inquiry, such as applied linguistics and foreign language assessment (c.f. Kramsch, 2000; Lightbown 1985; 2000; Long & Robinson, 1998).

Notes

[1] The edited volume is based on papers delivered at the 5th International Symposium on Processability, Bilingualism and Second Language Acquisition. The Symposium was held at Deakin University's Melbourne Campus, 26-28 September 2005.

[2] This section on the historical account of SLA draws largely on F. Mansouri, (2000), '*Grammatical Markedness and Information Processing in the Acquisition of Arabic as a Second Language*'. LINCOM EUROPA Academic Publishers: Munchen, Germany, pp73-77.

[3] Pienemann 1998, Pienemann, Di Biase & Kawaguchi, 2005

References

Anderson, S.R. (1991), 'Developmental sequences: the emergence of aspect marking in second language acquisition'. In T. Huebner and C. Ferguson (eds*), Cross-currents in second language acquisition and linguistics theories*. Amsterdam/Philadelphia: John Benjamins.

Brown, R. (1973), *A first language: The early stages*. Cambridge, Mass: Harvard University Press.

Burt, M. & Dulay, H. 1980, 'On acquisition orders', in S. Felix (ed) 1980a, *Second Language Development: Trends and Issues*. Tübingen: Gunter Narr.

DeVilliers, J. &. deVilliers, P. (1973), 'A cross-sectional study of the acquisition of grammatical morphemes in child speech'. *Journal of Psycholinguistic Research*, 2: 267-278.

Doughty, C. & Williams, J. (Eds.) (1998). *Focus on form in classroom second language acquisition*. Cambridge: Cambridge University Press.

Doughty, C. & Long, M. (Eds) (2003), *The Handbook of Second Language Acquisition*. The United Kingdom: Blackwell Publishing.

Dulay, H. M. Burt & Krashen, S. (1982), *Language Two*. New York: Oxford University Press.

Dulay, H. M & Burt, M. (1973), 'Should we teach children syntax?'. *Language Learning*. 23: 245-258.

Ellis, R. (1994), *The Study of Second Language Acquisition*. Oxford: Oxford University Press.

Givon, T. (1979a), *On understanding grammar*. New York: Academic Press.

Hakuta, K. 1974, 'A preliminary report on the development of grammatical morphemes in a Japanese girl learning English as a second language'. *Working Papers on Bilingualism,* 3: 18-43.

Hatch, E. (1978a), 'Discourse analysis and second language acquisition', in Hatch, E. (ed), *Second language acquisition: a book of readings*. Rowley, Mass: Newbury House.

Huebner, T. (1979), 'Order of acquisition vs. Dynamic paradigm: a comparison of method in interlanguage research'. *TESOL Quarterly*, 12:21-28.

Kramsch, C. (2000). Second language acquisition, applied linguistics, and the teaching of foreign language. *The Modern Language Journal*. 84, 3, Fall, 311-326.

Krashen, S. D. (1983), 'Newmark's ignorance hypothesis and current second language acquisition theory', in Gass, S. & Selinker, L. (eds), Language transfer in language learning. Mass: Newbury House.

Larsen-Freeman, D. & Long, M. (1991), *An Introduction to Second Language Classroom Research*. London: Longman.

—. (1975), *The acquisition of grammatical morphemes by adult learners of English as a second language*. Unpublished Ph.D. dissertation, University of Michigan.

Lightbown, P.M. (1985). 'Great expectations: second language acquisition research and classroom Teaching'. *Applied Linguistics*. 6, 2, 173-89.

—. (2000). 'Classroom SLA research and second language teaching'. *Applied Linguistics*. 21, 4, 431-462.

Long, M. & Robinson, P. (1998). 'Focus on form: theory, research and practice'. In C. Doughty & J. Williams (Eds.) *Focus on form in classroom second language acquisition*. Cambridge: Cambridge University Press, pp.15-41.

Macroy, G. (2000). 'Learning to teach grammar in the modern foreign languages classroom'. *Research in Education*. 64. 1-11.

Mansouri, F. (2000). *Grammatical markedness and information processing in the acquisition of Arabic as a second language*. Munchen, Germany: LINCOM EUROPA Academic Publishers.

Meisel, J.M., Clahsen, H. & Pienemann, M. (1981), 'On determining developmental stages in natural second language acquisition'. *Studies in Second Language Acquisition*, 3: 109-135.

Mitchell, R. (2000). 'Applied linguistics and evidence-based classroom practice: the case of foreign language grammar pedagogy'. *Applied Linguistics*. 21, 3, 281-303.

Pienemann, M. (1998). *Language processing and second language development: processability theory*. Amsterdam/Philadelphia: John Benjamins.

Wode, H. (1977), 'The L2 acquisition of /r/'. *Phonetica*, 34: 200-217.

CHAPTER 2

AN INTRODUCTION TO PROCESSABILITY THEORY

Manfred Pienemann

Basic outline of the theory

Processability Theory (Pienemann 1998) is a theory of second language development. The logic underlying Processability Theory (PT) (Pienemann 1998; 2005) is the following: at any stage of development the learner can produce and comprehend only those L2 linguistic forms which the current state of the language processor can handle. It is therefore crucial to understand the architecture of the language processor and the way in which it handles a second language. This enables one to predict the course of development of L2 linguistic forms in language production and comprehension across languages.

The architecture of the language processor accounts for language processing in real time and within human psychological constraints such as word access and human memory. The incorporation of the language processor in the study of second language acquisition therefore brings to bear a set of human psychological constraints that are crucial for the processing of languages. The view on language production followed in PT is largely that described by Levelt (1989), which overlaps to some extent with the computational model of Kempen and Hoenkamp (1987) which emulates much of Merrill Garrett's work (e.g. Garrett 1976, 1980, 1982) and on which the corresponding section of Levelt's model is based. The basic premises of that view are the following:

- Processing components operate largely automatically and are generally not consciously controlled;
- Processing is incremental;
- The output of the processor is linear, while it may not be mapped onto the underlying meaning in a linear way;
- Grammatical processing has access to a temporary memory store that can hold grammatical information. (cf. Pienemann 1998 for detail)

The core of PT is formed by a universal processability hierarchy that is based on Levelt's (1989) approach to language production. PT is formally modelled using Lexical Functional Grammar (LFG) (Bresnan 2001). PT is a universal framework that has the capacity to predict developmental trajectories for any second language. The notion 'developmental trajectory' implies a developmental dimension known as 'staged development' as well as a variational dimension accounting for individual differences between developmental trajectories as illustrated in Figure 1.

Figure 1 shows two different developmental trajectories, T1 and T2, which are based on the same set of developmental stages (indicated by the dotted horizontal lines). The two developmental trajectories differ with respect to the interlanguage varieties that are developed at each stage (indicated by vertical lines). As can be seen in Figure 1, there are many possible developmental trajectories based on the same stages of development.

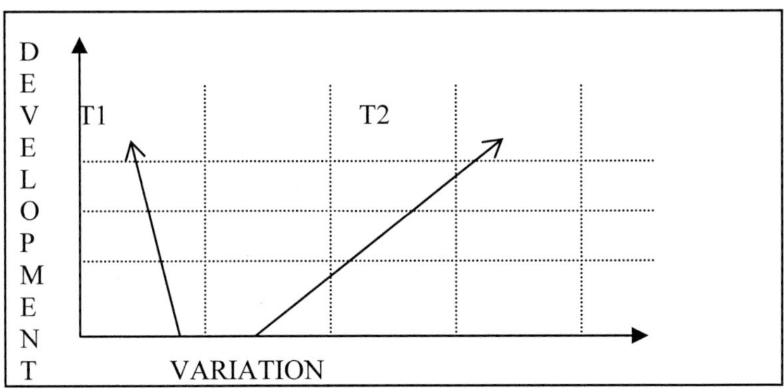

Figure 1: Different developmental trajectories

In this paradigm, each stage represents a set of grammatical rules that share certain processing routines, and each interlanguage variety represents a specific variant of the grammatical rules. For instance, in ESL question formation the following developmental sequence has been found (e.g. Pienemann, 1998):

Stage	Structure	Example
Stage 1	SVO question	He live here?
Stage 2	WH+SVO	Where he is?
Stage 3	Copula inversion	Where is he?
Stage 4	Aux-second	Where has he been?

Learners attempting to produce 'Aux-second' at stage 3 (i.e. before they are ready for this structure) have been found to produce the following interlanguage variants:

A Where he been?
B Where has been?
C Where he has been?
D He has been where?

Variants A to D have in common that they get around placing the auxiliary in second position after an initial WH-word. In other words, they constitute different solutions to the same learning problem. In Figure 1 each of the different solutions is represented by a vertical line. It is important to bear in mind that for each structural learning process there is a limited set of variable solutions. In the course of L2 development, the learner accumulates grammatical rules and their variants, allowing her or him to develop an individual developmental trajectory while adhering to the overall developmental schedule. In this way, PT defines a two-dimensional space for the formation of processable hypotheses. Both dimensions of this space (i.e. 'Hypothesis Space') are constrained by the processability hierarchy which can be applied to any L2 using Lexical Functional Grammar, a theory of language to be described later in this chapter.

The original version of PT (Pienemann 1998) focused solely on what is known as the 'developmental problem' (that is, 'why do learners follow universal stages of acquisition?'). The extended version of PT (Pienemann, Di Biase and Kawaguchi 2005) also starts to address the so-called 'logical problem' (that is, 'what is the origin of linguistic knowledge?' For instance, how do learners know that there are such things as nouns and verbs?). The developmental and the logical problem are the key issues of any theory of language acquisition, and PT addresses these issues in a modular fashion. One module deals with the developmental problem, a separate, but connected module deals with the logical problem. Both modules are based on LFG because LFG is designed to account for linguistic knowledge in a way that is compatible with the architecture of the language processor, and both these components are needed for PT to address the developmental and the logical problem. The developmental problem is addressed by describing the constraints the language processor places on development, and the logical problem is addressed using specific components of LFG that are summarized below.

The commitment of LFG to the interface between linguistic knowledge and language processing is illustrated very clearly in the following quotation:

> [Children] acquire knowledge and skills that enable them to produce and comprehend an infinite number of novel utterances... The major goal of psycholinguistic research is to devise an explanatory account of the mental operations that underlie these linguistic abilities.
> —Kaplan and Bresnan (1982:177)

As Kaplan and Bresnan (1982) point out, the various components of a theory of language acquisition can be studied separately as long as they ultimately fit together in a coherent model. In the PT framework the language processor is seen as the computational routines that operate on, but are separate from, linguistic knowledge (cf. Kaplan and Bresnan 1982).

The basic claim of the original version of PT is that language development is constrained by processability. This affects first and second language development (albeit in different ways). It also affects interlanguage variation and L1 transfer. The extended version of PT adds to this the claim that the initial form of grammar in SLA is determined by the default relationship between what is known as 'argument structure', that is, the ideas expressed in a sentence, and the way they are expressed by grammatical forms.

Key constructs and mechanisms underlying PT

The processability hierarchy

In Pienemann (1998) the processability hierarchy is based on the notion of transfer of grammatical information within and between the phrases of a sentence. For instance, in the sentence 'Little Peter goes home' the grammatical information 'third person singular' is present in the phrase 'Little Peter' and in 'goes'. This is commonly referred to as 'subject-verb agreement'. In LFG and in Levelt's model of language generation it is assumed that the language processor checks if the two parts of the sentence, 'Little Peter' and 'goes', contain the same grammatical information. To be able to carry out this checking operation, the procedures that build phrases in language generation need to have developed in the second language processing system. In our example learners need to have developed a procedure for building noun phrases such as 'Little Peter' and verb phrases such as 'goes home'. They also need to have developed a procedure for putting these two phrases together to form a sentence. In Levelt's (1989) model of language generation, it is assumed that the grammatical information 'third person singular' needs to be stored in the procedures that build the phrases in which this information is used, and that the two lots of information are compared within the procedure that puts the two phrases together to form a sentence. The learner of a language needs to develop procedures that can handle the job of storing and comparing grammatical information. This way, speakers can learn to decide which sentences are grammatically acceptable and which aren't. For instance, in the sentence '*Little Peter go home' the phrase 'little Peter' is marked for 'third person singular', but the verb isn't. This would be detected by a competent speaker when the noun phrase and the verb phrase are assembled to form a sentence. However, if the learner has not yet developed a fully functioning sentence procedure the mismatch will not be detected.

The same principle applies to grammatical information contained within phrases. For instance, in the noun phrase 'two kids' the grammatical information 'plural' is contained in the numeral 'two' and in the noun 'kids'. In language generation these two bits of information are compared when the noun phrase is assembled by the noun phrase-procedure. In the case of 'two' and 'kids' the two bits of grammatical information do match.

We can now see that in both examples grammatical information has to be matched between parts of the sentence. In Lexical Functional Grammar this process is called 'feature unification'. In non-technical language we might describe this process as information matching. LFG uses formal means to account for such processes. The fact that LFG has this capacity is one of the key reasons why PT uses LFG to model these psycholinguistic processes.

The two examples we used also serve to illustrate the processability hierarchy. It is easy to see that in the 'Little Peter' example grammatical information has to be matched between a noun phrase and the verb phrase and that this occurs when the two pieces are assembled to form a sentence. In contrast, in the second example the information matching occurs in the noun phrase procedure – *before* the sentence is assembled. In other words, there is a time sequence involved in the matching of grammatical information which forms the basis of the original processability hierarchy. Noun phrases are assembled before verb phrases which are assembled before the sentence. In addition, individual words belong to categories such as 'noun' and 'verb', and category procedures are the memory stores that hold grammatical information such as 'singular' or 'past'. Therefore category procedures appear before noun phrase procedures.

The following is an overview of the original processability hierarchy, following Pienemann (1998):

1. no procedure
2. category procedure
3. noun phrase procedure
4. verb phrase procedure
5. sentence procedure
6. subordinate clause procedure.

The basic hypothesis underlying PT is that learners develop their grammatical inventory following this hierarchy for two reasons: (1) because the hierarchy is implicationally ordered, i.e. every procedure is a necessary prerequisite for the next procedure; and (2) because the hierarchy mirrors the time-course in language generation. Therefore the learner has no choice other than to develop along this hierarchy. Phrases cannot be assembled without words being assigned to categories such as 'noun' and 'verb', and sentences cannot be assembled without the phrases they contain and so forth. The fact that learners have no choice in the path they take in the development of processing procedures follows from the time-course of language generation and the design of processing procedures. This is how the architecture of language generation constrains language development.

As mentioned above, the original version of the processability hierarchy focuses on information transfer within phrase structure. In the extended version of PT (Pienemann, Di Biase and Kawaguchi 2005) the processability hierarchy is extended to include further aspects of language generation, in particular the relationship between what is known as 'conceptual structure' and grammatical structure. Argument structure refers to the basic ideas conveyed in a sentence, i.e. who does what to whom. In other word, the extended version of PT also includes the relationship between what is intended to be said and the way this is expressed using grammatical forms. This extension is also modeled using Lexical-Functional Grammar. Details will be summarized later on.

Figure 2 illustrates the basic points of the processability hierarchy. Three examples of phrase structures are listed in the left-hand column. The second column specifies the type of information transfer possible at each stage. ESL morphological structures are given in the next column to exemplify the types of structures possible at each stage, and the information transfer involved in the generation of these structures is illustrated in the column on the right-hand side.

		Information Exchange		
↑	Stage	Locas of Exchange	Example	Illustration
	Sentence	Within sentense	Peter sees a dog	S; NPs, V; N, V NP; [3rd pers sg] [3rd pers sg, pres, non-cont.]
	Phrase	Within phrase only	Two kids	NP; Det [pl], N [pl]
	Category	No exchange	Talk-ed	V [past]

Figure 2: An illustration of the processability hierarchy focusing on 3 stages

Hypothesis Space

The processability hierarchy has been described as the sequence in which the fundamental design of the language processor develops in L2 acquisition, and it has been added that the learner is constrained to follow this sequence. At the same time, the processing procedures developed at every stage of the hierarchy do allow for some degree of leeway for the shape of the L2 grammar. Hypothesis Space is created by the interplay between the processability hierarchy and the leeway it generates at every level.

The constraining effect of the processability hierarchy is illustrated in Figure 2. As can be seen in Figure 2, at the stage 'phrase' grammatical information can be exchanged only within phrases, not beyond the phrasal boundary. Therefore grammatical structures requiring information exchange beyond the phrase boundary, such as subject verb-agreement cannot be processed at this stage. To recoup, learners have no choice other than to follow the processability hierarchy in their development of the L2 grammatical inventory because of the internal architecture of the language processor. At any given point in the hierarchy any grammatical operation requiring processing procedures that are beyond the current point of development are out of reach for the learners. In other words, processing procedures constrain the range of possible production grammars for every level.

At the same time, these constraints leave sufficient leeway for learners to find different solutions to structural learning problems. I illustrated this above with the example of the position of auxiliaries in English WH-questions. This position requires processing procedures at the sentence level in the hierarchy. L2 learners can nevertheless produce WH-questions. When they attempt to do this, learners have four structural options that avoid the placement of the auxiliary in second position. The options available are all processable using the resources available at the previous stage, and the number of options is limited because of the limited resources that are available. The fact that learners need to circumnavigate a structural problem (here Aux-second) is caused by the constraints inherent in the hierarchy. In this way, possible developmental trajectories are constrained by the processability hierarchy.

Developmental dynamics

Developmental trajectories within Hypothesis Space have their own dynamics that are a key component of language development. These dynamics are particularly visible in a comparison of first and second language development as shown in Table 2 which lists two sets of processing procedures and the differential developmental trajectories found in the acquisition of German as a first and as a second language (cf. Pienemann 1998b).

Processing procedures			
Constituent structure	Mapping	**L2 German**	**L1 German**
subordinate clause procedure		comp SOV [comp **S V O**]	comp **SOV**
use of S-procedure for storage across constituents in S	topicalisation of core arguments	X Vf S O Vi [(X) **S V O**]	X Vf **S O V**i
use of VP-procedure for storage across constituents in VP		X **S Vf O V**i	---
use of saliency principle to relax canonical order constraint	XP-adjunction	X **S V O**	---
category procedure	unmarked alignment	**S V O**	**S OV**
(both result in canonical order)			

Table 2: Developmental dynamics

To appreciate the developmental dynamics shown in Table 2, the reader needs to bear in mind the following descriptive facts about German word order.

- Affirmative main clauses follow a SVO pattern (as in English) except for sentences with a non-subject in initial position (e.g. 'Gestern ging er weg'. / 'Yesterday went he away').
- In sentences containing more than one verb the non-finite verb appears in final position (e.g. 'Er hat ihn gesehen' / 'He has him seen').
- In main clauses the inflected verb is always in second position.
- In embedded clauses the verb is in final position.

As can be seen in Table 2, L1 and L2 learners follow different developmental trajectories that both reach the same target containing all word order regularities listed above, and both trajectories are placed within the constraints defined by Hypothesis Space. Nevertheless, the two developmental trajectories are fundamentally different, mainly because they start with a different initial hypothesis, and the structure entailed in the initial hypothesis propagates through the entire developmental process (cf. Pienemann 1998b). L1 learners preserve the initial SOV order and modify it to fit the target language, whereas L2 learners preserve the SVO order and make adjustments on this basis that also leads to a close match of the target pattern. I will show below that these dynamics can be modeled using a formal approach to developmental dynamics called 'Generative Entrenchment' (Wimsatt 1986).

Empirical evidence in PT-based research

Given the focus of PT on developmental dynamics, the most suitable research design is a longitudinal or cross-sectional study with a large set of data relevant for the phenomena under scrutiny. 'Relevant data' does not equal a large data set. The data need to be relevant to the point to be studied. For instance, the study of subject-verb agreement marking requires a large set of contexts for subject-verb agreement marking. This will allow the researcher to decide if the verbal marker is supplied or not. If no context appears, no conclusion can be drawn. However, even the presence of a number of morphological markers is no guarantee that these are based on productive interlanguage rules. In order to exclude the use of formulae and chunks the researcher needs to check lexical and morphological variation (i.e. same morpheme on different words and same word with different morphemes). These descriptive methods are described in more detail in Pienemann (1998a).

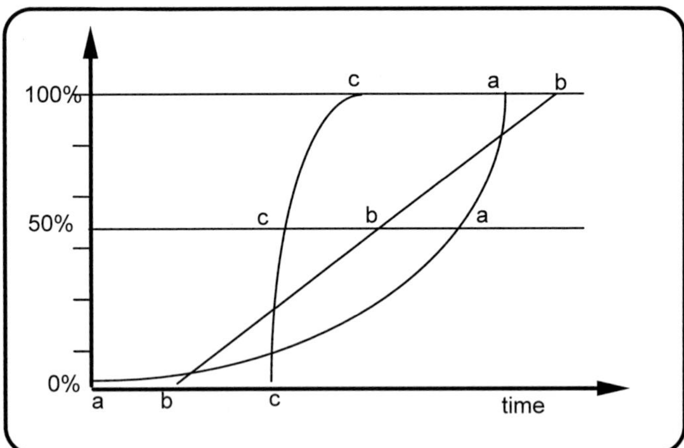

Figure 3: Accuracy and development

The interpretation of corpus data depends on the acquisition criterion that is used. In Pienemann (1998a) I make a case for the use of the emergence criterion. The basic point is this: accuracy criteria (e.g. 80% suppliance) are arbitrary. This is illustrated in Figure 3 which shows three different routes for the development of the rate of suppliance of grammatical structures. Obviously the three routes have a different gradient. Therefore the order of acquisition of the three structures is c > b >a using a 50% criterion and c > a > b using a 100% criterion. In other words, accuracy rates do not permit firm conclusions about the state of the interlanguage. Any test of the PT hierarchy would need to be based on the same definition of the acquisition criterion and on sufficiently large sets of relevant spontaneous production data. Naturally, spontaneous production data cannot be directly compared with other types of data, such as grammatical judgement data because both sets of data tap into different skills and /or types of knowledge.

The PT hierarchy is indeed highly falsfiable. Any set of data that demonstrates that learners produce level x structures at level x-1 (i.e. that stages can be skipped) constitutes a case of falsification. However, one needs to bear in mind that besides the transfer of grammatical information, language contains additional factors that also contribute to the order of acquisition of specific target language structures. One prime factor is form-function relationship. For instance, Dewaele and Veronique (2001) tested NP agreement in French adjectives focusing on levels of accuracy in gender assignment. PT is not a suitable conceptual framework for such a study because gender is a lexical feature and thus has to be acquired for every lexical item. Therefore a study of agreement in French adjectives tests more than just the learner's ability to exchange grammatical features within the NP. Any incorrect example may be due to one of two reasons: (1) either an inability to transfer information within the NP or (2) a lack of lexical learning. Therefore any empirical test of PT would also need to factor out additional complexity due to form-function relationships (cf. Pienemann 1998a for details).

Apart from corpus data, reaction time experiments also constitute a valid basis of a test of PT. For instance, the 1998 volume on PT (Pienemann 1998a) contains an on-line experiment based on reaction times in a sentence matching task. The design of the study was based on the comparative measure of reaction times in native speakers, non-native speakers with a specific skill (subject-verb agreement) and non-native speakers without that skill. PT predicts that 'skilled non-native speakers' and native speakers will process subject-verb agreement in a manner similar to each other and different from 'unskilled non-native speakers'. This hypothesis was confirmed in the above study.

Transfer of grammatical information and feature unification

As mentioned above, the original version of PT focused on phrase structure (which is called 'constituent structure' in LFG) and the transfer of grammatical information within it. This information transfer process is modelled using feature unification. The modelling of feature unification is based on the following notions and assumptions. Every entry in the learner's mental lexicon needs to be annotated for the specific features of the target language. For instance, the entry 'Peter' needs to be assigned to the lexical class 'noun'. It needs to be annotated as a proper noun, and the feature 'NUMBER' needs to have the value 'singular'. The lexical entry 'sees' needs to be assigned to the lexical class 'verb', and the features NUMBER, PERSON, TENSE and ASPECT need to have the following values:

NUMBER	= singular
PERSON	= 3
TENSE	= present
ASPECT	= non-continuous

To achieve subject verb-agreement in the sentence 'Peter sees a dog' the value of the features NUMBER and PERSON have to be matched. In LFG this is called 'feature unification'. Figure 2 illustrates the unification of the features NUMBER and PERSON between the noun phrase 'Peter' and the verb 'sees'. These features and their values '3rd' and 'singular' reside in the lexical entries of the noun 'Peter' and the verb 'sees'. This grammatical information is passed on to the noun phrase procedure (NP) and verb phrase procedure (VP) respectively. From there the two groups of information are passed on to the sentence procedure (S) where they are matched (or 'unified').

In the design of PT, the point of unification is related to the hierarchy of processability that reflects the time course of real time processing. The hierarchy that results from a comparison of the points of feature unification can be illustrated on the basis of Figure 2 which shows that the example structures illustrated in Figure 2 can be ordered as follows:

1. No exchange of grammatical information (= no unification of features),
2. Exchange of grammatical information within the phrase,
3. Exchange of grammatical information within the sentence.

Once one applies this hierarchy to ESL morphology, the following developmental trajectory can be predicted:

1. past –ed	which will appear before
2. plural –s	which in turn will appear before
3. third person –s.	

In order to appreciate the universal nature of PT it is crucial to consider that the hierarchy illustrated in Figure 2 is not language-specific and that, in principle, it applies to the transfer of grammatical information in any language. In contrast, the examples that were given for ESL morphology utilise this hierarchy and apply it to one specific target language. The application of the full processability hierarchy to the syntax and morphology of specific languages will, of course, involve more detail of the LFG formalism.

Lexically driven grammar

A lexically driven grammar stores grammatical information in the lexicon. For instance, the lexical entry for 'walked' is marked for past tense and it lists the core argument of the verb as 'agent'. This lexical information is required in the assembly of the sentence. The lexically driven nature of sentence generation is an integral part of Levelt's approach and is backed up by extensive empirical evidence. LFG also encodes syntactic properties primarily in the lexicon (cf. Schwarze 2002, 148-9). This makes LFG particularly suitable for the study of dynamic linguistic systems such as developing learner grammars, because LFG affords a formal account of the linguistic dynamics present in developing learner grammars.

The lexically driven nature of sentence generation is supported by a wide range of psycholinguistic empirical evidence including research on slips of the tongue and on-line experiments (cf. Levelt 1989) and was demonstrated again recently in experimental work on sentence production by Pickering, Branigan, and McLean (2002) which shows that 'constituent structure is formulated in one stage' and thus supports the architecture of LFG.

Pienemann (1998) showed that for every level of the PT hierarchy, processing procedures can be captured through feature unification in LFG which in turn shares key characteristics with Kempen and Hoenkamp's (1987) procedural account of language generation.

Generative entrenchment

The basic mechanism behind generative entrenchment is the principle that developmentally early decisions bias the further development of the interlanguage system. This percolation of structural properties in developmental processes is known in biology and philosophy and has been termed *generative entrenchment* by Wimsatt (1986, 1991).

The concept of generative entrenchment is exemplified, for instance, by the embryonic development of animals where sections of the fertilised egg take on more and more specialised structures. The segmentation of the body plan occurs very early in these processes for all animals. These structural features are maintained throughout the developmental process, and they do not have to be decided on every time a refinement of parts of the structure is made. One can say that these features are 'developmentally entrenched'.

We also know that incorrect information on the positioning of segments can have serious consequences for the ultimate shape of the organism. This sometimes unfortunate phenomenon illustrates the concept of the *depth* of generative entrenchment. The earlier a decision is made in structural development, the more far-reaching the consequences for the ultimate stage in structural development. However, once a decision has been made and a new structure has been added, it is very costly, if not impossible, for the developmental process to move to a different developmental path. In effect, changing the developmental path would mean that all developmental steps up to the node that gives access to the alternative path would have to be cancelled. As a result, a great deal of structural information would be lost in such a move. Many physical processes of development are indeed irreversible, as the example of developmentally malformed organisms shows.

The key explanatory point that can be derived from the concept of generative entrenchment for language acquisition is that a massive computational saving can be made if structural decisions do not have to be revised in the developmental process every time a structural change occurs. To illustrate this point, let's assume that a developmental process consists of ten stages and that potentially there are 10 different options for each stage. Wimsatt calculated that in order for the learners to get to the end of the developmental process they need 1.000.000.000 different trials if all structural decisions have to be revised for each stage and each option. However, if they can retain the solution found for every stage a mere 100 trials is needed.

In this model initial structural features propagate in the developing system and thus determine the ultimate structure without being invoked again and again. The basic 'body plan' stays the same. In other words, a computational saving is made by laying structures down and keeping them. The alternative would be a developing system in which all processes of structural refinement have to be orchestrated globally for every developmental step, and this would require far more computational resources than the preservation of structures once they have developed.

Lexical mapping

Lexical Mapping Theory is a component of Lexical-Functional Grammar (cf. Bresnan 2001). LFG has three independent and parallel levels of representation as shown in Figure 4 below: argument structure, functional structure and constituent structure. Argument structure describes who does what to whom in a sentence. It is based on a universal hierarchy of argument roles that includes roles such as 'agent' or 'patient'. The core argument roles for each verb are listed in the lexical entry of the verb. For instance, the argument roles of the English verb 'see' are 'experiencer' and 'theme'. The following notation is used for this:

see <experiencer, theme>.

In other words, the act of seeing requires someone who experiences the seeing and something that is seen.

As mentioned above, 'constituent structure' is basically another name for 'phrase structure' and describes the structure of the parts of sentences. This component consists of universal units (such as 'verb', 'noun phrase' etc.), but these are arranged in a way that is specific for every language. For instance, in some languages adjectives precede the noun, in other languages they follow the noun. Functional structure also consists of universal units (such as 'SUBJECT' or 'OBJECT') which are related to constituent structure in a language-specific way. Functional structure serves to connect argument structure and constituent structure.

This design of LFG as a theory of language ensures that universal argument roles can be expressed using a whole range of different grammatical forms. For instance, in English the argument role 'agent' can be expressed as a grammatical subject as can be seen in the active sentence 'Peter feeds his dog' or as a grammatical adjunct as can be seen in the passive sentence 'the dog is fed by Peter'. In other words, the relationship between argument structure and the other two levels of structure is variable in a specific language, and it also varies between languages. This variable relationship between what is intended to be said (argument structure) and the way it is expressed using grammatical forms creates expressiveness in language, but it also creates what Levelt (1981) called 'the linearisation problem'. As mentioned above, the output of the processor is linear, while it may not be mapped onto the underlying meaning in a linear way. This non-linear relationship can be seen, for instance, in subject verb-agreement where the information 'PERSON = 3' and 'NUMBER = singular' is present in two places in the output of the processor, and the two lots of information have to be assembled and co-ordinated by the speaker. In fact, this assembly can only be carried out if the learner has developed the necessary processing procedures.

The linearisation problem also applies to the relationship between argument structure and functional structure. As I showed for the active-passive alternation above, the relationship between the underlying meaning and the way it is expressed can be variable. Therefore, the type of expression that deviates from a simple match between underlying meaning and grammatical form (as in the passive) introduces a degree of non-linearity. Lexical Mapping Theory can formally model the different degrees of non-linearity in the relationship between argument structure and functional structure, and the extended version of PT utilises this capacity of Lexical Mapping Theory to incorporate it into the pocessability hierarchy.

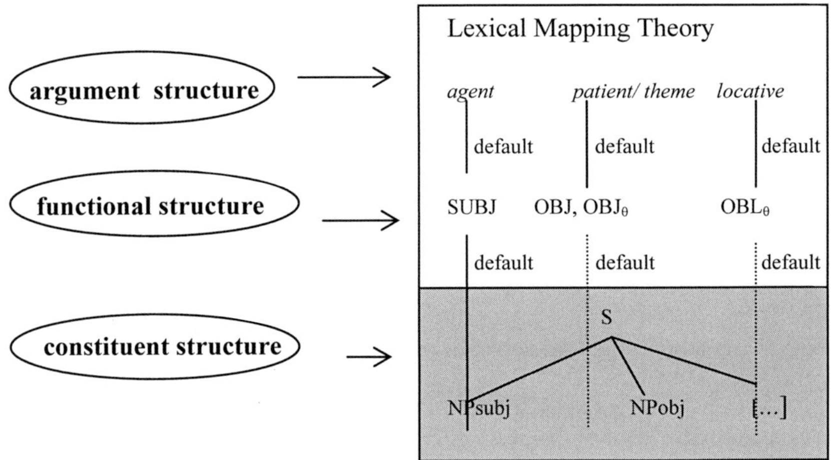

Figure 4: Unmarked alignment in LFG (from: Pienemann, Di Biase and Kawaguchi 2005)

As illustrated in Figure 4, Lexical Mapping Theory accounts for the mapping of argument structure onto functional structure. In PT the default mapping principle is unmarked alignment which is based on the one-to-one mapping of argument roles onto grammatical functions (for instance, 'agent' = SUBJECT). Naturally, target languages allow for a much wider range of relationships between argument structure and functional structure (including passives, topicalisation[1], among others), and these develop step-wise in second language acquisition. Principles of lexical mapping can account for these developmental processes.

In other words, *unmarked alignment* is the initial state of L2 development. It is based on the one-to-one mapping of the three parallel levels of representation onto each other. Unmarked alignment results in canonical word order[2]. For ESL this is SVO. *Unmarked alignment* simplifies language processing for the learner who, at this stage, will analyse the first noun phrase as the agent. This way, canonical word order avoids any kind of transfer of grammatical information during language processing.

PT implies that second language acquisition starts with a linear relationship between argument structure and functional structure and that changes of this linear relationship will require additional processing procedures that will be acquired later. Hence the *unmarked alignment hypothesis* implies a developmental prediction for L2 structures that affect the relationship between argument structure and functional structure. One example is the passive.

In the passive the relationship between argument roles and syntactic functions may be altered as can be seen in the supression of argument roles and altered function-assignment. These alterations for passives are illustrated in examples (1) – (4).

(1) Peter sees a dog.

(2) see <experiencer, theme>

| |

SUBJ OBJ

(3) A dog is seen by Peter.

(4) seen <experiencer, theme>

| | - - - - - - -

Ø SUBJ (ADJ)

Sentences (1) and (3) describe the same event involving two participants. The difference between the two is that in (3) the constituent *a dog* that is OBJECT in (1) is realised as SUBJECT, and the constituent *Peter* that is SUBJECT in (1) is realised as ADJUNCT. The respective mapping of arguments onto grammatical functions is shown in (2) and (4). In (2) the 'experiencer' is mapped onto SUBJECT and the theme onto OBJECT. In (4) it is the 'theme' that is mapped onto SUBJECT, and the 'experiencer' is mapped onto ADJUNCT.

These alterations of the relationship between argument roles and syntactic functions constitute a deviation from *unmarked alignment*. In order for this type of marked alignment to be possible, the function of a noun phrase (SUBJECT, OBJECT or ADJUNCT among others) can be established only by assembling information about the constituents in the sentence procedure. This means that the passive is based on a non-linear relationship between argument structure and functional structure, and this construction requires the sentence procedure, i.e. the highest level in the processability hierarchy.

The TOPIC Hypothesis

As mentioned above, *unmarked alignment* ties together in a linear way the three parallel levels of representation, argument structure, functional structure and constituent structure. Lexical Mapping Theory specifies the relationship between argument structure and functional structure, and PT derives developmental predictions from the language-specific relationship between argument structure and functional structure using Lexical Mapping Theory. Similar predictions can also be derived from the relationship between functional structure and constituent structure. One set of such predictions is entailed in the TOPIC Hypothesis. To account for developmental dynamics in the relationship between functional structure and constituent structure Pienemann, Di Biase and Kawaguchi (2005) propose the TOPIC hypothesis which predicts that learners will initially not differentiate between SUBJECT and other grammatical functions in sentence-initial position (e.g. TOPIC). In this context it is important to note that in LFG TOPIC is a grammatical function. For instance in the sentence '*Anne*, he likes' *Anne* has two functions, OBJECT and TOPIC. The TOPIC function is assigned to a constituent in sentence-initial position other than the SUBJECT that introduces new information to the discourse (for instance *Anne* in the above example[3]). When the learner is able to add a constituent before the subject position, this will trigger the differentiation of the grammatical functions TOPIC and SUBJECT.

The TOPIC hypothesis predicts that TOPIC will first be assigned to so-called non-core functions which do not relate to arguments listed in the lexical entries of verbs such as ADJUNCTS. Later they will also be assigned to core-functions such as OBJECTS. The reason for this is that that the assignment of TOPIC to core-functions creates a higer degree of non-linearity. In other words, the TOPIC hypothesis predicts three overall stages in the mapping of functional structure onto constituent structure:

1. TOPIC and SUBJECT are not differentiated.
2. The initial constituent is an ADJUNCT or a question-word. TOPIC is differentiated from SUBJECT.
3. The TOP function is assigned to a core argument other than SUBJECT.

Typological plausibility

The goal of an explanatory theory of SLA must, of course, be to provide a mechanism which has the capacity of making predictions for any human language. It would therefore be desirable to demonstrate the applicability of the proposed theory for a range of typologically different languages. If it can be demonstrated that the actual course of L2 development follows the route predicted by the theory (stated in universal terms), then the status of that theory must be beyond a mere generalisation of observational facts.

Examining the typological plausibility of PT is the overarching theme of the volume edited by Pienemann (2005). First steps in this direction were made in Pienemann (1998) by demonstrating that the developmental trajectories found in the acquisition of Swedish and Japanese as second languages follows the course predicted by PT. The research on Swedish SLA was based on an extensive overview of the majority of studies carried out on Swedish SLA over a period of more than two decades (cf. Pienemann and Håkansson 1999).

Glahn, Håkansson, Hammerberg, Holmen, Hvenekilde and Lund (2001) tested this framework with specific reference to affixation in attributive and predicative adjectives in Scandinavian languages (cf. also Hammerberg 1996). When intervening variables, such as gender assignment, are 'factored out' (cf. Pienemann 1998:159 ff.) the data strongly support the predictions made by the theory.

The research on Japanese SLA reported in Pienemann (1998) was based on Kawaguchi's initial work which is presented in more detail in Di Biase and Kawaguchi (2002). Kawaguchi (2005) extended this framework. The application of PT to Japanese SLA constitutes a crucial test case for the theory because all other languages PT had been applied to (German, English and Swedish) are closely related to each other and share a number of typological features. For instance, they are all configurational languages with verb-second constraints. In contrast, Japanese is a non-configurational, agglutinative language. The crux of the typological plausibility test for PT is to demonstrate that the universal architecture of grammatical information flow entailed in PT can make testable and correct predictions for the course of Japanese L2 development. Kawaguchi demonstrated that the developmental predictions she made for Japanese as L2 on the basis of PT are bourne out by longitudinal and cross-sectional learner data.

Most studies of Japanese SLA focused on adult university learners of Japanese. However, recent PT-based studies also have included natural learners. For example, Itani-Adams (2003) studies bilingual first language acquisition of a Japanese-Australian child. Her work utilises the developmental trajectory of English as a second language established by Pienemann (1998) and the developmental trajectory of Japanese as a second language established by Di Biase and Kawaguchi (2002). Itani-Adams found that both languages develop following the hierarchy predicted by PT (lexical > phrasal > inter-phrasal). She used PT as a matrix for a comparison of language development across the two first languages of the informant. She found the three different types of morphology (i.e., lexical, phrasal and inter-phrasal morphology) did not develop in synchrony in two languages. This finding supports De Houwer's (1990) Separate Development Hypothesis. Iwasaki (2003) studied the acquisition of Japanese morphosyntax by a seven-year-old Australian boy in a naturalistic environment and found the same developmental trajectory as Di Biase and Kawaguchi (2002).

Zhang (2001, 2002, 2004, 2005) applied PT to modern standard Chinese, another language that is typologically distant from Germanic languages. Modern standard Chinese is an isolating and topic-prominent language. Zhang identified five grammatical morphemes and related them to three different PT levels. Her data show that the morphemes are acquired in the sequence predicted by PT.

Gao (2004) is an extensive empirical study of the acquisition of key grammatical morphemes and topic marking in Mandarin as a second language by adult language learners in formal and informal contexts with a range of different source languages. This study replicates the Zhang study using data from a number of typologically different source languages. This study also includes additional aspects of Mandarin grammar, especially topic marking. All of these aspects of Mandarin are positioned within the PT framework, and the resulting developmental trajectory is supported by the data.

Di Biase (cf. Di Biase and Kawaguchi 2002) applied the PT hierarchy to Italian as L2. One important corollary of his research is the conclusion that the mechanics of subject-verb agreement may vary between typologically different languages. This analysis is not only congruent with the data presented by Di Biase and with his implementation of PT into Italian, but also with Cross-linguistic on-line studies of agreement in English and Romance languages by Vigliocco, Butterworth and Garrett (1996) and Vigliocco, Butterworth and Semenza (1995).

Harada (2004) explores the relationship between the acquisition of modality and PT stages of development in three Japanese learners of English L2. She finds that only lexical modality (e.g. as expressed in 'maybe' or 'I think') appears in early learners' language (stage 1 and 2) while modal verbs (e.g. can + lexical verb) seem to coincide with the appearance of the VP procedure.

Empirical research carried out in the PT framework yielded precise descriptions of ESL and other developmental trajectories and of learner variation. This research has been used as an objective psycholinguistic basis of measurement in educational evaluation studies. For instance, Keßler (in press) compared levels of attainment in primary and secondary ESL programs in German schools utilising PT-based descriptions of ESL development.

The study by Berti and Di Biase (2002) shows the effectiveness of L2 teaching based on a syllabus infomed by the PT hierarchy in conjunction with form-focused teaching method. PT has also been used as a basis for profiling natural and formal L2 learners of Italian as L2 (Bettoni and Di Biase, 2005).

Håkansson, Salameh and Nettelblatt (2003) produced a highly innovative application of PT that capitalises on its Cross-linguistic capacity. Håkansson et al. studied the acquisition of Swedish-Arabic bilingual children with and without specific language impairment. Based on the above PT hierarchy for Swedish, Mansouri's (2000) Arabic PT levels and further development of this research by Håkansson and Mansouri, these authors (Håkansson, Salameh and Nettelblatt, 2003) were able to measure language development of bilingual informants using compatible scales for both languages. This was possible because of the universal nature of the underlying PT framework. In other words, this approach to the measurement of bilingual language development affords us a description of the current state of the learner's bilingual system in which both languages can be compared on the same developmental scale despite their typological distance. The application of PT to Arabic is discussed in Mansouri (2005).

Özdemir (2004) applies the comparative approach developed by Håkansson et al. to the study of trilingual language development in Turkish-German children learning English. She uses the existing PT hierarchies for English (L3) and German (L2) and develops a Turkish PT hierarchy. All three languages are profiled on the basis of PT hierarchies. This permits a comparison of their levels of development across all three languages.

References

Andersen, R. 1984. The one-to-one principle. *Language Learning* 34: 77-95.

Bettoni, C. and Di Biase, B. 2005. Sviluppo obbligato e progresso morfosintattico – un caso di Processabilità in italiano L2. *ITALS (Italiano Lingua Seconda)*

Bresnan, J. 2001. *Lexical-functional syntax.* Malden, MA: Blackwell.

Clahsen, H. 1984. The acquisition of German word order: A test case for cognitive approaches to L2 development, pp. 219-242. In R. Anderson (ed.), *Second languages*. Rowley, MA: Newbury House.

Cook, V. 2001. Second language learning and language teaching. 3rd Edition. Arnold: London

Dewaele, J.-M. & Veronique, D. 2001. Gender assignment and gender agreement in advanced French interlanguage: a cross-sectional study. Bilingualism. Language and Cognition 4:3, 275-297.

Di Biase, B. & Kawaguchi, S. 2002. Exploring the typological Plausibility of Processability Theory: Language development in Italian second language and Japanese second language. *Second Language Research, 18*, 274-302.

Gao, X. 2004. Noun phrase morphemes and topic development in L2 Mandarin Chinese: A processability perspective. PhD thesis, Victoria University of Wellington, New Zealand.

Garrett, M. F. 1976. Syntactic process in sentence production. In R. Wales & E. Walker (eds.), New approaches to language mechanisms, 231-256. Amsterdam: North Holland.

—. 1980. Levels of processing in sentence production. In B. Butterworth (ed.), *Language production: Vol. 1. Speech and Talk*, pp. 177-220. London: Academic Press.

—. 1982. Production of speech: observations from normal and pathological language use. In A.W. Ellis (ed.), *Normality and pathology in cognitive functions,* pp. 19-76. London: Academic Press.

Glahn, E., Håkansson, G., Hammarberg, B., Holmen, A., Hvenekilde, A., & Lund, K. 2001. 'Processability in Scandinavian second language acquisition.'. *Studies in Second Language Acquisition* 23: 389-416.

Håkansson, G., Salameh, E.-K. & Nettelbladt, U. 2003. 'Measuring language development in bilingual children: Swedish-Arabic children with and without language impairment'. *Linguistics* 41: 255-288.

Hammarberg, B. 1996. Examining the processability theory: the case of adjective agreement in Swedish. In Kellerman, E., Weltens, B. & T. Bongaerts (eds.). EUROSLA 6. A selection of papers. *Toegepaste talwetenschap in artikelen* 55. 1996:2, 75-88.

Harada, A. 2004. The acquisition of English modal verbs by Japanese learners. MA dissertation. University of Western Sydney.

Itani-Adams, Y. 2003. From word to phrase in Japanese -English bilingual first language acquisition. Paper presented at The MARCS seminar, 15 September 2003, University of Western Sydney.

Iwasaki, J. 2003. The acquisition of verbal morphosyntax in JSL by a child learner. Paper presented at 13th Biennial Conference of the JSAA, July 2-4, 2003, Brisbane.

Jordan, G. 2004. Theory construction in second language acquisition. Benjamins: Amsterdam.

Kaplan, R. & Bresnan J. 1982. Lexical-Functional Grammar: a formal system for grammatical representation. In Bresnan, J. (ed.), *The mental representation of grammatical relations,* pp. 173-281. Cambridge, MA: The MIT Press.

Kawaguchi, S. 2005. Argument structure and syntactic development in Japanese as a second language. In: Pienemann, M. (ed.) 2005. *Cross-linguistic aspects of Processability Theory*. J. Benjamins: Amsterdam/ New York. 253-298.

Kempen, G. & Hoenkamp, E. 1987. An incremental procedural grammar for sentence formulation. *Cognitive Science, 11*, 201-258.

Keßler, Jörg-U. 2006. Assessing EFL-development online: A feasibility study of Rapid Profile. In: Fethi Mansouri (ed.) 2006. *Bilingualism and theory-driven second language acquisition research.* Cambridge Scholars Press.

Levelt, W.J.M. 1989. *Speaking. From intention to articulation*. Cambridge, MA: MIT Press.

Mansouri, F. 2000. Grammatical Markedness and Information Processing in the Acquisition of Arabic as a Second Language, pp. 1-260, *LINCOM EUROPA* Academic Publishers, Munchen, Germany.

—. 2005. Agreement morphology in Arabic as a second language: Typological features and their processing implications. In: Pienemann, M. (ed.). *Cross-linguistic aspects of Processability Theory*. John Benjamins: Amsterdam. 117- 153.

Meisel, J. M. 1983.Strategies of second language acquisition: More than one kind of simplification". In R. W. Andersen (ed.). *Pidginisation and crelisation as language acquisition.* Rowley. Mass.: Newbury House. 120-157.

Meisel, J. M., Clahsen, H. and Pienemann, M. 1981. Determining developmental stages in natural second language acquisition. *Studies in Second Language Acquisition*. 3. 109-135.

Özdemir, B. 2004. Language development in Turkish-German bilingual children and the implications for English as a third language. MA thesis. University of Paderborn, Germany.

Pickering, M.J., Branigan, H.P. and McLean, J.F. 2002. Constituent Structure is Formulated in One Stage. Journal of Memory and Language, 46, 586-605.

Pienemann, M. 1981. *Der Zweitspracherwerb ausländischer Arbeiterkinder.* Bonn: Bouvier.

—. 1998. *Language Processing and Second Language Development: Processability Theory*, John Benjamins, 366p.

—. (ed.) 2005a. Cross-lingistic aspects of Processability Theory. John Benjamins: Amsterdam/ New York.

—. 2005 b. An outline of Processability Theory. In: Pienemann, M. (ed.) (in press a). Cross-lingistic aspects of Processability Theory. John Benjamins: Amsterdam/ New York

—. 2005 c. Discussing PT. In: Pienemann, M. (ed.) (in press a). Cross-linguistic aspects of Processability Theory. John Benjamins: Amsterdam/ New York.

Pienemann, M. and Håkansson, G. 1999. A unified approach towards the development of Swedish as L2: A processability account. *Studies in Second Language Acquisition*, 21, 383-420.

Pienemann, M., Di Biase, B. and Kawaguchi, S. 2005. Extending Processability Theory. In: Pienemann, M. (ed.) 2005 a. Cross-linguistic aspects of Processability Theory. John Benjamins: Amsterdam/ New York

Pienemann, M., Di Biase, B. Kawaguchi, S. and Hakansson, G. 2005. L1 transfer typological distance and processability. In: Pienemann, M. (ed.) 2005a. Cross-linguistic aspects of Processability Theory. John Benjamins: Amsterdam/ New York

Pienemann, M., Di Biase, B., Kawaguchi, S. and Håkansson, G. 2005. Processing constraints on L1 transfer. In J. F. Kroll & A. M. B. DeGroot (Eds.). Handbook of Bilingualism: Psycholinguistic Approaches. New York: Oxford University Press.

Schwarze, C. 2002. Representation and variation: On the development of Romance auxiliary syntax. In M. Butt & T. Holloway King (Eds.), *Time over Matter: Diachronic Perspectives in Morphosyntax.* .Stanford, California: CSLI Publications

Slobin, D.I. 1973. Cognitive prerequisites for the development of grammar. In: C.A. Ferguson and D.I. Slobin (eds.) Studies of child language development. New York: Holt, Rinehart and Winston. 175-208.

Taylor R. 2004. Spanish L2 from a Processability perspective: two developmental case studies. BA (Honours) dissertation. University of Western Sydney.

Vigliocco, G., Butterworth, B. & Garrett, M.F. 1996. Subject-verb agreement in Spanish and English: differences in the role of conceptual constraints. Cognition, 61, 261-298.

Vigliocco, G., Butterworth, B. and Semenza, C. 1995: Constructing subject–verb agreement in speech: the role of semantic and morphological factors. *Journal of Memory and Language 34,* 186–215.

White, L. 1991. Second language competence versus second language performance: UG or processing strategies?. In L. Eubank (ed.), Point -

counterpoint: Universal grammar in the second language, pp. 67-189. Amsterdam: John Benjamins.

Wimsatt, W.C. 1986. Developmental constraints, generative entrenchment and the innate-acquired distinction. In W. Bechtel (ed.), Integrating scientific disciplines, pp. 185-208. Dordrecht: Martinus Nijhoff.

—. 1991. Generative entrenchment in development and evolution. MS Dept of Philosophy, University of Chicago.

Zhang, Y. 2001. *Second language acquisition of Chinese grammatical morphemes: A processability perspective*. PhD thesis. The Australian National University, Canberra.

—. 2002. A processing approach to the L2 acquisition of Chinese grammatical morpheme. In B. Di Biase (ed.), *Developing a second language. Acquisition, processing and pedagogy of Arabic, Chinese, English, Italian.*

—. 2004. Processing constraints, categorial analysis and the second language acquisition of the Chinese adjective suffix *-de*(ADJ). *Language Learning*, 54/3, 437-468.

—. 2005. Processing and formal instruction in the L2 acquisition of five Chinese grammatical morphemes. In: Pienemann, M. (ed.). *Cross-linguistic aspects of Processability Theory.* John Benjamins: Amsterdam/ New York, 155-177.

CHAPTER 3

LEXICAL MAPPING IN PROCESSABILITY THEORY: A CASE STUDY IN JAPANESE

Satomi Kawaguchi

The impact of the interplay between principles of discourse information and linguistic structure in the learner's system is one of the central issues in recent studies in second language acquisition (SLA) (e.g. Dimroth and Starren 2003). This chapter aims to introduce the Unmarked Alignment Hypothesis and the Lexical Mapping Hypothesis in current extensions of Processability Theory (Pienemann 1998 Pienemann; Di Biase & Kawaguchi 2005) and presents a preliminary empirical study from Japanese as a second language (JSL) in order to support these hypotheses. The two hypotheses are designed to explain second language development of argument-function mapping at the Syntactic-Pragmatic interface. I will show how the Lexical Mapping Theory (Bresnan and Kanerva 1989; Bresnan 2001, Dalrymple 2001) within the framework of Lexical Functional Grammar (LFG; Bresnan 2001) contributes to explaining this interface, using Japanese as an example.

Processability Theory (Pienemann 1998, Pienemann et. al. 2005) is a processing-oriented approach to second language development. In the original version of Processability Theory (1998), the concept of "feature unification" explains the developmental sequence of L2 morphosyntax where the acquisition proceeds the following order: single words (no morphological variation) > lexical operation> phrasal operation> interphrasal operation. For example, in English, marking of past tense on the verb (i.e., *-ed*) belongs to lexical operations, as it does not require any feature unification with any other constituent in the encoding process. On the other hand NP/VP agreement requires phrasal unification between the head and its modifier. An example of NP agreement is the plural marker *–s* in such noun phrases as *two dogs*. An example of VP agreement is the auxiliary verb and the appropriate participial form of the main verb (i.e., "be" auxiliary and *–ing*, "have" auxiliary and *–ed/ -en*). Further, an English example of inter-phrasal operation is *–s* on verb, indicating that the attribute of its subject is "third person" and "singular". This subject-verb agreement requires inter-phrasal operation between NP_{SUBJ} and VP in the encoding process. Thus, Processability Theory predicts the following acquisitional trajectory and empirical studies (e.g. Pienemann 1998) have supported this prediction: *-ed* (Past) > *-s* (plural) / *be + -ing* / *have + ed* > *-s* (third person singular).

Processability Theory has been applied to various languages so far, such as German (Pienemann 1998), Swedish (Pienemann and Håkansson 1999), Italian (Di Biase and Kawaguchi 2002), Japanese (Di Biase and Kawaguchi 2002; Kawaguchi 2005a & b, Iwasaki 2003, Itani-Adams 2003), Chinese (Zhang 2001, 2002, 2004, 2005), Arabic (Mansouri 1997, 2002, 2005) and Spanish (Taylor 2004), and has contributed to characterizing L2 development. However, PT's predictive range for L2 morphosyntax has been mainly concerned with accounting for obligatory operations such as agreement phenomena and word order rules. The extension of PT (Pienemann et. al. 2005) adds the developmental dimension of speaker-induced discourse-pragmatic choices (e.g., passive, topicalization) and their marking in syntactic and morphological structure. This extension of PT is especially useful in characterizing development of higher stages of L2 development, that is, after the establishment of canonical order. In this chapter, I will introduce two hypotheses from the extension of PT, the Unmarked Alignment Hypothesis and the Lexical Mapping Hypothesis, and show how these hypotheses contribute to explaining thematic argument-grammatical function (GF) mapping in second language acquisition.

The remaining sections are organized as follows: In Section 2, the issue of pragmatic-syntax interface is discussed. Section 3 summarizes PT-based hypotheses, the Unmarked Alignment Hypothesis and the Lexical Mapping Hypothesis. Section 4 presents the structural outcome in Japanese L2 based on the two new hypotheses, while Section 5 presents a preliminary empirical study supporting these hypotheses.

Pragmatic-syntax interface

The same eventuality can be mapped onto various syntactic forms because the speaker takes a certain perspective on the conceptual structure to be expressed, out of one or more alternatives (Levelt 1989). Let us consider the event where Peter is patting a dog. If the speaker wants to express what Peter did, then one possible structural outcome would be "Peter pats the dog". But this is not the only possible way to express the event that the sentence is describing. If the speaker answers the question "what happened to the dog?", then it is quite likely that the speaker will take up the dog as the grammatical subject and construct a sentence like "the dog was patted by Peter" as "the dog" is already established as the topic of the discourse.

Also, different formulations with different lexical verbs may express the same thematic structure, for example, *Peter gave a bone to the dog* and *the dog received a bone from Peter*. According to Levelt (1989) these different formulations of the same thematic structure are due to different perspectives. The former example with the verb *give* is expressed from the agent's point of view, whereas the latter one with *receive* is from the recipient's viewpoint. Levelt added that "(a) speaker must decide not only which roles in a scene he wants to express (he may want to ignore the agent completely…) but also which of those roles are to be foregrounded" (97). Although the selection of one formulation over the other may enhance the speaker's expressivity (such as by choosing to foreground or background certain information), the choice of a certain verb such as *receive* may impose learning difficulty on the learner since such verbs are claimed to be "exceptional" verbs (Pinker 1984), because a recipient, but not the usual agent, occupies the highest thematic role of the argument. One L1 acquisition study reports that "exceptional" verbs are acquired later (Slobin 1985). This may be true with the acquisition of L2 as well. PT predicts that syntactic formulations using "exceptional" verbs such as *receive* and *please* show delayed acquisition, due to non-canonical argument-function mapping (see Section 3).

Further, language-specific constraints may affect the structural outcome. For example, it is perfectly natural to say "a typhoon smashed the house" in English. But the inanimate agentive subject is not preferable in many languages. A solution for avoiding inanimate agents as the grammatical subject with these languages is to employ passive construction where *the house* becomes the clause subject, resulting in such sentences as "the house was/got smashed because of a typhoon". Alternatively, the intransitive verb may be selected as in "the house collapsed because of a typhoon". In these sentences "typhoon" is encoded not as a verb's argument but as an adjunct. Thus, native speakers use a range of (more or less language-specific) devices in order to mark a particular entity or event/state in the message as being of particular importance. Discourse and pragmatic factors affect such choices concerning information distribution over the sentence structure: the speaker's perspective-taking, matters of topicality, agency, humanness/animacy, foregrounding/backgrounding of information, etcetera.

According to Levelt (1989), there are at least three ways in which languages encode the entity/event/state of conceptual importance:

1. attribution of a grammatically prominent function, that is, the subject function
2. attribution of a syntactically prominent position: initial, or early in the sentence

3. attribution of prosodic prominence

The first point in the above list concerns the mapping between thematic roles and grammatical function (i.e., mapping between a(rgument)-structure and f(unctional)-structure, in the terminology of LFG). An example of this type is active/passive alternation, that is, where the active construction maps the agent role to the subject function while the passive maps the patient role to the subject function. The second point concerns the linear organization of the sentence (i.e., mapping between f(unctional)-structure and c(onstituent)-structure, in the terminology of LFG). For example, topicalization and object scrambling are good linguistic devices for placing a constituent of conceptual prominence to the sentence initial position. As for the third point, pitch accent can be utilized. This chapter focuses on the attribution of a grammatically prominent function (i.e., the first point in the above list). See Zhang's chapter in this volume discussing the attribution of a syntactically prominent position (i.e., the second point in the above list).

According to Levelt's discourse model (1989), the most prominent entity in the Conceptualizer activates its lemma in the Formulator. Consequently, its lemma becomes available first and is encoded in a syntactically prominent function/position in the sentence, namely the grammatical subject, and/or early in the sentence. Levelt believes such organization is effective because it is easier for the interlocutor to process information when he/she has a chance to know the topic which is going to be talked about at the beginning of the sentence. Choice of a specific grammatical construction over another ensures effective communication. On the other hand, this may create structural complexity and impose learning difficulty. Therefore, the choice of a specific grammatical structure may not be available for the learner when he/she has not developed the needed procedural skill. The extension of PT (Pienemann et. al. 2005) explores this pragmatic-syntactic interface and adds the developmental dimension of speaker-induced discourse-pragmatic choices and their marking in syntactic and morphological structure.

Lexical Mapping and Processability Theory

In the above section, I explained that grammar allows more than one form for expressing a target linguistic context. Also, all languages have various linguistic devices for directing attention by promoting or demoting the participant/entity. This sort of operation is explained by the mapping between thematic roles and grammatical function. Many linguists (e.g. Jackendoff 1972; Foley & Van Valin 1984; Givón 1984) have suggested a universal hierarchy of thematic roles, as in (1). This hierarchy orders the relative prominence of the argument of a predicator: the higher the level, the more prominent. So the most prominent role is universally the agent. This means that the agent is more likely to be encoded as the verb's core-argument rather than non-argument (Bresnan 2001). On the other hand, the locative role, located at the bottom of the hierarchy, is less prominent and likely to be encoded as non core-argument rather than core-argument.

(1) Thematic hierarchy (Bresnan 2001, 307)
Agent > Beneficiary > experiencer/goal > Instrument > Patient/Theme > Locative

Grammatical functions also have a hierarchical relationship according to their prominence, as in (2). All core argument functions are more prominent than non core-argument functions.

(2) relational hierarchy[1] (Keenan and Comrie 1977, referred in Bresnan 2001, 96)

core (SUBJ > OBJ > OBJ_θ) > noncore (OBL_θ > COMPL > ADJUNCT)

SUBJ > OBJ > OBJ_θ > OBL_θ > COMPL > ADJUNCT

Pienemann et al. (2005) propose thematic role-grammatical function mapping as a second set of principles for PT in addition to the principle of "unification". The inclusion of this new principle expands the range of syntactic structures covered by the PT hierarchy, including passive, raising and causative, which were not included in the PT hierarchy in Pienemann (1998). Let us look at the mapping of the two sentences, *Peter patted the dog* and *the dog was patted by Peter*. Using a simplified version of Jackendoff's (1983) representation of conceptual structure, the eventuality described with these two sentences is represented in Figure 1 as below.

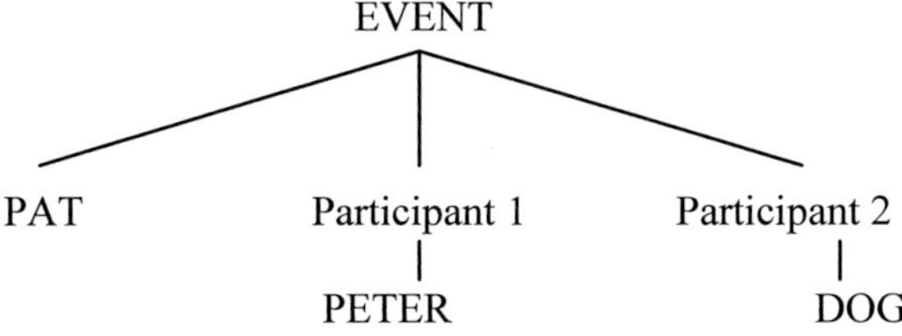

Figure 1. Conceptual structure of Peter patting a dog

An event PAT involves two participants, namely Participant 1 "PETER" and Participant 2 "DOG". Different linguistic realisations of this conceptual structure depend on the speaker's perspective: how to associate the participant's thematic role with the grammatical function. This sort of grammatical mapping operation is formalized by Lexical Mapping Theory (LMT) within the framework of Lexical Functional Grammar (LFG; Alsina 1996; Bresnan 2001; Bresnan and Kanerva 1989). In LMT, the mapping between the thematic role and the grammatical function is referred as a(rgument)- to f(unctional)-structure mapping while the mapping between the syntactic element and grammatical function as c(onstituent)- to f(unctional)-structure mapping. The association of these two arguments in the three different, but parallel levels of representation is schematically shown below, where "x" and "y" in the parentheses correspond to Participant 1 and Participant 2 respectively.

(3)

a. Association of three different levels of representations for *Peter patted the dog*.

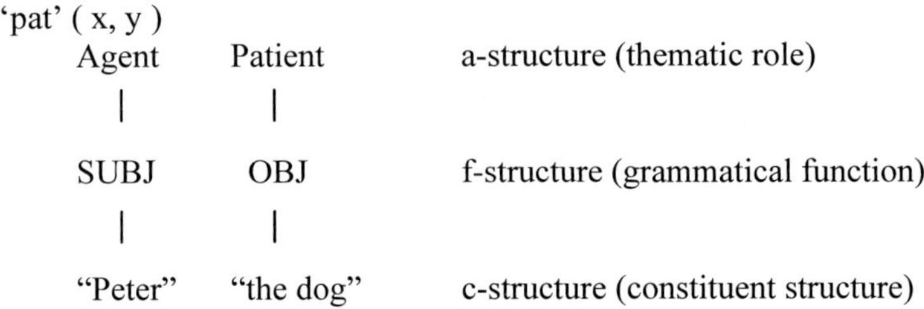

b. Association of three different levels of representations for *the dog was patted by Peter*.

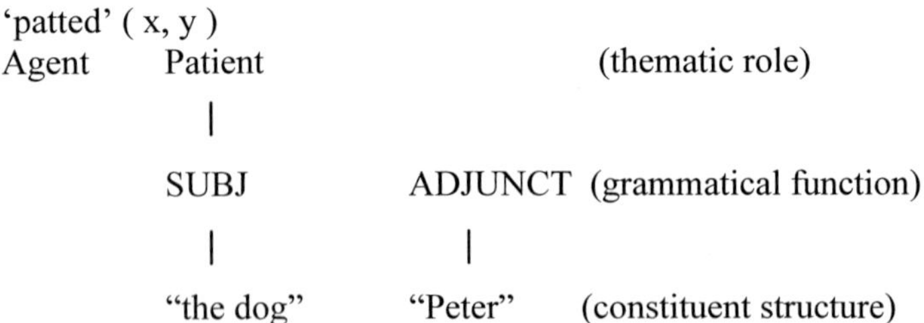

The example (3a) shows that the verb *pat* takes two arguments "x" and "y" at the conceptual levels, which fulfil the thematic roles of the agent and the patient. These two roles are mapped onto the subject and the object respectively. On the other hand, with the verb *patted* in (3b), the passive counterpart of (3a), the patient, but not the agent, is linked to the subject function. Further, the agent of the eventuality is demoted, and realized not as core-argument but as an oblique. Therefore, the passive construction is a linguistic device to give more prominence to the patient role rather than the agent role. Now look at this association from the view of the hierarchical relation of prominence described in (1) and (2). Notice that the relative hierarchy of the two thematic roles, Agent and Patient, and their associated grammatical roles, SUBJ(ect) and OBJ(ect), coincide in (3 a): Agent > Patient and SUBJ > OBJ. However, it is not the case in (3 b): Agent > Patient but ADJUNCT < SUBJ.

According to Pinker's linking rule (1984), canonical mapping occurs when the lexical entry of the verb specifies thematic roles for its arguments that are associated with their grammatical function without crossing the links between the two tiers in Figure 2. Therefore, (3 a.) is canonical mapping but (3 b.) is not.

SUBJ	OBJ	OBLIQUE	(grammatical functions)
Agent	theme/patient	goal/source/location	(thematic relations)

Figure 2. Canonical mapping following Pinker (1984: 298-307)

More precise mechanisms of the linking rule in Lexical Mapping Theory are found in Bresnan and Kanerva (1986), Bresnan (2001, 302-321) and Dalrymple (2001, 202-215).

The choice of different structural mappings (e.g., active/passive alternation) is useful for encoding discourse information, by promoting and demoting prominence on a particular argument role in the linguistic structure. However, although the choice is available to the mature speaker of a language, this may not the case with the L2 learner. This is because a particular mapping may yield some syntactic complexity which the learner may not be able to handle, due to lack of the processing resources required. PT predicts that the learner initially can handle only canonical, default, mapping because it is the least costly way of organizing syntax. As a result, the language beginner produces only the canonical order. Then gradually he/she acquires the resources to handle non-canonical mapping.

In the following Section, I introduce PT's (Pienemann et. al. 2005) two new hypotheses; (1) the Unmarked Alignment Hypothesis which explains the initial syntax in SLA and; (2) the Lexical Mapping Hypothesis which explains gradual development of attributing prominence to a particular thematic role as well as suppressing a thematic role in non-default mapping.

The Unmarked Alignment Hypothesis

This hypothesis explains initial syntax in language acquisition and is defined as follows:

> In second language acquisition learners will initially organise syntax by mapping the most prominent semantic role available onto the subject (i.e. the most prominent grammatical role). The structural expression of the subject, in turn, will occupy the most prominent linear position in c-structure, namely the initial position (Pienemann, et. al., p229).

Like many other approaches to explaining language acquisition (e.g., Meisel, 1991; Pinker 1984, 1989; Slobin, 1985) PT predicts "canonical order" as the initial syntactic alignment. This is language-specific. For example, the canonical order in English, German, Italian, and others, is SVO, while it is SOV in Japanese, Turkish, Korean and others. In LFG this may be viewed as an optimal, unmarked alignment of the most prominent role in the argument structure hierarchy (the "agent" role) mapping onto the universally most prominent grammatical function (the subject) occupying the most prominent position in surface structure (initial) as in Figure 3 below (see the universal thematic hierarchy in (1) and the [functional] relational hierarchy in (2)).

pat < *x, y* >

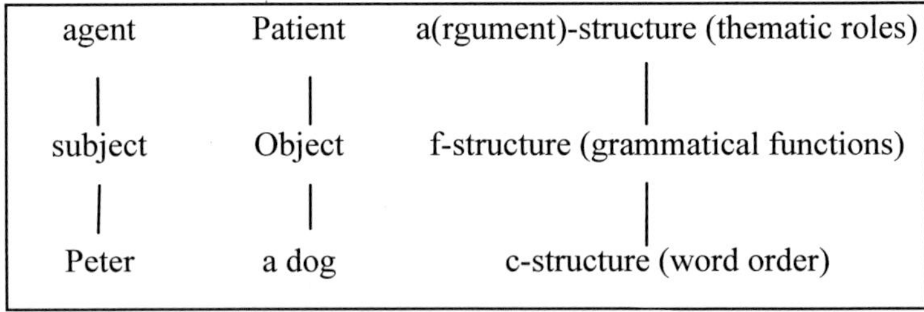

Figure 3. Canonical mapping: Peter pats a dog

The mapping of this canonical sentence resulted from a default linking between the thematic role and the grammatical function. In terms of discourse information, this sentence is neutral in the sense that no NP receives an emphatic expression (provided no accent pitch is placed on any constituent of the sentence). In processing terms, canonical order is computationally the least costly means of organizing syntax (Pinker, 1984, 1989). This is evident from Sasaki's (1998) study showing that both Japanese native speakers and learners of Japanese L2 exhibited the shortest latencies and highest accuracy rate for identifying the agent in the canonical (active) order sentence compared to non-canonical sentences (in terms of both word order and voice). Sasaki attributed this result to the lower processing load involved for the task in canonical sentences. Concerning the unmarked or canonical order, Choi (1999, 29) wrote:

> The unmarked or canonical order is the order which is not contextually restricted or constrained. In other words, the unmarked order is context-neutral. This can be interpreted as meaning that the unmarked order, or the phrase structure which results in that order, is determined only by sentence-internal information, i.e., the morphological or syntactic properties of the component elements of the sentence, and is not influenced by sentence-external factors such as discourse-contextual information.

As in Choi's (1999, 2001) claim, canonical order is context-neutral. Therefore, in discourse non-canonical order may be a preferable option for the mature speaker of a language, because such sentences may be able to encode such information as topic, focus, foreground/background, definite/indefinite, thus fulfilling discourse expressiveness. However, the Unmarked Alignment Hypothesis predicts that the syntax which the second language learner can process is limited to canonical order initially. In other words, the language beginner lacks the procedural skills to encode pragmatic factors by utilising non-canonical mapping. As the Lexical Mapping Hypothesis below explains, non-canonical mapping requires functional assignment to the NPs. This procedure is placed higher in PT stages (i.e., sentence-procedure).

Lexical Mapping Hypothesis

This hypothesis concerns subsequent syntactic development after the establishment of canonical order in relation to discourse information based on non-default mapping of semantic argument roles onto grammatical structure (technically, the association between argument-structure and functional-structure). According to Kawaguchi and Di Biase (2005) the hypothesis is defined as:

> L2 learners initially map the most prominent thematic role onto SUBJ and gradually learn how to attribute prominence to a particular thematic role, e.g., promoting the patient (rather than the agent) role to SUBJ, first in single clauses such as in passive constructions and later in complex predicates such as Causative constructions (e.g., in Japanese or Romance).

Thus, acquisition of procedural skill for non-canonical mapping gives the learner more structural choices which reflect pragmatic factors. Pinker (1984) points out non-canonical mapping occurs from at least two different sources: (1)

intrinsically non-canonical "exceptional" verbs such as *receive* and *please*, which do not conform to a canonical association between argument structure and grammatical functions and; (2) non-basic verb forms such as passives. We look at these two different sources of non-canonicity in turn, below.

According to Levelt (1989), the message structure underlying the sentences "Tanya gave the book to Martin" and "Martin received the book from Tanya" is the same. However, the choice of one sentence over the other is related to: "(w)hether the speaker will formulate the one or the other sentence in the presence of this semantic structure depends on, among other things, whether TANYA or MARTIN is the topic" (95). Superficially, both sentences are of the SVO linear order. But in terms of lexical mapping, the former sentence exhibits canonical and the latter non-canonical association.

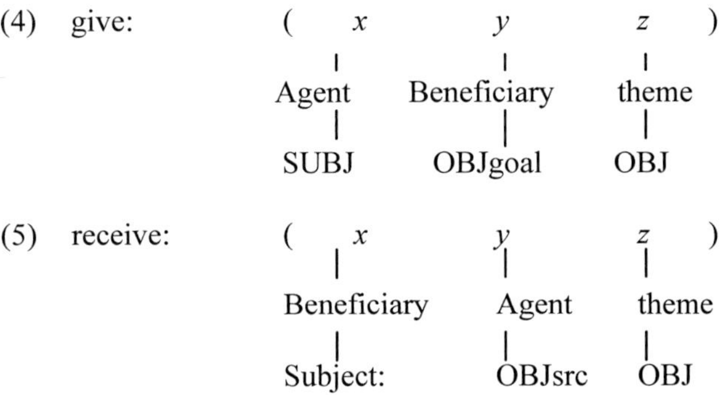

The verb *give* has three participants, *x*, *y* and *z*. The most prominent participant role *x* is linked to the most prominent thematic role, Agent, and it is mapped onto the most prominent grammatical function, SUBJ. This mapping signifies canonical association. As for the verb *receive*, on the other hand, the less prominent thematic role, Beneficiary, links to the most prominent argument *x*, which is mapped onto the most prominent grammatical function, SUBJ. Obviously, this association is not canonical. It is reported that in first language learning, the verbal lexicon which requires intrinsically non-canonical mapping is acquired later. For example, Slobin (1985) observed that the Japanese verb *morau* ("receive") whose recipient argument maps onto the subject (and takes nominative case) is acquired late by Japanese children. In experiments, Marantz (1982) found that three and four year-old children could easily learn made-up verbs whose agent and patient arguments were expressed as subjects and objects respectively. However, the same informants had difficulties learning verbs with opposite correspondences.

The second type is non-basic verb forms. An example of this is the passive, of which I have shown its non-canonical association of argument-function in the previous Section (see example (3 b.)). Another example is the causative verb in Japanese and Romance languages. Both verb forms include what LMT calls "morpholexical operations". "Morpholexical operations affect lexical argument structures by adding and suppressing thematic roles" (Bresnan & Kanerva 1989, 26). For example, the passive suppresses the highest thematic argument (i.e., agent). In the case of the causative, it adds an extra thematic role. According to Matsumoto (1996), Japanese coercive causatives involve causer-controlled sub-events where the logical subject of the embedded clause is fused to the patient of the matrix clause. Consequently, the Japanese causative involves an embedded sub-event at the a-structure level, but this is realized as a single clause in f-structure. Alsina (1996) assumes that the causative verb and the base verb undergo predicate composition yielding one, single, complex, a-structure (186). The sentence in (6 a.) exemplifies the Japanese causative sentence. In (6 a.) *musume* (daughter) is the recipient-patient of the causative verb as well as the agent of the base verb. Thus, two thematic roles are fused into one, in the f-structure. As a result, the causative verb and the base verb behave like one single predicate in the light of case assignment (Alsina, 1996). The resulting a-onto f-structure mapping looks like (6 b.):

(6) a. *Yumiko-ga musume-ni susi-o tukur-ase-ta*
Yumiko-NOM daughter-DAT sushi-ACC make-CAUS-PAST
"Yumiko get her daughter to make sushi"

b.
'cause < Agent, Recipient-Patient, make <Agent Patient>>' a-structure
SUBJ OBJ OBJpatient f-structure

Causative construction involves non-linear mapping due to the fusion of thematic roles in the event and sub-event in the a(rgument)-structure. Therefore, the production of causative structure requires appropriate functional assignment.

Thus, LMT serves as a basis for explaining the linearity/non-linearity of the mapping of a-structure onto f-structure. In summary, in canonical order sentences, the highest thematic role of the predicate is mapped onto SUBJ. This can be done by the canonical association between thematic roles and grammatical functions. However, in non-canonical order sentences such as passivisation, the initial argument of the predicator is suppressed. The Agent function is linked to the non-initial argument. This triggers the non-linearity of lexical mapping and S-procedure is required for construction of the sentence functional assignment. Figure 4 below summarizes the Lexical Mapping Hypothesis.

a- to f- structure mapping	*Structural outcomes*
Non-default mapping (single clause)	Passive Complex predicates e.g. Causative
↑	↑
Default mapping, i.e., Most prominent thematic role is mapped onto SUBJ	Canonical Order

Figure 4 Lexical Mapping Hypothesis (after Pienemann, Di Biase and Kawaguchi 2005, 246)

Prediction in Japanese L2 based on the two hypotheses

This subsection presents predictions in Japanese L2 based on the two hypotheses, the Unmarked Alignment Hypothesis and the Lexical Mapping Hypothesis. Major typological characteristics of Japanese are as follows: Japanese is typologically head-last and its canonical order is SOV. Unlike English, word order in Japanese itself does not play a major role in encoding syntactic relations. Instead, similarly to other head last languages like Korean, the NP's grammatical or semantic relation to the predicate is indicated by the post nominal case particle such as *–ga* (nominative), *-o* (accusative) or *–wa* (topic). Japanese is typologically a NOM-ACC language (Shibatani 1990) and usually NOM marks both transitive and intransitive SUBJ while ACC marks transitive OBJ. Another important typological character is nominal ellipsis. Japanese uses extensive nominal ellipsis. In spoken Japanese, redundant elements tend to be omitted, and all constituents including nouns, postpositional nominal particles and verbs can be omitted as long as they are recoverable from the context (Hinds 1982). Therefore, ellipsis is normally used where a pronoun is typically used in English.

	The Unmarked Alignment Hypothesis	**The Lexical Mapping Hypothesis**	**Predicted structural outcomes in Japanese L2**
Later syntax (Sentence procedure)	Marked orders	Non-default argument mapping: 'Exceptional' verb Non-basic verb form	'Exceptional' verb Non-basic verb form (morpho-lexical operation: passive and causative, complex predicate: benefactives)
↑	↑	↑	↑
Initial syntax (Canonical order procedure)	Canonical order	Canonical order (agent-like role = SUBJ, patient-like role = OBJ)	Canonical order (i.e., (S)OV, TOP_{SUBJ} OV)

Table 1. Prediction of structural outcomes in Japanese L2 based on the Unmarked Alignment Hypothesis and the Lexical Mapping Hypothesis

The predictions based on the Unmarked Alignment Hypothesis and the Lexical Mapping Hypothesis are summarized in Table 1. The second and the third columns show the predictions for the initial and the later syntax in L2 acquisition respectively, based on the two hypotheses. The fourth column shows predictions on the structural outcomes specific to Japanese L2. The initial syntax produced by the learner is restricted to the canonical order, SOV; this applies even when discourse context favours non-canonical mapping. The learner develops non-canonical mapping only after the establishment of canonical order.

In the following, I briefly show the formal representation of Japanese structures. Firstly, Japanese canonical order is SOV, as exemplified in (7). But this includes the null realization of SUBJ in (8), which is a typological characteristic of Japanese.

(7) *Mariko-ga susi-o tabeta.*
Mariko-NOM sushi-ACC eat-PAST
"Mariko ate sushi"

(8) *susi-o tabeta.*
"(she) ate sushi"

I believe that Japanese canonical order includes the TOP(ic)-OBJ-Verb order, where the clausal subject is marked with the topic particle *–wa*. Bresnan (2001, p. 98) claims "the subject is often identified as the default TOP of the clause". In fact, according to LFG, SUBJ is quite unique in the fact that it is both a grammaticised discourse function (like TOP and FOCUS) and an argument function (like OBJECT, OBJ, etc.). Also, Lambrecht (1994) points out that the strong correlation between SUBJ and TOP seems to be a universal feature across language typology. There is a tendency, Lambrecht says, to "equate grammatical subject-predicate structure with pragmatic topic-comment sentence" (136). Therefore the subject is the unmarked expression of the topic.

In some languages such as English, TOP is positionally encoded and appears in the most prominent position (i.e., sentence initial). In Japanese also, TOP tends to appear sentence initially. However, it is also morphosyntactically grammaticised: TOP is indicated by the postnominal particle *–wa*. At the beginning of syntactic acquisition, in fact, lemma access and category procedure do not permit the recognition of grammatical functions of NPs in a sentence. This implies that the second language (L2) learner lacks resources for linking TOP to another grammatical function (such as SUBJ or OBJ). The learner identifies the agent-like semantic function as a default topic and does not differentiate these two (i.e., SUBJ and TOP) functionally. Therefore, Japanese canonical word order in learners' nominal marking may be realized as:

(9)	agent	patient	action	———	a-structure
	ı	ı	ı	———	
	N-*ga/wa*	N-*o*	V		c-structure
	NOM/TOP	ACC			

So the most prominent participant of the eventuality is marked either *–wa* (TOP) or *–ga* (SUBJ) without functional distinction at this stage, as in (10) as well as in (7) and (8).

(10) *Mariko-wa* *susi-o* *tabeta*
Tanaka-TOP susi-ACC eat-PAST
"Mariko ate sushi"

The structure S → SOV is achieved with the phrase structure rule (11) below (after Matsumoto, 1996, p. 57).

(11) S →	XP*	{V, A}
	(↑GF)=↓	↑=↓

The noun marked as TOP coincides with SUBJ and the sentence pattern remains SOV, which is the canonical word order in Japanese. Hence, it is hypothesized to emerge at the stage where canonical mapping is in control (i.e., the Categorial procedure).

The Lexical Mapping Hypothesis predicts various structural outcomes of non-canonical mapping after the establishment of canonical order. Examples of such structures are the passive and the causative, which involve morpholexical operations. I have already shown the mechanism of the passive and the causative in the previous section using Japanese examples (the mapping mechanisms of these structures are universal). Also, the marked mapping mechanism of an "exceptional" verb, *receive*, which is similar to a Japanese verb *morau* "receive" is presented above. Among the structures listed in Table 1, one structure which I have not touched upon yet is the benefactive construction in Japanese, which is shown below.

The auxiliary verbs of giving and receiving are collectively referred to as "benefactives" following Backhouse (1993). In benefactive constructions, the main verb precedes the benefactive auxiliary that contributes the benefactive role. The following three examples represent Japanese benefactives.

(12) a. Give-schema
Mariko-ga kodomo-ni hon-o yon-de ageta
Mariko-NOM child-DAT book-ACC read-COMP give-PAST
"Mariko read a book to the child"

b. Give-schema
Tomodachi-ga musume-ni seetaa-o ande-kureta
friend-NOM my daughter-DAT sweater-ACC knit-COMP give-PAST
"My friend knitted a sweater for my daughter"

c. Receive-schema
*Kodomo-ga Mariko-ni hon-o yon-de mora*tta.
child-NOM Mariko-DAT book-ACC read-COMP receive-PAST
"The child received the favour of Mariko reading a book."

According to Backhouse (1993, 124-125), Japanese benefactive predicates are translated as follows: (a) V-*te ageru*; "(I/we, etc.) do (something for someone)", (b) V-*te kureru* "(someone) does (something as a favour to me/us)" and; (c) V-*te morau* "(I/we, etc.) receive the favour of (someone doing something for us)".

In his LFG analysis, Ishikawa (1985) proposed that Japanese benefactive constructions are functionally biclausal and showed overwhelming supporting evidence, including the insertion of quantifier-like particles such as *–dake* (only) and *–sae* (even) between the main verb and the benefactive auxiliary. Later work by Matsumoto (1996) as well as Shibatani (1994) also supported Ishikawa's analysis. Following Ishikawa's (1985, 152) and Matsumoto's (1996, 48) representation of lexical entry and f-structure respectively, the above three examples of benefactive construction are represented below:

(13) a. lexical entry of *ageru* "give" and f-structure of (12 a.)
lexical entry ageru (give): V
(↑PRED)='*ageru* (give) <benefactor, beneficiary, beneficial event>
(SUBJ) (OBJgoal) (XCOMP)

f-structure

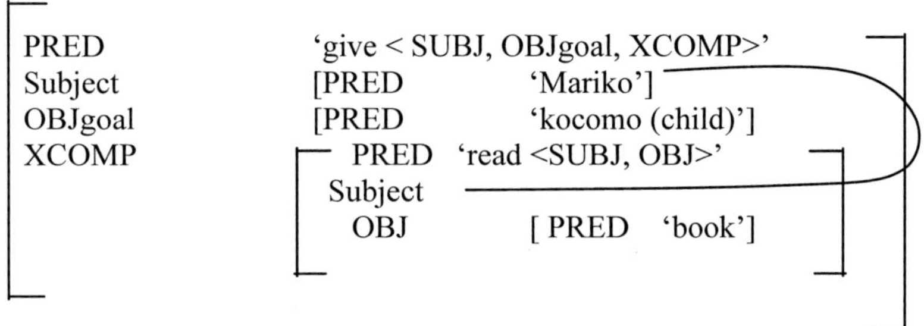

b. lexical entry of *kureru* "give" and f-structure of (12 b.)
kureru (give): V
(↑PRED)='*kureru* (give) <benefactor, beneficiary, beneficial event>
(SUBJ) (OBJgoal) (XCOMP)
I/one of us

f-structure

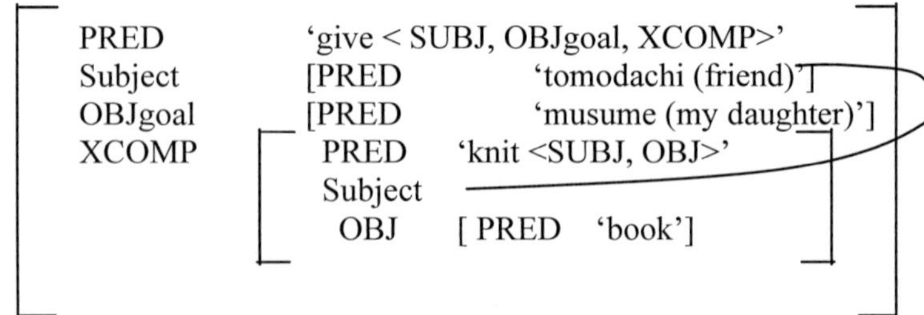

c. lexical entry of *morau* "receive" and f-structure of (12 c.)
receive: V
(↑PRED)='*morau* <beneficiary, benefactor, beneficial event>
(SUBJ) (OBJsource) (XCOMP)

f-structure

PRED	'receive < SUBJ, OBJsrc, XCOMP>'	
Subject	[PRED	'kodomo (child)']
OBJsrc	[PRED	'Mariko']
XCOMP	PRED	'read <SUBJ, OBJ>'
	Subject	
	OBJ [PRED	'book']

All three benefactive predicates take SUBJ, OBJ and XCOPM as arguments. With the two give-schema benefactives in (13 a.-b.), XCOMP's SUBJ is liked to the same function, namely SUBJ, in the matrix clause. This linking is indicated by the line in the f-structure representation. Although these two benefactives take the same argument structure, the lexical entry of the auxiliary *kureru* adds one constraint, which states that the beneficiary is either "I" or the person from "in-group"[2]. With the receive-schema benefactive in (13 c.), XCOMP's SUBJ is linked to the OBJ function rather than the SUBJ in the matrix clause. Notice that the benefactive auxiliary *morau*, "receive" takes an intrinsically non-canonical argument structure, similar to the case when the Japanese benefactive auxiliary verb *morau* functions as the main verb (see 5). Based on the lexical entry and f-structure representations above, lexical mappings between the verb specific semantic role and the grammatical function involved in (12 a.-c.) are informally represented as follows:

(14)

a. Lexical mapping of the sentence *Mariko-ga kodomo-ni hon-o yon-de ageta* "Mariko read a book to the child".

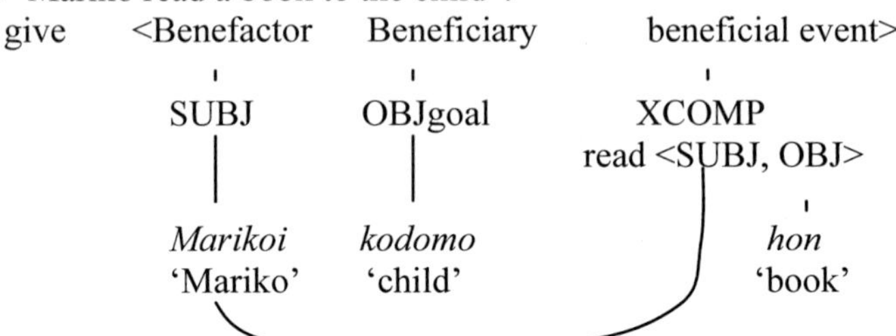

b. Lexical mapping of the sentence *Tomodachi-ga musume-ni seetaa-o ande-kureta* "My friend knitted a sweater for my daughter".

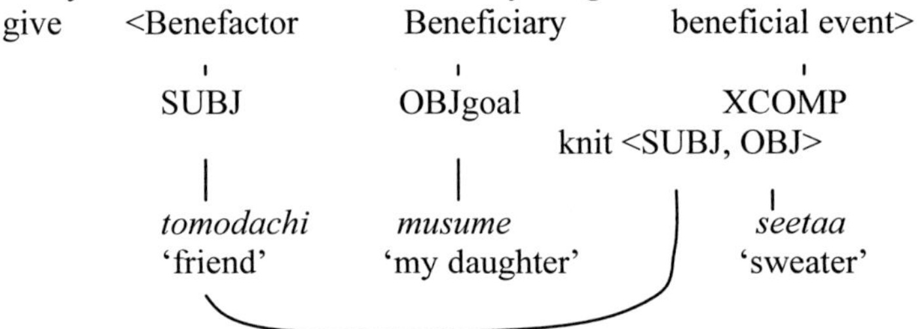

c. Lexical mapping of the sentence *Kodomo-ga Mariko-ni hon-o yon-de moratta* "The child received the favour of Mariko reading a book".

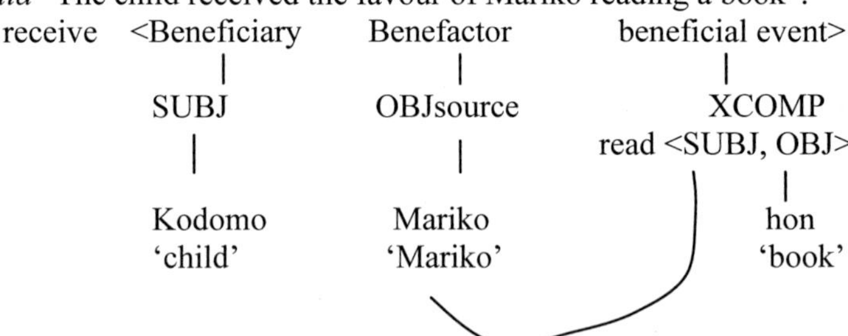

Although all three benefactives in (12 a-c) are superficially SUBJ- OBJ θ - OBJ linear order, which characterizes Japanese canonical order, they are obviously not canonical mapping because they involve a complex predicate where the f-structure of SUBJ in XCOMP is identified with the value of an argument function in a higher matrix. Therefore, all three Japanese benefactives involve non-canonical mapping and thus PT predicts that the learner produces these structures when he/she acquires the skill of s-procedure.

Notice that the sentences (12 a) and (12 c) above express the same eventuality. Most accessible entities (i.e., the currently activated entry) at the conceptual level tend to occupy the sentence initial (or early in the sentence) position. Then the subsequent sentence should be constructed accordingly. The task for the Japanese L2 learners with the benefactive structure includes: assignment of correct grammatical function to the NPs by attaching appropriate case particles, and selection of an appropriate benefactive auxiliary (either give-schema or receive-schema) in order to express the intended meaning. For example, in (12 a-c), the assignment of the case marker to the first NP restricts the subsequent linguistic form: if the speaker starts from *Mariko-ga* (Mariko-NOM) when describing an event, Mariko reading a book for the child, then the subject function is already attributed to the NP and, consequently, it has to receive the benefactor role by choosing a give-schema benefactive, V-*te ageru*. On the other hand, if CHILD is the most accessible entity at the conceptual level and the speaker starts the sentence with the NP, *kodomo-ga* (child-NOM), then the speaker has to choose a receive-schema benefactive, V-*te morau* as its predicate in order to assign the beneficiary role to the NP. However, the L2 learner may not be able to handle this sort of functional assignment in non-canonical mapping when he/she is at the early stage of Japanese L2 learning. It is also possible that the L2 learner tends to choose the V-*te ageru* construction over V-*te kureru* and V-*te morau* and/or that the learner's constructions of V-*te kureru* and V-*te morau* show lower accuracy rates due to an additional processing task: V-*te kureru* involves non-canonical mapping plus an additional constraint on mapping (i.e., the beneficiary role should be linked to "I/one of us") and; V-*te morau* involves non-canonical mapping plus an intrinsically non-canonical argument structure, which imposes an additional speech processing load.

Empirical evidence for the hypotheses from a Japanese L2 study

This section reports a preliminary analysis of argument-function mapping from a three year longitudinal study in Japanese L2. The learner's data are compared with the predictions based on the PT's two hypotheses: the Unmarked Alignment Hypothesis and the Lexical Mapping Hypothesis. Although cross-linguistic experimental studies are necessary in order to validate the universality of these hypotheses, analysis of the longitudinal study shows several strengths. Firstly, it reveals the pattern of developmental sequences across time, showing emergence and periods of increase and decrease, of a particular linguistic phenomenon. It also shows correct and incorrect uses, as well as avoidance at a certain point of second language acquisition. Further, it provides opportunities to investigate the relationship between discourse environment and speech production. Therefore, my analysis here provides an excellent ground for future experimental studies although it aims primarily to serve as support evidence for the two hypotheses.

1. Informant

The informant for the three year-longitudinal study, Linda, is a university student in Sydney, Australia. She is a native speaker of English and was 18 years old at the beginning of the study. She received six hours of instruction from two different instructors for 12 weeks per semester. Data collection started four weeks after she commenced her Japanese studies. Data collection was conducted monthly. Free conversation (between the informant and a native speaker of Japanese) and various tasks including picture story telling tasks and spot the difference tasks were utilized for speech elicitation. Thus, the data is sampled in a close to naturalistic setting. Each session, consisting of between 20 and 30 minutes, was tape-recorded, transcribed and transliterated[3].

2. Method of analysis

Data analysis follows the procedure described below. In order to look at Linda's speech production involving canonical mapping and non-canonical mapping in each session, the frequency of clauses produced by the learner is counted according to the following categories:

a) number of clauses with the canonical transitive verb.
b) number of clauses with the canonical intransitive verb.
c) number of clauses with an "exceptional" verb which intrinsically requires non-canonical mapping (e.g., *morau* "receive", *kariru* "borrow", etc.).
d) number of clauses with the non-basic verb form involving passive, causative or benefactives.

Among the four categories above, a) and b) require canonical mapping while c) and d) require non-canonical mapping. The pattern of a learner's use of verbs belonging to the four different categories is examined across time. Also, the learner's errors concerning argument-function mapping are analysed. Further, as for the clauses with non-basic verb form, a detailed analysis of argument-function mapping is carried out in conjunction with its discourse.

3. Results

Frequency of the clause involving canonical and non-canonical order in Linda's speech

Table 2 represents the distribution of canonical mapping and non-canonical mapping structures observed in the learner's speech production. The learner produced a total of 351 clauses with lexical verbs[4] during the three-year longitudinal study, where 330 and 21 clauses were realized in canonical and non-canonical mapping respectively. The early syntax the learner produced up to Time 3 was restricted to canonical mapping. It is at Time 4, which is around the seventh month after the commencement of learning Japanese L2, that the learner produced a clause involving non-canonical mapping for the first time. Although the frequency is not great, Linda produced non-canonical mapping structures once or more thereafter, except at Time 6.

Time	Total No. of clauses with lexical verb	Canonical mapping	Non-canonical mapping
1 (1st year 1st semester)	1	1	0
2 (1st year 1st semester)	9	9	0
3 (1st year 2nd semester)	12	12	0
4 (1st year 2nd semester)	23	22	1
5 (2nd year 1st semester)	28	26	2
6 (2nd year 1st semester)	22	22	0
7 (2nd year 2nd semester)	11	9	2
8 (2nd year 2nd semester)	43	42	1
9 (3rd year 1st semester)	53	51	2
10 (3rd year 1st semester)	35	29	6
11 (3rd year 2nd semester)	56	54	2
12 (3rd year 2nd semester)	58	53	5
Total	351	330	21

Table 2. Frequency of canonical and non-canonical order in Linda's speech

Figure 2 shows the distribution of canonical mapping with the canonical transitive and canonical intransitive, and non-canonical mapping with "exceptional" verbs: passive, causative and benefactive. Further, Table 3 presents the detailed figures of canonical and non-canonical mappings. In the table, two numbers are listed before and after slash ("/"). The number after the slash indicates the total occurrence of clauses with respective verb type while the number before the slash indicates the frequency of successful deployment of argument–function mapping. But when both of them are zero, simply "0" (zero) is entered in the cell. Therefore, the gap between these numbers before and after the slash indicates the frequency of unsuccessful mapping[5]. Further, the ratio of successful mapping against the total occurrence is listed in parentheses.

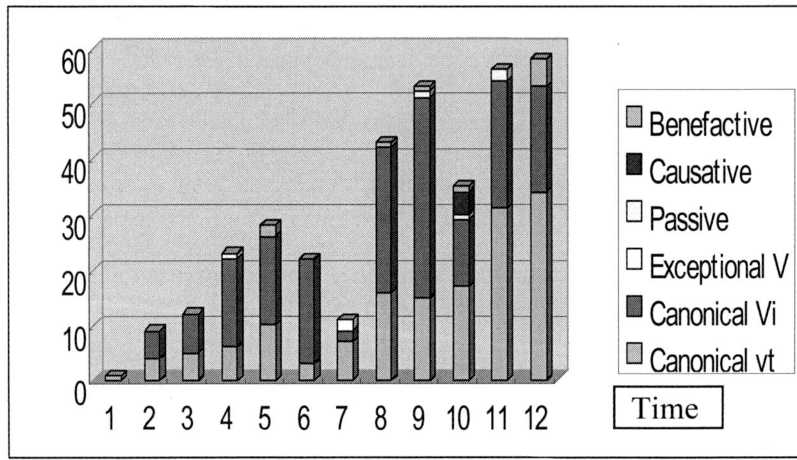

Figure 2. Distribution of clauses with different predicate types in Linda's data

Inter-view No	Total No. of clause	Canonical mapping		Non-canonical mapping			
		Clauses involving transitive verb	Clauses involving intransitive verb	Clauses involving intrinsic-ally non-canonical mapping (i.e., 'exceptional verb')	Non-basic verb form		
					passive	Causa-tive	Bene-factive
Time 1	1	1/1 (1)	0	0	0	0	0
Time 2	9	4/4 (1)	5/5 (1)	0	0	0	0
Time 3	12	4/5 (.8)	7/7 (1)	0	0	0	0
Time 4	23	6/6 (1)	16/16 (1)	1/1 (1)	0	0	0
Time 5	28	10/10 (1)	16/16 (1)	0	0	0	1/2 (.5)
Time 6	22	2/3 (.67)	19/19 (1)	0	0	0	0
Time 7	11	7/7 (1)	2/2 (1)	1/2 (.5)	0	0	0
Time 8	43	16/16 (1)	25/26 (.96)	0	0	0	0/1 (.5)
Time 9	53	15/15	35/36 (.97)	0	1/1 (1)	0	1/1 (1)
Time 10	35	17/17 (1)	11/12 (.92)	0	0/1 (0)	4/4 (1)	1/1 (1)
Time 11	56	31/31 (1)	23/23 (1)	0	2/2 (1)	0	0
Time 12	58	33/34 (.97)	19/19 (1)	0	0	0	3/5 (.6)
Total	351	146/149 (.98)	178/181 (.98)	2/3 (.67)	3/4 (.75)	4/4 (1)	6/10 (.60)

Table 3. Distribution of canonical mapping and non-canonical mapping according to different predicate types

From a glance at Figure 2 and Table 3, we can see that the learner's production was limited to canonical mapping initially and then she gradually became able to produce a variety of constructions involving non-canonical mapping according to the time. In the following, we look at the data in terms of argument-function mapping with the canonical transitive and intransitive verbs, "exceptional" verbs, the passive, the causative and the benefactives, one by one.

a) Canonical transitive verbs and intransitive verbs

The dominant use of canonical mapping structures with both transitive and intransitive verbs is observed throughout the longitudinal study. At the first three interviews (i.e., in the first six months of learning Japanese), she produced canonical mapping only. In Time1, Linda produced many copula sentences but only one lexical verb, as in the following example (15). Although the subject was realized as null, its reference, "I", is recoverable from the context as this utterance was produced when Linda was introducing herself.

(15) *eigo to.. um chotto um nihongo (laugh) -o hanasu hanasimasu*
English and a little Japanese -ACC speak speak-POL.
"(I) speak English and a bit of Japanese"

In the example (15), Linda used the canonical transitive verb *hanasimasu*, "speak". This verb requires Agent and Theme, and these thematic arguments are mapped onto the elliptic subject[6] and the object canonically, as shown below in (16).

(16)

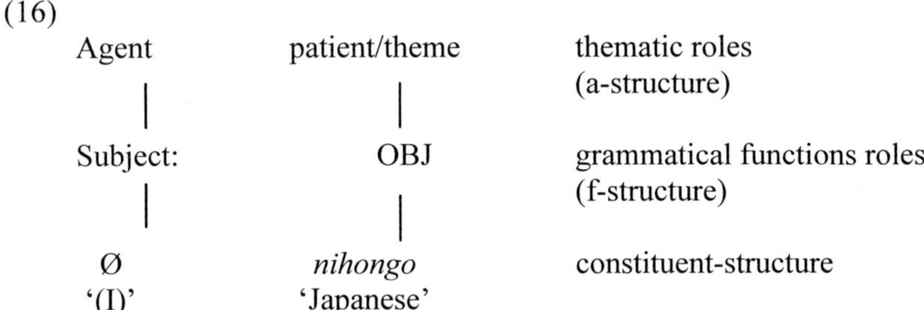

The informant started to produce sentences with (canonical) intransitive verbs from T2. The canonical intransitive verbs Linda used at T2 are *okimasu* "wake up", *nemasu* "sleep" and *ikimasu* "go". All of these verbs require Agent as the sole argument. Linda mapped the agent role canonically onto the grammatical subject in all cases.

More obvious canonical mapping with the *overtly* expressed NP_{SUBJ} was found in the later interviews. Example (17) is taken from Time 4. In this case, the agent, *okaasan* "mother," and the theme, *aisukuriimu* "icecream", are canonically mapped onto the SUBJ and the OBJ respectively.

(17) (T4) *er um (long pause) um okaasan-wa aisukuriimu-o kaimasita*
mother-TOP icecream-ACC buy-PAST.POL.
"My mother bought an icecream"

The most prominent thematic role (i.e., Agent) is linked to the most prominent grammatical function (i.e., Subject) and occupies the most prominent location of the sentence (i.e., the sentence initial). In terms of Optimal LFG (Sells 2001, Lee 2001), this mapping constitutes the most harmonious linking. According to Pinker's (1984) linking rule, the sentence above constitutes a canonical linking because the predicate's argument roles are connected to their grammatical functions without crossing links between the tiers.

b) "Exceptional" verbs

The first non-canonical mapping Linda produced was with the "exceptional" verb *moraimasita* receive-POL.PAST "received" at Time 4 as in example (18). This verb intrinsically requires non-canonical mapping, where the receiver rather than the giver is encoded as a first thematic argument of the predicate.

(18)
(T4) *er* (long pause) *um saakasu-no kippu-o um.. -wa ryoosin ni moraimasita*
Circus GEN ticket-ACC -TOP parents-DAT receive-POL.PAST
"I received a ticket of circus from my parents"

Linda used "exceptional" verbs only three times throughout the longitudinal study. The other examples beside example (18) both occurred at T7: that is, (19) and (20). In both cases, the verb *kariru* "borrow" is used. The verb *kariru* has an a-structure, represented in (21) below, where its first thematic argument is the recipient of the action rather than the agent who initiates the action; thus, it intrinsically involves non-canonical mapping.

(19) (T7) *mm. hito hito -wa hon-o hon-o kari-tai-desu*
people people-TOP book-ACC book-ACC borrow-DES-POL
"People want to borrow books"

(20) (T7) **demo dakara librarian (long pause) hon-o (long pause)*
but so librarian book-ACC

mhm.. karimasu
borrow
(lit) "but so the librarian borrows the books."
(intended) "but so librarian lends the books."

(21) *kariru* (recipient, agent, theme)

The above examples (19) and (20) were produced consecutively when Linda was performing a picture task, looking at several pictures which describe what the librarian does in a day. In example (19), Linda showed a successful assignment of two thematic roles onto the grammatical functions: the recipient role (i.e., *hito* "people") is mapped onto the topic-subject and the theme role (*hon* "book") onto the object. The sentence (20), on the other hand, displays unsuccessful mapping, as in (22).

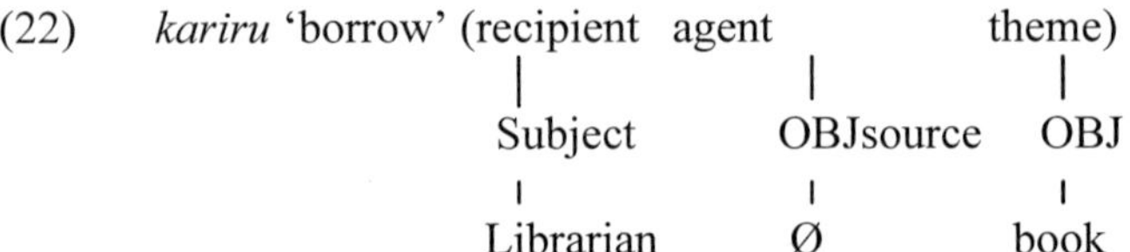

Therefore, the literal translation of the sentence (20) would be "so the librarian borrows the book (from the people)". However, this is not what Linda was intended to say, as the picture depicts a scene where the librarian lends out books to the people. So obviously, the functional assignment in (22) is wrong. In this case, the error could be fixed by choosing the verb *kasu* "lend" instead of *kariru* "borrow". Two Japanese verbs, *kariru* and *kasu* require the same thematic roles, namely agent, recipient and theme, as their arguments. However, unlike *kariru* "borrow", *kasu* "lend" exhibits a canonical argument structure, where the agent role rather than the recipient role is placed as its highest-ranked argument, as in (23).

(23) *kasu* "lend" (agent, recipient, theme)

Thus the verb *kariru* "borrow" requires a goal-possessor or recipient and *kasu* "lend" requires a source-possessor. As the long pauses after the words *librarian* and *hon-o* (book-ACC) in (20) may indicate, Linda was searching for the appropriate verb. As Pinker (1984) points out, acquisition of "exceptional" verbs seems to pose some problems for the L2 learner.

c) non-basic verb form

Linda started to produce the syntactic structures involving non-basic verb forms much later than canonical operations emerged. She started to produce benefactive constructions in her second year and passive and causative constructions in her third year of learning Japanese L2. I will briefly look at the production of each structure.

Passive Sentences

Table 4 lists all the passive constructions Linda produced in her longitudinal study and Table 5 exhibits the detailed analysis of SUBJ and ADJ(unct) in passive sentences produced by her. In the first row in the table, all the possibilities are listed as to how SUBJ and ADJ(unct) are encoded. For example, NP_{SUBJ} in passive can: (a) be marked with *-ga* (NOM), (b) be marked with *-wa* (TOP), (c) have no morphological marking on NP, (d) be elliptic, or (e) be marked with a wrong particle. Only (e) is ungrammatical, while the others are all possible grammatical choices in Japanese. I scored the frequency according to the above possibilities.

T9	64 *densya-ni notta toki doroboo-ni saihu-o tor-are-masita* Train-on ride-PAST time robber-DAT wallet-ACC steal-PASS-POL-PAST 'When (she) got on the train, (she) had her wallet stolen by a thief'
T10	90 *demo inu-wa* (long pause) *watasi-ni* (long pause) *kami-rare-masita*? but dog TOP I-DAT bite-PASS-POL-PAST (Lit) 'But a dog (long pause) was bitten by me' (Intended) 'But I was bitten by a dog'
T11	42 *mmn* (long pause) *kooreika-no geein..-wa igaku-ga* aging GEN cause-TOP medical science-NOM *sinposita koto-ga age-rare-masu* (long pause) *progress* fact-NOM mention-POL.PASS 'Progress of medical science is mentioned as a cause of (Japanese) ageing (society)' 44 *soreni atarasii kusuri-ga kaihatus-are-masita* (long pause) in addition new medicine NOM develop-PASS-POL-PAST 'In addition, new medicine was developed'

Table 4. Passive constructions produced by Linda

		SUBJ					ADJ				
Time	**(total)**	**NP-*ga***	**NP-*wa***	**NP-Ø**	**Ø**	**wrong P**	**NP-*ni***	**NP-*wa***	**NP-Ø**	**Ø**	**wrong P**
T9	(1)	0	0	0	1	0	1	0	0	0	0
T10	(1)	0	0	0	0	1(**ni*)	0	0	0	0	1(*wa)
T11	(2)	2	0	0	0	0	0	0	0	2	0

Table 5. Case-marking in passive sentences in Linda's corpus
The particle in parentheses indicates the one Linda used

The first passive construction in Linda's corpus is observed at T9. At this interview she produced one passive sentence, and this contains the agent realised as ADJ, as below:

(24)

(T9) *densya-ni notta toki doroboo-ni saihu-o tor-are-masita*
train on ride-PAST time robber-DAT wallet-ACC steal-PASS-POL-PAST
"When (she) got on the train, (she) had her wallet stolen by a thief."

In (24), the nominal element for the subject is omitted but the adjunct, which is linked to the agent role, is present and case-marked as DAT. The presence of ADJ(unct) reinforces the passive construction because it shows demotion of the agent to non-subject status. Therefore, this passive sentence at T9 exhibits sufficient evidence for non-default mapping given this is a "marked" construction compared to the prevalence of canonical mapping of the subject as *-ga* (NOM) or *-wa* (TOP). In the next interview, T10, Linda produced one passive structure, as in (25). But this time, her case marking for SUBJ and ADJ is incorrect: the Agent is marked as TOP and the Patient is marked as DAT (Adjunct). But in the passive, the patient should be realised as SUBJ (NOM) or TOP and, agent may be realised as ADJ (DAT) or may be suppressed altogether (see Section 3).

(25)

(T10) **demo inu-wa (long pause) watasi-ni* (long pause) *kami-rare-masita?*
but dog TOP I-DAT bite-PASS-POL-PAST
(Lit.) "But a dog (long pause) was bitten by me."
(Intended) "But I was bitten by a dog."

In (25), long pauses after the two NPs may indicate that Linda attempted to process a well-formed sentence by unifying information between NPs and their predicates at the S-node, but that unification was unsuccessful. Therefore, this ungrammatical passive sentence is considered as evidence against the acquisition of S-procedure. At T11 Linda produced two passive sentences and in both cases the ADJ argument was suppressed, as below, which is probably the less costly operation in terms of processing.

(26) (T11) (Talking about aging society in Japan)
mmn (long pause*) kooreika-no geein..-wa igaku-ga*
aging GEN cause-TOP medical science-NOM

sinposita koto-ga age-rare-masu (long pause)
progress fact-NOM mention-PASS.POL

"Progress of medical science is mentioned as a cause of (Japanese) ageing (society)."

(27)
(T11) *soreni atarasii kusuri-ga kaihatu-sare-masita* (long pause)
in addition new medicine NOM develop-PASS-POL-PAST
"In addition, new medicine was developed."

Causative Sentences

Linda produced causative constructions at only one interview, T10, where she successfully produced this construction four times. Three of these were intransitive causatives one a transitive causative. These examples exhibit evidence of the acquisition of S-procedure by the informant. First, let us look at examples of intransitive and transitive causative sentences from the session at T10.

a. Intransitive causative

(28) (T10) *sosite go-zi-ni* (long pause) *bosu-wa watasi-o*
and five-o'clock-at boss-TOP I-ACC
zangyoos-ase-masita
work overtime-CAUSE-POL-PAST
"Then at five o'clock my boss made me work overtime."

b. Transitive causative

(29) (T10) *demo watasi-no okaasan-wa watasi-ni*
but I-GEN mother-TOP I-DAT

yasai-o tabe-sase-masu
vegetable-ACC eat-CAUSE-POL-PRES
"But my mother makes me eat vegetables."

The main verbs in the two examples above, *zangyoosuru* ("work overtime") and *taberu* ("eat"), are intransitive and transitive respectively. In both sentences the noun *watasi* ("I") is included and both of them are semantically the "causee". Table 6 lists all the causative constructions Linda produced in her longitudinal study and Table 7 exhibits the frequency count of Linda's case marking for causative constructions according to whether they are transitive or intransitive. These tables are laid out in a similar manner to Tables 4 and Table 5 for the passive. The cells for $OBJ_{patient}$ for intransitive causative are shaded because the intransitive causative does not include $OBJ_{patient}$ as its argument.

Transitive	64 *demo watasi-no okaasan-wa watasi-ni yasai-o tabe-sase-masu* but I-GENmother-TOP I-DAT vegetable-ACC eat-CAUSE-POL. 'But my mother makes me eat vegetables' 78 *uh bosu-wa watasi-ni itumo kopii-o sase-masu* boss-TOP I-DAT always photocopy-ACC do. CAUSE-POL. 'my boss always asks me to make photocopy' 80 *sosite bosu-wa watasi-ni koohii-o tukur-ase-masu* and boss-TOP I-DAT coffee-ACC make-CAUSE-POL. 'and my boss asks me to make a coffee'
Intransitive	84 *sosite go-zi ni (long pause) bosu-wa watasi-o zangyoo-sase-masita* and five-o'clock-at boss-TOP I-ACC work overtime-CAUSE-PAST.POLITE 'Then at five o'clock my boss made me work overtime'

Table 6. Intransitive and transitive causative constructions produced by Linda at T10

		SUBJECT					OBJECT						OBJpatient				
	Total	NP-*ga*	NP-*wa*	NP -Ø	Ø	Wrong P	NP -*o*	NP-ni	NP-*wa*	NP-Ø	Ø	Wrong P	NP-*o*	NP-*wa*	NP -Ø	Ø	Wrong P
Intransitive	(1)	0	1	0	0	0	1	0	0	0	0	0					
Transitive	(3)	0	3	0	0	0	0	3	0	0	0	0	3	0	0	0	0

Table 7. Frequency count of case-marking in causative sentences at T10 in Linda's corpus data

The Japanese case marking system is not straightforward in terms of the grammatical function and thematic roles of the NP which the case-marking particle is attached to. When the Vstem of the causative predicate is intransitive, the "causee" is case-marked as ACC (i.e., *-o*), whereas when it is transitive it is marked as either ACC (i.e., *-o*) or DAT (i.e., *-Ni*)[7]. In order to achieve the correct case marking for different verbal types, the learner needs to work out the role of the NP at three levels: grammatical function, thematic role, and appropriate case marking. Linda's case marking for both intransitive and transitive causatives was all correct. Therefore, the available data of Linda's causative production shows her ability to use S-procedure (thus, the operation of non-canonical mapping) at T10.

Benefactive structures

Now we look at Linda's production of benefactive structures. Recall from Section 4 that there are different Japanese benefactive predicates, namely the give-schema and the receive-schema. Linda produced the following three benefactives: (1) V-te *ageru*; (2) V-te *kureru* and; (3) V-te *morau*. Both (1) and (2) belong to the give-schema but (2) requires the beneficiary to be "I" or "one of us". On the other hand, (3) belongs to the receive-schema where the beneficiary role but not the agent role (i.e., verb-specific semantic role is "benefactor") is mapped onto the SUBJ function. Table 8 lists all the benefactive constructions Linda produced throughout her longitudinal study.

Time	Turn number and benefactive constructions with translation and English gloss
T5	68 **Bobu-san-ga purezento-o er* (long pause) *tetudatte er moraimasita* (long pause) Bob-Mr-NOM present-ACC help-COMP receive-PAST.POL (Lit.) 'Bob received the favour of helping (carrying) the present' (Intended) '(I) received the favour of Bob (carrying) the present for me' 82 *er ie-e kaeru toki. er okaasan-wa er keeki-o tukutte. tukette er kuremasita* home-to return when mother-TOP cake-ACC make-COMP give-PAST 'When (I) return(ed) home, my mother made a cake for me'
T8	13 *Sosite um. otoosan-wa mm (long pause) okaasan ni tetudatte agemasita* then father-TOP mother-DAT help-COPM give-PAST 'Then father helped mother'
T9	72 *Sorekara er Zyon-san-ni aisukuriimu-o katte.. agemasita* then John-Mr-DAT ice cream-ACC buy-COMP give-PAST 'Then (I) bought an ice cream for John'
T10	22 *er watasi-no ryoosin-wa* (long pause) *er* (long pause) *doosei* (XX) I-GEN parents-TOP living together *um mitomete kure kuremasu* accept-COMP give-PRES ' My parents will accept (me) living together (with my boyfriend) for me'

T12	54 *Demo.. er nihonzin-ni er tetudatte agemasita* but Japanese-DAT help-COMP give-PAST 'But I helped Japanese (person)' 60 *er watasi-wa um gomennasai. um demo.. er nihonzin-ni er tetudatte agemasita* I-TOP sorry but Japanese-DAT help-COMP give-PAST 'er I um sorry. But I helped Japanese (person)' 90 *Dakara Risa-san-wa totemo um kanasikatta node atarasii huku o katte agemasita* so Lisa-Mss-TOP very sad-PAST because new cloth-ACC buy-COMP give-PAST (Intended) 'So (her boyfriend) bought a cloth for her because Lisa was very sad' 100 *Demo. um.. sensei-wa suisenzyoo-o katte kaite agemasita* but teacher-TOP recommendation letter-ACC write-COMP give-PAST 'But the teacher wrote a recommendation letter (for him)' 104 * *er.. er urm* (long pause) *um Kurisu-san-wa sensei-ni um hokano suisenzyoo-o* Chris-Mr-TOP teacher-DAT other recommendation letter-ACC *kaite um..* (long pause) *kaite... ageta hoogaii-desu* write-COMP write-COPM give-PAST better-COP 'it is better that Chris get his teacher to write a recommendation letter (for him)'

Table 8. Benefactive constructions produced by Linda
The asterisk "*" next to the utterance indicates that the following sentence involves a mismatch between the argument-function mapping and the predicate.

The benefactive constructions were taught just before the interview T5. Linda produced some of the benefactive constructions at T5, but their use became more continuous only later, at T8, T9, T10 and T12. By T8, she produced all three different benefactive structures. At T5 she produced the benefactives twice, but one of these instances shows incompatibility of the case marking of NPs and the predicate in order to express the intended meanings in (30). This sentence was produced when Linda was describing a picture with a scene where a boy named Bob is helping his girlfriend carry the birthday presents which she received from her friends. The predicate Linda chose to use in order to express this scene is *tesudat-te moraimasita* (help-COMP receive-

POL-PAST), which involves the receive-schema benefactive auxiliary verb. The argument structure of this predicate is shown in (31.a), which requires non-default, non-canonical mapping. On the other hand, NPs in the sentence are linked to the argument and the function in (31.b). However, the Recipient role is assigned to *Bob*, who is actually the benefactor (i.e., Agent role) of the event. Thus, the resulting linguistic structure fails to express the intended meaning.

(30) (Linda T5, 68)
**Bobu-san-ga purezento-o er* (long pause) *tetudatte er moraimasita* (long pause)
Bob-Mr-NOM present-ACC help-COMP receive-POL-PAST

(Lit.) "Bob received the favour of helping (carrying) the present."
(Intended) "(I) received the favour of Bob (carrying) the present for me."
Or "Bob gave a help of carrying the present (for me)"

(31) a. *tetsudatte morau*
receive <Beneficiary, Benefactor, Beneficial event>

b.argument-function mapping expressed in the sentence in (30)

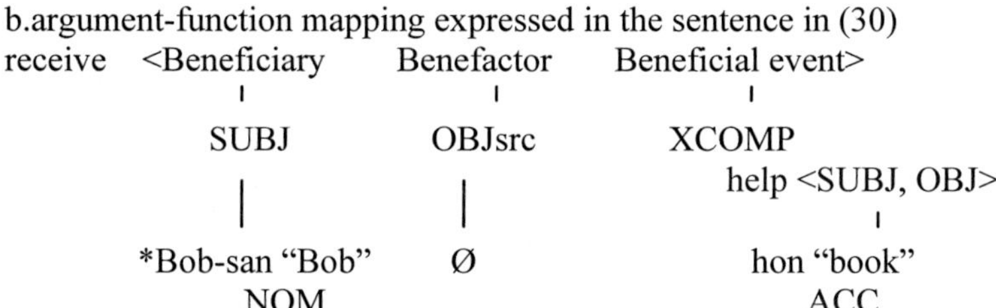

The above example (30) is ill-formed because of the mismatch between the functional assignment of NPs (indicated by the case particle[8]) and the choice of benefactive auxiliary for expressing the intended meaning. The intended meaning can be expressed by either changing the functional assignment of NPs as in (32) OR by changing the choice of benefactive auxiliary to the give-schema, as in (33).

(32) *Bobu-san-<u>ni</u> purezento-o tetudatte er moraimasita*
Bob-Mr-DAT present-ACC help-COMP receive-POL-PAST
"(I) received the help of carrying the present from Bob."

(33) *a. Bobu-san-ga purezento-o er tetudatte er kuremasita*
Bob-Mr-NOM present-ACC help-COMP give-POL-PAST
"Bob gave a help of carrying the present (for me)."

Therefore, (30) produced at T5 shows an example of lack of unification between NPs and VP within the construction. Hence, it is evident that the operation involving non-default, non-canonical mapping was insufficiently developed in the learner's interlanguage. Over the next two interviews, T6 and T7, Linda did not produce any instances of benefactives or other structures involving morpholexical operation. Given that the benefactive constructions were introduced in her class right before the interview T5, it is reasonable to suspect that Linda's productions of benefactive constructions at T5 were "trials" of a structure which had been freshly taught in the class. The next benefactive construction appeared in Linda's corpus at T8. Linda produced one benefactive sentence at this interview:

(34) (T8)
sosite um. otoosan-wa mm (long pause) okaasan-ni tetudat-te agemasita
then father-TOP mother-DAT help-COMP give-POL-PAST
"Then the father helped the mother."

In (34) the benefactor (i.e., *otoosan* "father" in this case) is marked as TOP and the beneficiary (i.e., *okaasan* "mother" in this case) is marked as DAT. However, while the auxiliary is correctly produced, the case-marking of the beneficiary, *-ni* in *okaasan-ni*, is an error, that comes from overgeneralization. In the give-schema benefactives in Japanese, the beneficiary role mapped onto OBJgoal is case marked as DAT. However, when the beneficiary is the direct object of the sentence, the second object is omitted (Makino and Tsutsui 1986). Such verbs involve *tetudau* ("to help"), *miokuru* ("see (someone) off") and *nagusameru* ("console"). This is due to the fact that the patient of *tetudau* ("to help") equals the beneficiary of the event of *"tetsudatte ageru"* (i.e., "help *mother* for the benefit of the *mother*" in case of (34)). In such cases where there are only two arguments in the benefactive construction, the beneficiary (*okaasan* "mother" in the case of (34)) should be marked with ACC but not DAT. Although the case marking of the beneficiary was unlike the target language, (34) forms positive evidence of successful functional assignment. Linda just did not know the limitation of rule application, and therefore this should be considered a developmental error.

At T9 Linda produced one benefactive, where the grammatical functions of the semantic role are incorrectly assigned, as (35) shows:

(35) (Linda T9) 72

* *sorekara er Zyon-san ni aisukuriimu o katte.. agemasita*
then John-Mr-DAT ice cream-ACC buy-COMP give-POL-PAST
(Lit.) "Then er (she) bought an ice cream for John."
(Intended) "Then John received the favour of (me) buying an ice cream."
or "Then (I) bought an icecream for John"

The source of error is the mismatch between the predicate *katte ageru* (buy-COMP give) "buy (something for the benefit of someone)") and the NP's argument-function mapping similar to the example (30).

At the next interview, T10, the informant produced another benefactive construction with a different benefactive auxiliary, *kureru*. This sentence shows a piece of evidence for successful non-default mapping, as NP case marking and VP are compatible. At T12, there were five instances of benefactive construction, as shown in Table 8. On one occasion, the beneficiary was marked with non target *-ni* (DAT), as in (36).

(36) (Linda T12) 54

* *demo.. er nihonzin-ni er tetudatte agemasita*
but Japanese-DAT help-COMP BENE(give)-POL-PAST
"But I helped Japanese (woman)."

This benefactive sentence involves the verb *tetudau* ("to help"). This is a "special" verb in the sense that the direct object of the predicate and the beneficiary happen to be the same as explained above. So this sentence should be considered as positive evidence of S-procedure.

At the same interview in T12, there is a case where the case assignment to NPs and the benefactive predicate do not match (evidence against S-procedure). In the example (37) below, *Kurisu-san* (Chris) should be the goal but not the source of the benefit involved in the event of his teacher writing a recommendation letter. Similarly to (30), (37) needs to change NP case marking in accordance with the currently used benefactive auxiliary *ageru* ("give the favour") or else changing selection of the benefactive auxiliary to *morau* ("receive the favour") in accordance with the current grammatical function assigned by the nominal marking of *sensei-ni* (OBJ_{θ}).

(37) (Linda T12) 104

er.. er urm (long pause) *um Kurisu-san-wa sensei-ni um hokano*
Chris-Mr-TOP teacher-DAT other

suisenzyoo-o kai-te um.. (long pause) kai-te ... ageta hoogaii-desu
recommendation letter-ACC write-COMP write-COMP BENE(give)-PAST
better-COP

(Lit.) "It is better that Chris write another recommendation letter to the teacher."
(Intended) "It is better that Chris get his teacher to write another recommendation letter (for him)."

In sum, T12 shows clear evidence of acquisition of S-procedure as the informant exhibited three instances of positive evidence, even though she failed to produce well-formed benefactive constructions twice.

The following Table 9 summarizes the frequency score of the use of benefactive constructions according to V-*te ageru*, V-*te kureru* and V-*te morau*. These structures are listed at the top row. The two benefactive structures listed in the second and the third columns involve the give-schema. On the other hand, the structure listed in the fourth column, V-*te morau*, is the receive-schema. The numbers before and after the slash indicate the frequency count of successful and unsuccessful deployment of non-canonical mapping. When both of them are zero, "0" is simply listed in the cell.

Time	**V-*te ageru* (Agent, Recipient, Theme)**	**V-*te kureru* (Agent, Recipient, Theme) Recipient = I or one of us**	**V-*te morau* (Recipient, Agent, Theme)**
T5	0	1/0 (1.0)	0/1 (0)
T8	1/0 (1.0)	0	0
T9	0/1 (0)	0	0
T10	0	1/0 (1.0)	0
T12	4/1 (0.8)	0	0
Total	5/2 (0.7)	2/0 (1.0)	0/1 (0)

Table 9 Frequency of the benefactive constructions
The number before the slash = the frequency of successful a- to f- structure mapping
The number after the slash = the frequency of unsuccessful a- to f- structure mapping
The number in the parenthesis indicates accuracy rate

Although the frequency is small across three benefactive structures, this summary table reveals some interesting patterns. First, the learner used the benefactive construction with V-*te ageru* most frequently (i.e., seven times), far more than the other two benefactives. As for argument mapping with this benefactive structure, most cases (i.e., five cases out of seven) are correct. Second, although the learner attempted the benefactive structure with V-*te kureru* much less (only twice), the structures in both cases were well-formed. Last, the learner attempted the benefactive structure with V-*te morau* only once at T5 just after she learned this construction in the class. But this production was ill-formed. Therefore, the acquisition seems to follow the following order: V-*te ageru* > V-*te kureru* > V-*te morau*. The relative acquisitional order of V-*te kureru* and V-*te ageru* found here is parallel to the findings reported by Yanagimachi (1997, cited in Tanaka 2001) and Pizziconi (2000) with English L1 learners and Tanaka (2001) with English L1, Korean L1, Chinese L1 and Indonesian/Malay L1 learners. Further, in the area of first language acquisition, Clancy (1985) reported that Japanese children's production of V-*te morau* is much smaller than V-*te kureru*. Therefore, the acquisitional order observed here seems to be the reflection of the processing load defined by PT.

The benefactive structure with V-*te ageru* requires non-canonical mapping. The benefactive structure, V-*te kureru,* requires non-canonical mapping similar to V-*te ageru* but with one additional specification (i.e., the Recipient has to be "I" or "one of us"). Therefore, the learner has an additional task for producing this structure. On the other hand, the benefactive structure with V-*te morau* itself is an "exceptional" verb requiring non-canonical mapping. In addition, further non-canonicity is involved, due to the fact that XCOMP's subject needs to be linked to the object source in the matrix clause. This operation adds further complexity in on-line speech production. Therefore, PT predicts that this benefactive structure would be acquired later than the other two.

Conclusion

In this chapter, I have presented two new hypotheses from current developments of Processability Theory (Pienemann, et. al. 2005): the Unmarked Alignment Hypothesis and the Lexical Mapping Hypothesis. These hypotheses predict the universal L2 development of argument-function mapping at the discourse-syntax interface. I have shown how these hypotheses can be interpreted in special reference to Japanese L2. I have also presented an analysis of a three-year longitudinal study of a university student learning Japanese L2. The data showed the dominant use of canonical structures all the time during the study. The early data up to the third interview (i.e., the sixth month of learning Japanese L2) included canonical mapping only. This is what the Unmarked Alignment Hypothesis predicted. Then the learner gradually started to produce non-canonical structures. The first non-canonical mapping was observed in the fourth interview (i.e., the seventh month), involving an "exceptional verb". The first non-basic verb form was in the fifth interview (i.e., 13th month) with the benefactives. Once non-canonical structures appeared at the fourth interview, the informant continuously produced the structures of non-canonical operations except in one interview, Time 6. The variety of non-canonical structures increased in time: "exceptional verbs", the benefactive, the passive, and the causative constructions, although the argument-function mapping of these structures was not always successful. Thus, information organization is an important factor for the acquisition of a second language.

As Levelt (1989) explains, the speaker tends to map the most accessible entity in the discourse onto the SUBJ (or TOP). Then the linear organization of the sentence needs to be constructed accordingly. However, in some cases, the learner shows obvious mismatch between the syntactic coding of the noun and the required predicate. This is especially true with the complex predicate of the benefactive. PT's Lexical Mapping Hypothesis predicted this situation where the L2 learner acquires non-canonical mapping later than canonical mapping due to the higher processing load. Further, my analysis on the development of the Japanese benefactive has indicated that there might be a hierarchical relationship among three different benefactive structures. However, it requires further empirical study to test this claim.

Notes

[1] OBJθ refers to secondary object.
[2] In Japanese culture, the family members and the company members are considered to be "in-group".
[3] The Kunrei-style Romanisation system is used here, except for long vowel sounds which I have chosen to transcribe as double vowels (i.e., aa, ee, ii, oo, uu) in place of the usual bar above the vowel.
[4] Presentational constructions involving iru "exist" for the animate entity and aru "exist" for the inanimate entity are excluded from this analysis as "its communicative function is not to predicate a property of a given entity but to introduce a new entity into a discourse" (Lambrecht 1994, 39).
[5] An example of unsuccessful mapping produced by my Linda is as follows:

90 demo inu-wa (long pause) watasi-ni (long pause) kami-rare-masita?
but dog TOP I-DAT bite-PASS-POL-PAST
(Lit) "But a dog (long pause) was bitten by me."
(Intended) "But I was bitten by a dog."

[6] Linda quickly learned nominal ellipsis, especially at the subject position when the subject is the first person in the affirmative sentence and the second person in the question sentence.
[7] The o-version implies more coercive causation than the ni-version (Shibatani 1990 p.309).
[8] See Nordlinger (1998) for the constructive case within the framework of LFG where the case morphology contributes to construct the f-structure which it belongs to. Also, see Di Biase and Kawaguchi (2002) for acquisition of functional assignment in Japanese L2.

References

Alsina, A. (1996). *The role of argument structure in Grammar*. Stanford, CA: CSLI Publications.

Backhouse, A. (1993). *The Japanese language: An introduction*. Oxford, New York and Toronto: Oxford University Press.

Bresnan, J. (2001). *Lexical-functional syntax*. Malden, MA: Blackwell Publishers.

Bresnan, J. & Kanerva, J. (1989). Locative inversion in Chichewa: A study of factorization in Grammar. *Linguistic Inquiry,* 20, 1-50.

Choi, Hye-Won (2001). Phrase structure, information structure, and resolution of Mismatch. In P. Sells (Ed.) *Formal and Empirical Issues in Optimality Theoretic Syntax,* (pp. 17-62). Stanford, California: CSLI Publications.

—. (1999). *Optimizing structure in context – Scrambling and information structure*. Stanford, California: CSLI Publications.

Clancy, P. M. (1985). The acquisition of Japanese, In D. I. Slobin (Ed.), *The crosslinguistic study of language acquisition, Vol. 1: The Data.* pp. 373-524. Hillsdale. NJ: Lawrence Erlbaum.

Dalrymple, M. (2001). *Syntax and Semantics Volume 34: Lexical Functional Grammar*. San Diego: Academic Press.

Di Biase, B. & Kawaguchi, S. (2002). Exploring the typological plausibility of Processability Theory: language development in Italian L2 and Japanese L2. *Second Language Research*, 18 (3), 274-302.

Dimroth, C. & Starren, M. (Eds.). (2003). *Information structure and the dynamics of language acquisition.* Amsterdam, Philadelphia: John Benjamins.

Foley, W. & Van Valin, R. (1984). *Functional syntax and universal grammar.* Cambridge: CUP.

Givón, T. (1984). *Syntax: A functional-typological introduction.* Amsterdam: John Benjamins.

Ishikawa, A. (1985). *Complex predicates and lexical operations in Japanese.* Unpublished doctoral dissertation. Stanford: Stanford University.

Itani-Adams, Y. (2003). *From word to phrase in Japanese -English bilingual first language acquisition.* Paper presented at The MARCS seminar, University of Western Sydney, 15 September.

Iwasaki, J. (2003). *The acquisition of verbal morpho-syntax in JSL by a child learner*. Paper presented at 13th Biennial Conference of the JSAA, Brisbane, July 2-4.

Jackendoff, R. (1972). *Semantic interpretation in generative grammar.* Cambridge, Mass: MIT Press.

—. (1983). *Semantics and cognition.* Cambridge, MA: MIT PRESS.

Kawaguchi, S. (2005a) Argument structure and syntactic development in Japanese as a second language. In M. Pienemann. (Ed.). *Cross-linguistic aspects of Processability Theory*. pp. 253-298. Amsterdam and Philadelphia: John Benjamins.

—. (2005b). Processability Theory and Japanese as a second language. Acquisition of Japanese as a Second Language, 9. *Acquisition of Japanese as a Second Language*, 9.

Keenan, E. O. and Comrie, B. (1977). Noun phrase accessability and Universal Grammar. *Linguistic Inquiry, 8.* 63-99.

Lambrecht, K. (1994). *Information structure and sentence form: Topic, focus and the mental representation of discourse referents.* Cambridge: CUP.

Lee, H. (2001). Markedness and word order freezing. In P. Sells (ed.), *Formal and empirical issues in optimality theoretic syntax*, pp. 63-127. Stanford, CA: CSLI Publications.

Levelt, W. J. M. (1989). *Speaking. From intention to articulation.* Cambridge, MA: MIT Press.

Mansouri, F. (1997). From emergence to acquisition: Developmental issues in Arabic interlanguage morphology. *The Australian Review of Applied Linguistics,* 20 (1), 83-104.

—. (2002). Exploring the interface between syntax and morphology in second language development. In B. Di Biase (ed.), *Developing a second language: Acquisition, processing and pedagogy of Arabic, Chinese, English, Italian, Japanese, Swedish,* pp. 59-72. Melbourne: Language Australia.

—. (2005). Agreement morphology in Arabic as a second language: Typological features and their processing implications. In M. Pienemann. (Ed.). *Cross-linguistic aspects of Processability Theory.* pp. 117-154. Amsterdam and Philadelphia: John Benjamins.

Marantz, A. (1982). On the acquisition of grammatical relations. *Linguistische Berichte: Linguistik als Kognitive Wissenschaft* 80/82: 32-69.

Matsumoto, Y. (1996). *Complex predicates in Japanese - A syntactic and semantic study of the notion 'word'.* California and Tokyo: CSLI Publications and Kurosio Publishers.

Miesel, J. (1991). Principles of universal grammar and strategies of language use: On some similarities and differences between first and second language acquisition. In L. Eubank (ed.), *Point – counterpoint. Universal grammar in the second language*, pp. 231-276. Amsterdam and Philadelphia: John Benjamins.

Pienemann, M. & Håkansson, G. (1999). A unified approach towards the development of Swedish as L2: A processability account. *Studies in Second Language Acquisition*, 21, 383-420.

—. (1998). *Language and second language development Processability Theory.* Amsterdam and Philadelphia: John Benjamins.

Pienemann, M., Di Biase, B. & S. Kawaguchi (2005). Extending Processability Theory. In M. Pienemann (ed.). *Cross-linguistic aspects of Processability Theory.* pp. 199-251. Amsterdam and Philadelphia: John Benjamins.

Pinker, S. (1984). *Language Learnability and Language Development.* Cambridge, Mass.: Harvard U.P.

—. (1989). Language Acquisition. In D. N. Osherson & H. Lasnick (Eds.), *An invitation to cognitive science: Vol. 1 Language.* Cambridge, MA.: MIT Press.

Pizziconi, B. (2000). The acquisition of Japanese communicative style: the yarimorai verbs, *BATJ Journal*, 1, 1-16.

Sasaki, Y. (1998). Processing and learning of Japanese double-object active and causative sentences: an error-feedback paradigm. *Journal of Psycholinguistic Research*, 27 (4), 453-479.

Sells, P. (Ed.) (2001). *Formal and empirical issues in optimality theoretic syntax.* Stanford, California: CSLI Publications.

Shibatani, M. (1994). Benefactive constructions: a Japanese-Korean comparative perspective. In N. Akatsuka (Ed.). *Japanese/Korean Linguistics Vol. 4*, pp. 39-74. CSLI Publications.

Slobin, D. I. (1985). *The Crosslinguistic Study of Language Acquisition.* Vols. 1 & 2. Hillsdale, N.J.: Lawrence Erlbaum.

Tanaka, M. (2001). *The acquisition of point of view and voice in Japanese as a foreign/second language: The case of adult learners of English, Korean, Chinese and Indonesian/Malay.* Unpublished doctoral dissertation, International Christian University, Tokyo.

Taylor, R. (2004). *Spanish L2 from a processability perspective: Two developmental case studies*. BA (Honours) Dissertation, University of Western Sydney.

Yanagimachi, T. (1997). *The acquisition of referential form use in L2 oral narrative discourse by adult English-speaking learners of Japanese*. Unpublished doctoral dissertation, The University of Minnesota, MN.

Zhang, Y. (2001). *Second language acquisition of Chinese grammatical morphemes: a processability perspective*. Unpublished doctoral dissertation, Canberra: Australian National University.

—. (2002). A processability approach to L2 acquisition of Chinese grammatical morphemes. In B. Di Biase (ed.), *Developing a second language: Acquisition, processing and pedagogy of Arabic, Chinese, English, Italian, Japanese, Swedish*, pp. 29-44. Melbourne: Language Australia.

—. (2004). Categorial analysis, processing demands, and L2 acquisition for the Chinese adjective suffix *-de* (ADJ). *Language Learning*, 54 (3), 437-468.

—. (2005). Processing and formal instruction in the L2 acquisition of five Chinese grammatical morphemes. In M. Pienemann. (ed.). *Cross-linguistic aspects of Processability Theory*. pp. 155-178. Amsterdam and Philadelphia: John Benjamins.

CHAPTER 4

PROCESSABILITY THEORY APPLIED TO WRITTEN AND ORAL SWEDISH

Gisela Håkansson and Catrin Norrby

According to Processability Theory (Pienemann 1998) second language learners go through levels of development where the computational mechanisms for processing the second language are created in a gradual manner. The structural options are constrained at a given time: learners cannot learn or produce linguistic structures that they are not able to process. The level of grammatical processability is assumed to be steady across different tasks as long as these tasks are 'based on the same skill type in language production' (Pienemann 1998:273).

This 'steadiness hypothesis' provides a view on second language acquisition that is different from positions that perceive learner language as variable and subjected to external influence. In the well-known Monitor Model suggested by Krashen (1981, 1985) learners are hypothesized to be able to monitor their performance and reach a higher level of grammatical accuracy when there is time for planning, the focus is on form and the grammatical rule is known. According to Krashen, all these conditions are present in grammar tests and this is the reason why many learners perform better in grammar tests than in communicative situations.

Results from empirical studies of learner variation have revealed a more complex relationship between learner performance and monitoring. Some studies have shown that monitoring gives different results for different linguistic structures, e.g. increases accuracy for 3rd person – s, but not article use in English (Tarone 1985), for regular but not irregular past in English (Ellis 1992), for noun-modifier agreement but not article use in Spanish (Ortega 1999). Disentangling Krashen's suggested conditions time, form focus and rule knowledge, Hulstijn & Hulstijn (1984) found attention on grammatical form to outweigh the others. The learners in their study performed an oral story retelling task under four conditions: time pressure and grammar focus, time pressure without grammar focus, no time pressure but grammar focus, and finally, no time pressure and no grammar focus. The results were given as percentages in obligatory contexts and demonstrated that time pressure by itself did not have any effect on Dutch word order, but learners performed better when their attention was on form rather than content. Explicit knowledge of the grammatical rule did not play a role.

The differences found in learner language production, have been explained as a function of allocation of resources, i.e. if the focus is on the form or on the meaning of the utterance. Second language learners find it more difficult than native speakers to focus on form and content at the same time, and therefore they need to decide what to give priority (e.g. Yuan & Ellis 2003). The underlying assumption seems to be that learners have access to grammatical rules but sometimes do not apply them because of 'stress or overload due to fatigue or distraction' (Sharwood Smith 1994:109). Yuan & Ellis (2003:7) propose that planning time 'allows the speaker to search his/her linguistic resources, especially grammatical, during the formulation stage more thoroughly'. Ortega (1999:119) suggests that extra time for planning removes the cognitive load and gives the learner room to use 'the upper limits of their IL grammar'.

In most studies of variation in learner production the data has been analyzed in terms of fluency (e.g. speech rate), complexity (e.g. subordination) and/or accuracy in learner language. Generally, the influence of planning time has shown to be considerable for fluency and complexity (e.g. Foster & Skehan 1996, Mehnert 1998, Ortega 1999, Segalowitz & Hulstijn 2005), but the results are not so convincing when it comes to accuracy (Ortega 1999). In measuring accuracy, the question is usually not whether learners are able to produce a structure or not, but rather how consistent they are in their application of a certain grammatical rule. This means that the focus lies on mastery of a specific grammatical structure instead of on when the structure emerges in the developing interlanguage. Furthermore, when using group mean values instead of the performance of individual learners some of the developmental dimension of language acquisition is lost.

In the present study we will use the framework of Processability Theory and base the analyses on when grammatical structures emerge in the individual learners' production, written and oral.

Processability Theory

Processability Theory (Pienemann 1998) is predicated on Levelt's (1989) model of spoken language production. A basic principle is that the conceptual message has to be encoded through the formulator to get a grammatical form. For this the learner needs new automatized processes in the target language, and these are created incrementally. One important feature in the learner's development of the grammar is the concept of 'unification of grammatical features' from Lexical-Functional Grammar (LFG) (Bresnan 1982). In the first stages there is no grammatical exchange between elements and the learner has to rely on bare words alone, but as the grammar develops there are more and more unification points. The different stages are acquired in an implicational order, i.e. it is impossible to reach a certain stage without having automatized the preceding one.

In Pienemann and Håkansson (1999) Swedish grammar was provided with an LFG treatment leading to a hierarchy of processing complexity where five stages can be identified, as shown in table 1 and described below.

Processing Prerequisite	Outcome: Swedish grammar
Level 5 • clause boundary	sub-clause placement of negation
Level 4 • S procedure	subject-verb inversion; predicative agreement
Level 3 • phrasal procedure	NP agreement
Level 2 • category procedure	verb suffix: present, past; noun suffix: plural
Level 1 • word / lemma	'words'

Table 1. Hierarchy for the morpho-syntactic development of Swedish

The first step for the learner is to identify and acquire the words of the target language (Level 1). The next step is to organize the lexicon into categories using the morphological evidence of tense suffixes for verbs and number suffixes for nouns. This is the level of lexical morphology (Level 2), which is the first indication of the learner being able to make a distinction between different forms for different functions (e.g. one form for singular and another for plural). A grasp of lexical morphology is a necessary prerequisite for phrasal morphology (Level 3) to be processable. The processing of phrasal morphology allows the learner to unify the features of heads and modifiers in a phrase, e.g. agreement between article, adjective and noun in the Swedish noun phrases. The next step extends the processing to include not only unification of features between words within one single phrase, but also across phrases, such as the subject noun phrase and the verb phrase in a clause (Level 4). This level implies that the grammatical functions in a clause will be accessible to the learner, and feature unification between subject and predicate is possible. At this level, the rule that regulates subject-verb inversion in Swedish is processable to the learner. Finally, when main clause word order is automatized, the learner can apply different word order rules in Swedish main and subordinate clauses and place the negation differently (Level 5).

As should be clear, each level in the sequence builds on the preceding level, which implies that the development of levels is implicational. The prediction is that a learner at Level 5 will be able to process the grammatical information captured in all the preceding levels. In other words, learners should not be able to skip any of the steps in the hierarchy. Swedish structures are expected to emerge in the learner's production in the following implicational order (‘>‘ means ‘implies’):

Sub-clause neg+v > inversion, predicative agreement >NP agreement > lexical suffixes

Evidence for this hierarchy has been found in oral data from adults (Glahn et al. 2001, Håkansson & Norrby 2005) and children (Håkansson 2001, 2005) acquiring Swedish as a second language. However, the relationship between oral and written production has not been reported before. A comparison between writing and speech within a developmental framework poses new questions and the following hypothesis:

Is it possible for written and oral performance to differ if the processing constraints decide which grammatical structures are open to the learner? In other words, can learners control structures in writing that they cannot process in speech? Our hypothesis is that the processability constraints are equally applicable for learners' spoken and written language production, when the aim is to communicate meaning.

Data and method

This study is part of the project ‘Swedish inside and outside Sweden’ (Håkansson, Norrby & Bruzaeus 2004, Håkansson & Norrby 2005). For the present analyses data from 20 learners are used. All learners had studied Swedish for about 150 hours at the start of data collection. Nine learners were foreign language learners, studying Swedish at Melbourne University, Australia. Eleven subjects were second language learners, studying Swedish at Malmö University, Sweden. The Melbourne students had English as their first language, and the Malmö students had Albanian, Arabic, Arabic/German, Hungarian/Romanian, Romanian/Ukrainian, and Russian as first languages. The learners are given code-names: Mal 1 – Mal 11 for the second language learners in Malmö, Mel 1 – Mel 9 for the foreign language learners in Melbourne.

For the present study written data from two different times of collection was used, Time I in the beginning of the academic year and Time II eight months later. The data consists of written compositions and translation tasks. The compositions are free essays with no further instructions but to observe the set length of approximately 200 words each. The translations from English to Swedish are approximately 175 words long and written specifically to elicit levels 2–5 of the PT hierarchy.

The oral data consists of communicative tasks specifically designed to elicit structures that are relevant to PT levels 3-5, i.e. attributive agreement, predicative agreement and subordinate clause word order. These tasks have been used earlier in studies of L1 and L2 Swedish (Glahn et al. 2001, Håkansson & Hansson 2000). To elicit attributive agreement a sheet with small and scattered objects in different colours was shown to the learners. The informant was asked to tell the colour with a sentence in response to a stimulus question (e.g. *Vad finns bredvid päronet?* 'What is there beside the pear?') The informant was to locate the right illustration and answer according to the picture (e.g. *Två gula äpplen* 'Two yellow apples'). The same procedure was used for predictive agreement. The test administrator asked a question (e.g. *Vilken färg är de små kopparna?* 'what colour are the small cups? – *De är bruna.* They are brown.'). Because there were many items on each sheet and the sequence of questions was not predictable, the informants had to concentrate on keeping the information in memory while searching for the right item. This was intended to make them focus on the identification of items and colours rather than on the morphological forms of the adjectives. The attributive adjective test contained 14 items (4 singular uter, 6 singular neuter, and 4 plural) and the predicative adjective test contained 16 items (5 singular uter, 5 singular neuter, and 5 plural).

The placement of negation in main and subordinate clauses was elicited in a communicative game. This game is played with 12 illustrated cards that depict the performance, or non-performance, of various activities. There are also larger playing boards, each containing six pictures that match those on the separate cards. The players take cards in alternative turns and place them on top of the matching illustrations on the boards. The person who gets his or her board(s) filled up first wins the game. As an introduction to the game and to the vocabulary used, each activity was described by the interviewer, with the informant giving the negated counterpart. This introduction made it possible to check whether the subjects knew the placement of negation in main clauses (after the finite verb), which is different from its placement in subordinate clauses (in front of the finite verb). The participants then drew a card and were asked to describe its content (e.g. *Vilket kort fick du?* 'Which card did you get?' – *Jag fick fågeln som kan flyga* 'I got the bird who can fly'). Then the interviewer drew a card and asked the informant to describe that card (e.g. *Vilket kort fick jag?* 'Which card did I get?' – *Du fick fågeln som inte kan flyga* 'You got the bird which can not fly'). By this method, 12 negated subordinate clauses, 6 clauses with main verbs, and 6 clauses with auxiliary and main verb were produced by the informants. The use of problem solving and a game to elicit the relevant structures had the advantage of diverting the subjects' attention from the formal aspects of language, by engaging them in a communicative situation.

The oral data was collected at the end of the study, at the time of the last written data collection (Time II). All tasks, both written and oral were tested on a group of native speakers to ensure that the target structures were used.

For the analysis an emergence criterion was used. This means that we analyzed the first productive example from each learner as an instance of rule application. However, in order to ensure that the structure in question was processed by the learner and not only part of a mono-morphemic chunk, the learner had to produce more than one case of that structure (Pienemann 1998:145). If a learner produced only one example, this result is put within parentheses. The occurrences of the target structure were calculated in percentages of obligatory contexts.

Results

Development over time: the Malmö group

The analyses are based on written data collected at two periods in time with approximately eight months interval. In Table 2, numbers of occurrences for structures of levels 2-5 are shown first as numbers out of obligatory contexts, then as percentage. As mentioned above, more than one example of a structure at a certain level must be produced in order for the learner to be given credit for that level, in order to minimize the risk of the example being a memorized chunk.

Time I writing						**Time II writing**				
Name	Level 2	Level 3	Level 4	Level 5		Name	Level 2	Level 3	Level 4	Level 5
Mal 1	17/17 1.	7/7 1.	15/15 1.	4/5 .8		Mal 3	24/24 1.	10/10 1.	13/13 1.	3/3 1.
Mal 2	15/15 1.	7/7 1.	12/15 .8	2/3 .7		Mal 4	29/30 1.	9/9 1.	12/12 1.	7/7 1.
Mal 3	13/13 1.	5/5 1.	15/15 1.	2/2 1.		Mal 7	23/23 1.	6/6 1.	8/9 .9	5/5 1.
Mal 4	16/16 1.	6/7 1.	9/10 .9	2/2 1.		Mal 1	25/25 1.	9/9 1.	7/7 1.	2/2 1.
Mal 5	16/16 1.	4/7 .6	8/14 .6	3/5 .6		Mal 2	24/24 1.	8/8 1.	18/18 1.	2/2 1.
Mal 6	18/18 1.	1/1 1.	7/10 .7	1/1 (1.)		Mal 8	28/28 1.	8/9 .9	13/13 1.	5/6 .9
Mal 7	16/16 1.	5/5 1.	10/14 1.	1/2 (.5)		Mal 11	26/26 1.	3/3 1.	5/8 .9	2/4 .5
Mal 8	9/10 .9	8/9 .9	8/11 .7	1/3 (.3)		Mal 10	25/25 1.	6/6 1.	5/5 1.	1/2 (.5)
Mal 9	17/17 1.	6/6 1.	13/13 1.	1/4 (.3)		Mal 9	28/28 1.	8/8 1.	9/9 1.	1/3 (.3)
Mal 10	6/6 1.	2/2 1.	8/8 1.	0/1 0		Mal 6	24/24 1.	6/6 1.	7/8 .8	1/3 (.3)
Mal 11	14/14 1.	3/5 .6	3/7 .4	0/2 .0		Mal 5	29/29 1.	6/6 1.	17/19 .9	1/2 (.5)

Table 2. Occurrences of structures out of obligatory contexts from the Malmö learners at two data collection points, Time I and Time II. Single examples are placed within parentheses.

As illustrated in Table 2 five learners are already at the top level (i.e. produce more than one example of structures at level five) at the time of the first data collection. One of them, Mal 5 seems to backslide. Three learners (Mal 7, 8 and 11) progress one level (from level four to level five), and three learners stay at the same level (Mal 6, 9 and 19). There are no gaps in the implicational scale, which means that when there is a development, it follows the PT predictions. From the point of view of emergence, we find that at Time I all learners produce structures of levels 2, 3 and 4. The production of level 5 structures is more limited, only five learners give more than one example and two learners never produce the structure. At Time II the level 5 structure has emerged in more learners, but there are still four learners that only produce single examples.

Development over time: the Melbourne group

The results from the Melbourne group are analyzed and presented in the same way. A summary is given in Table 3.

Time I writing						**Time II writing**				
Name	Level 2	Level 3	Level 4	Level 5		Name	Level 2	Level 3	Level 4	Level 5
Mel 1	17/17 1.	5/6 .8	9/11 .8	5/5 1.		Mel 1	29/29 1.	9/9 1.	8/8 1.	4/4 1.
Mel 2	18/18 1.	10/10 1.	10/11 .9	3/5 .6		Mel 8	28/28 1.	10/10 1.	11/11 1.	3/3 1.
Mel 3	17/17 1.	6/6 1.	8/12 .6	1/2 (.5)		Mel 7	29/29 1.	15/16 .9	13/1 .9	2/2 1.
Mel 4	14/17 .8	5/6 .9	6/10 .6	0/2 (0)		Mel 3	28/28 1.	13/15 .9	9/11 .8	2/2 1.
Mel 5	17/17 1.	6/6 1.	21/21 1.	0/2 0		Mel 2	29/29 1.	10/10 .9	14/14 .9	2/3 .7
Mel 6	17/17 1.	18/18 1.	16/17 .9	0/2 0		Mel 6	29/29 1.	13/13 1.	13/14 .9	1/3 (.3)
Mel 7	14/18 .8	6/7 .9	12/15 .8	0/1 (0)		Mel 5	26/26 1.	6/7 .9	14/17 .8	1/3 (.3)
Mel 8	23/27 .9	6/6 1.	11/11 1.	0/1 (0)		Mel 4	28/28 1.	15/16 .9	13/14 .9	0/3 0
Mel 9	12/14 9	7/9 .8	1/15 .1	1/3 .3		Mel 9	28/28 1.	8/10 .8	7/14 .5	0/2 0

Table 3. Occurrences of structures out of obligatory contexts from the Melbourne learners at two data collection points Time I and Time II. Single examples are placed within parentheses.

As in the data from Malmö, the data from Melbourne demonstrates that there are no gaps in the implicational scale, which means that the foreign language learners in Melbourne follow the PT predictions, just as the second language learners in Malmö do. At Time I, all learners except Mel 9 produce more than one example of structures of level 4. Only two of the learners produce more than single instances of level 5 structures. At Time II five of the learners produce more than one example of the level 5 structure, the negated subordinate clause.

Comparison written – spoken production: the Malmö group

The written and spoken production in the same individual was analysed in terms of Processability Levels 3, 4 and 5. The results for the Malmö group are summarized in table 4.

Time II - written					Time II - oral			
Name	Level 3	Level 4	Level 5		Name	Level 3	Level 4	Level 5
Mal 3	10/10 1.	13/13 1.	3/3 1.		Mal 3	12/13 1.	12/12 1.	8/8 1.
Mal 4	9/9 1.	12/12 1.	7/7 1.		Mal 2	14/14 1.	14/15 1.	12/12 1.
Mal 7	6/6 1.	8/9 .9	5/5 1.		Mal 8	14/14 1.	15/15	11/11 1.
Mal 1	9/9 1.	7/7 1.	2/2 1.		Mal 1	14/14 1.	16/16 1.	3/3 1.
Mal 2	8/8 1.	18/18 1.	2/2 .8		Mal 4	13/14 .9	13/13 1.	4/5 .9
Mal 8	8/9 .9	13/13 1.	5/6 .9		Mal 7	13/14 .9	/	10/12 .8
Mal 11	3/3 1.	5/8 .9	2/4 .5		Mal 10	14/14 1.	6/15 .5	1/12 (.1)
Mal 10	6/6 1.	5/5 1.	1/2 (.5)		Mal 5	12/12 1.	14/14 1.	/
Mal 9	8/8 1.	9/9 1.	1/3 (.3)		Mal 11	9/9 1.	14/16 .9	/
Mal 6	6/6 1.	7/7 1.	1/3 (.3)		Mal 6	13/13 1.	13/14 .9	0/3 0
Mal 5	6/6 1.	17/19 .9	1/2 (.5)		Mal 9	14/14 1.	12/15 .8	0/7 0

Table 4. Occurrences of structures out of obligatory contexts from the Malmö learners at Time II, written and oral production. A slash (/) means that there are no contexts for the structure in question.

At the group level, there is a slight difference between written and oral production. Seven Malmö learners produce level 5 in writing but only six learners produce level 5 in speech. There are three cases of missing contexts, once for level 4, predicative agreement, and twice for level 5, subordination.

The result for the individuals demonstrates that most Malmö learners produce structures at the same level in speech as in writing. There is only one learner, Mal 11, who produces level 5 in writing but not in speech. However, this does not make a strong case, since it is not a question of violating the rule for negative placement in subordinate clauses, but lacking the context for the structure, subordination. (This means that the learner answers the question 'Which card did you get?' with 'The boy does not paint' instead of 'I got the boy who does not paint').

Comparison written – spoken production: the Melbourne group

We turn now to the Melbourne data and the comparison between written and oral production.

Time II - written					Time II Oral			
Name	Level 3	Level 4	Level 5		Name	Level 3	Level 4	Level 5
Mel 1	9/9 1.	8/8 1.	4/4 1.		Mel 2	12/12 1.	15/15 1.	11/11 1.
Mel 8	10/10 1.	11/11 1.	3/3 1.		Mel 5	13/13 1.	0/1 (0)	11/11 1.
Mel 7	15/16 .9	13/14 .9	2/2 1.		Mel 1	14/14 1.	/	5/11 .5
Mel 3	13/15 .9	9/11 .8	2/2 1.		Mel 3	12/12 1.	8/13 .6	1/11 (.1)
Mel 2	10/10 1.	14/14 .9	2/3 .7		Mel 6	10/10 1.	15/15 1.	/
Mel 6	13/13 1.	13/14 .9	1/3 (.3)		Mel 8	13/14 .9	14/16 .9	/
Mel 5	6/7 .9	14/17 .8	1/3 (.3)		Mel 7	12/13 .9	11/15 .7	0/4 0
Mel 4	15/16 .9	13/14 .9	0/3 0		Mel 4	7/12 .	/	0/11 0
Mel 9	8/10 .8	7/14 .5	0/2 0		Mel 9	5/13 .4	5/10 .5	0/8 0

Table 5. Occurrences of structures out of obligatory contexts from the Melbourne learners at Time II, written and oral production. A slash (/) means that there are no contexts for the structure in question.

As with the Malmö group, there is a slight difference between writing and speech at the group level. Five learners produce level 5 in writing but only three learners do so in speech. However, the difference is mainly due to lack of contexts. For example, Mel 8, who uses structures at level 5 in writing, provides no such contexts in speech. There are only two learners (Mel 3, Mel 7) that perform at a higher level in writing than in speech, and only for Mel 7 is it a question of zero production in speech. An example from the performance of learner Mel 7 in writing and speech is given below:

Example (1) Mel 7

Written production (Level 5):	Oral production (below Level 5):
En röd Volvo som **inte** hade varit jättedyr	*Jag fick den som kan **inte** klättra
A red Volvo that not had been expensive	I got the one that cannot climb

Another learner (Mel 5) shows the opposite pattern, a higher level in speech than in writing. This learner produces the level 5 structure in all eleven contexts in speech, but gives only one single example out of three contexts in writing.

Summarizing the results for both groups, we find that for the comparison over time, there are no gaps in the implicational scaling (i.e. the learners follow the predicted pattern). For the difference between writing and speech, we find that there is a lack of contexts in oral production: seven learners (Mal 5, 7, 11, Mel 1, 4, 6, 8) use contexts in writing that they do not use in speech.

Discussion

In this study we investigated the development of Swedish morpho-syntax from a PT perspective in two groups of learners and compared their written and oral production. PT is designed for on-line speech production and it could have been expected that the written mode, which allows time for planning and monitoring, might give different results. However, the learners in our study followed the PT hierarchy both in speech and writing. Apart from the fact that the Malmö group was slightly more advanced the pattern was the same. Both groups followed the implicational sequence, i.e. there were hardly any gaps in the scales.

The development between Time I and Time II was small in terms of emergence of structures; only seven of the twenty learners showed a progress from one level to another. However, the development was considerable from a perspective of mastery of the structures. At Time I only two Malmö learners had 100% of the level 5 structures, and there were occasional errors also on the earlier levels. At Time II five learners produced 100% of the level 5 structures and the number of learners with 100% on the other levels increased. The development in the Melbourne group demonstrated the same trend; only one learner already had full supply of level five at Time I, but four learners had 100% at Time II, and the percentages increased overall.

On-line oral production demands automatized procedures, whereas writing allows time for the learners to use declarative knowledge and monitor their own production. If it were possible to stretch the PT levels by monitoring, we would have found learners to be able to produce more levels in writing than in speech. However, with very few exceptions, our informants did not produce higher levels in writing than in speech. This is in accordance with our hypothesis that the same processing constraints would guide oral and written production when the focus is on message and not on form. In all tasks there was a conceptual message that had to be encoded into a grammatical structure, and learners used the same levels of processability, irrespective of the time for planning. However, in Krashen's original conceptualization of monitoring three conditions had to be met in order for monitoring to take place: planning time, focus on form and rule knowledge. In our study, two of these conditions were held constant, i.e. focus and rule knowledge and the only difference between the oral and written tasks was therefore the difference in planning time. The results show that time alone does not give differences in levels of processability. This confirms the findings from the Hulstijn & Hulstijn (1984) study. The only context where their learners were able to change their grammatical performance was when they were explicitly told to focus their attention on formal aspects of the target language.

Language complexity is different from grammatical processability, and it is analyzed in terms of sentence length and degree of subordination. The very occurrence of subordinate clauses is therefore an indication of complexity, whereas the differentiation of main clause and subordinate clause word order patterns (in languages where there is such a difference, e.g. Swedish) is a sign of a high level of grammatical processability (Norrby & Håkansson submitted). As mentioned above, variation in learner performance has been found to occur more consistently in studies of complexity than in studies measuring grammatical accuracy (Ortega 1999). A tendency to have a more complex language in written than in oral production was found also in the present study. Seven learners used contexts in writing that they did not use in speech. One of the contexts was the NP-copula-adjective. In the oral task, three learners (Mal 7, Mel 1, Mel 4) did not produce the copula verb, thereby lacking a context for predicative agreement. The other structure was subordination. Four learners, two in the Malmö group (Mal 5, Mal 11) and two in the Melbourne group (Mel 6, Mel 8) consistently used main clauses instead of subordinate clauses in the oral task, despite the 12 obligatory contexts for subordination given in the communicative game. This is striking, considering that the type of subordinate clause that is elicited, the relative clause, is very common in spoken Swedish. Furthermore, exactly the same task, when used in a study of young Swedish three-year olds, generated the target subordinate clauses by the children (Håkansson & Hansson 2000). The fact that our adult learners avoided subordination in the oral tasks supports the results from other studies on the effect of planning time on language production, namely that language complexity is sensitive to external conditions such as planning time.

In conclusion, the present study demonstrated that the PT predictions are followed in both oral and written production of Swedish learner language. There is an implicational order of structures and no gaps in the hierarchy. The planning time that is allowed in writing does not seem to have an influence over processability of structures. With few exceptions, the learners are not able to stretch their interlanguage to include more levels in writing than in speech. However, the lack of complex structures such as subordination in speech suggests that planning time does have an influence on language complexity.

References

Bresnan, J. (1982). *The Mental Representation of Grammatical Relations.* Cambridge, MA: MIT Press.

Ellis, R. (1992). *Second Language Acquisition and Language Pedagogy.* Clevedon: Multilingual Matters.

Foster, P. & Skehan, P. (1996). 'The influence of planning and task type on second language performance'. *Studies in Second Language Acquisition.* 18: 299-323.

Glahn, E., Håkansson, G., Hammarberg, B., Holmen, A., Hvenekilde, A. & Lund, K. (2001). Processability in Scandinavian Second Language Acquisition. *Studies in Second Language Acquisition.* 23: 389–416.

Håkansson, G. (2001). 'Tense morphology and verb-second in Swedish L1 children, L2 children and children with SLI'. *Bilingualism: Language and Cognition.* 4: 85-99.

—. (2005). 'Similarities and differences in L1 and L2 development. Opening up the perspective: including SLI'. In Pienemann, M. (ed.), *Cross-linguistic Aspects of Processability Theory.* Amsterdam. John Benjamins.

Håkansson, G. & Hansson, K. (2000). 'Comprehension and production of relative clauses: a comparison between Swedish impaired and unimpaired children'. *Journal of Child Language.* 27: 313-333.

Håkansson, G., Norrby, C. & Bruzaeus, L. (2004). 'Svenska i och utanför Sverige. Grammatiska och pragmatiska mönster i inlärarspråket'. [Swedish inside and outside Sweden. Grammatical and pragmatic patterns.] In Ekberg, L. & Håkansson, G. (eds.) *Nordand 6. Sjätte konferensen om Nordens språk som andraspråk.* 78-89.

Håkansson, G. & Norrby, C. (2005) 'Grammar and pragmatics – Swedish as a foreign language'. In Foster-Cohen, S., Garcia-Mayo, M. & Cenoz, J. (eds). *EUROSLA Yearbook 5.* Amsterdam. John Benjamins. 137-161.

Hulstijn, J. & Hulstijn, W. (1984) 'Grammatical errors as a function of processing constraints and explicit knowledge'. *Language Learning.* 34: 23-43.

Krashen, S. D. (1981). *Second Language Acquisition and Second Language Learning.* Oxford: Pergamon.

—. (1985). *The Input Hypothesis: Issues and Implications.* London: Longman.

Levelt, W. (1989). *Speaking: From Intention to Articulation.* Cambridge, MA: MIT Press.

Mehnert, U. (1998), 'The effects of different lengths of time for planning on second language performance'. *Studies in Second Language Acquisition*. 20: 52-83.

Norrby, C. & Håkansson, G. (submitted) *The Interaction of Complexity and Grammatical Processing – The Case of Swedish as a Foreign Language.*

Ortega, L. (1999). 'Planning and focus on form in L2 oral performance'. *Studies in Second Language Acquisition*. 21: 108-148.

Pienemann, M. (1998). *Language Processing and Second Language Development: Processability Theory.* Amsterdam: Benjamins.

Pienemann, M. & Håkansson, G. (1999). 'A unified approach towards the development of Swedish as L2: a processability account'. *Studies in Second Language Acquisition*. 21: 383–420.

Segalowitz, N. & Hulstijn, J. (2005). 'Automaticity in bilingualism and second language learning'. In Kroll, J. & A. De Groot (eds.), *Handbook of Bilingualism.* New York: Oxford University Press. 371- 388.

Selinker, L. (1972). 'Interlanguage'. *International Review of Applied Linguistics*. 10: 209-231.

Sharwood Smith, M. (1994). *Second Language Learning: Theoretical Foundations.* London: Longman.

Tarone, E. (1985). 'Variability in interlanguage use: a study on style-shifting in morphology and syntax'. *Language Learning*. 35: 373-404.

—. (1988). *Variation in Interlanguage*. London: Edward Arnold.

Yuan, F. & Ellis, R. (2003). 'The effects of pre-task planning and on-line planning on fluency, complexity and accuracy in L2 monologic oral production'. *Applied Linguistics*. 24: 1-27.

CHAPTER 5

CONCEPTUALISING INTRA-STAGE SEQUENCING IN THE LEARNER LANGUAGE

Fethi Mansouri and Gisela Häkansson

In recent years, second language acquisition (SLA) research has been concerned with the developmental features of the learner language at different points in time during the acquisition process. It is now well documented that the interlanguage system develops gradually and continuously in an essentially cumulative manner as the target language structures are tested and either confirmed or discarded. A core objective of SLA research, therefore, remains to describe the learner language as systematically as is conceptually possible. In studies undertaken from a Processability Theory perspective, for example, the emphasis is mostly on the predictability power of the theory for language-specific acquisition stages. For example, DiBiase & Kawaguchi (2002), Glahn et al (2001), Håkansson (2001), Mansouri (2000) and Pienemann (1998), were all concerned, partially or totally, with the order of acquisition stages among individual learners of Italian, Japanese, Swedish, Arabic, German and English respectively.

Internal sequencing within specific stages or intra-stage sequencing are increasingly viewed as additional explanatory tools to that may be needed to account for language-specific typological features in the target language. In the case of Arabic as a second language (ASL) for example, such features may include humanness-animacy and definiteness marking. The logic behind the idea of intra-stage sequencing is this: the order in which structures belonging to the same developmental stage emerge is not arbitrary and in many cases can be highly predictable because these are motivated by. In this paper, we will focus on definiteness markers as part of phrasal morphology in ASL and Swedish as a second language (SSL) and will show that certain typological features such as cancelling the definiteness marker in certain patterns of noun phrases can be explained in terms of differing patterns of information exchange and differing processing requirements.

The question of form-function relations in the acquisition of definiteness (or article system) has been discussed in the SLA literature albeit almost exclusively in the context of ESL. In fact Anderson (1984) proposed the One to One Principle which claims that '*acquisition of a new form is facilitated when there is a clear and unique correspondence between form and meaning*', which is not the case even for English articles (Young, 1996).

The discussion of PT is undertaken elsewhere in this volume by Pinemann in chapter 2, so in this chapter the focus will be on the relevant structures in Arabic and their predicted intra-stage hierarchy.

Acquisition Criteria

PT argues for the application of the emergence criterion and its emphasis on morphological and lexical variation for the production of structures by the learner. This reflects the position taken in this study where there is at least one minimal pair of a given structure is produced before a judgment on emergence or lack of it can be formulated. PT categorises quantitative observations of the learner language into four types namely: '(1) no evidence; i.e. no linguistic contexts, (2) insufficient evidence; i.e. very small number of contexts, (3) evidence for non-application; i.e. non-application in the presence of contexts for rule x, (4) evidence of rule application; i.e. examples of rule application in the presence of contexts' Pienemann (1998:146) .

In line with this approach, the analysis here will rely primarily on type (4) observations as the empirical basis for applying the emergence criterion. The figures reported in the data tables below indicate the number of linguistic contexts for rule application and the corresponding number of suppliance. A ratio is also included in the same cell indicating the learner's developmental progression along the time axis.

Before dealing with definiteness marking in Arabic and their developmental features, let us outline briefly PT's general predictions for interlanguage morphology. PT argues that processing procedures and the capacity for the exchange of grammatical information are acquired in an essentially implicational sequence. The following table outlines this implicational sequence which should be testable in any learner language irrespective of the L2-specific typological features:

	Processing procedures	T1	T2	T3	T4	T5
5	**S'-procedure** (EmbeddedS)	-	-	-	-	+
4	**S-procedure**	-	simplified	simplified	inter-phrasal information exchange	inter-phrasal information exchange
3	Phrasal procedure	-	-	phrasal information exchange	phrasal information exchange	phrasal information exchange
2	**category procedure (lex. categ.)**	-	lexical morphemes	lexical morphemes	lexical morphemes	lexical morphemes
1	**word/ lemma**	+	+	+	+	+

Table 1. Hypothetical hierarchy of processing procedures

If the above hierarchy is to be universally applicable to language acquisition, then it needs to be applicable in relation to grammatical structures of individual languages. This is achieved by interpreting the processability hierarchy through a theory of grammar which is typologically and psychologically plausible. The focus of this chapter is on Stage 3 only (phrasal morphology) in terms of a hierarchy of typological patterns of form-function mappings and agreement relations. First a sketch of the structures to be investigated in ASL and SSL is provided below, followed by a discussion of the mpirical findings and a brief theoretical reflection on their importance for the processability theory overall.

Arabic Noun Phrases

Arabic is a non-configurational Semitic language with an agglutinative morphological system which also exhibits certain fusional features. As a result, it is the morphology that is used to indicate grammatical functions, through case marking, and not word order which is quite flexible. Noun phrases in Arabic consist of a head noun that may be preceded by determiner and definite marker and followed by one or more modifiers. Phrasal agreement refers to information exchange between a source head and its target modifier whereby key morpho-syntactic features (such as number, case, definiteness) are unified. Arabic noun phrases may be either post-nominal or pre-nominal as illustrated in the following two structures (Kremens, 2000:13):

a. Q-Dem-Ord-Card-Adj-**(Det)-N-(Gen)**

b. **(Det)-N-(Gen)**-Adj-Card-Ord-Dem-Q

The head noun within a noun phrase can have any combination of modifiers both preceding (pre-nominal) and following it (post-nominal). However, the basic sequence (Det)-N-(Gen)-Adj 'is a fixed combination that cannot be split. Different agreement rules govern pre-nominal and post-nominal agreement in Arabic NPs. Given that the focus of this chapter is not linguistic analysis *per se* but rather the learner language, the following analysis will not include the full spectrum of NP combinations and their complex agreement patterns. Noun-adjective agreement is not always a 'strict' feature-copying process (i.e., features being identically marked on both the noun and its modifier). In fact, there are many linguistic situations where the noun-adjective agreement is 'deflected' with features not merging as a block (Kihm, 2001:5). Before undertaking an analysis of the rule 'cancel definiteness marker', let us consider the marking of (in)definiteness in Arabic nominal morphology. This system is depicted in the following table using the noun */qalam/* (pen):

	Indefiniteness	**Definiteness**
Nom	qalam-u-**n**	**al**-qlama-u
Acc	qalam-a-**n**	**al**-qalam-a
Gen	qalam-i-**n**	**al**-qalam-i

Table 2. Marking Indefiniteness/Definiteness in Arabic

Because of the limited scope of this chapter, the following section will focus on an analysis of definiteness marking in noun-phrase structures followed by the implications of such patterns for second language acquisition.

The basic sequence (Det)-N-(Gen)-Adj in post-nominal NPs will be the main structure investigated in this analysis. Let us consider the following illustrative examples and their corresponding formalized linguistic analyses for the relevant NP structures:

(a) [DEF-Noun ====→ DEF-Adj]

(1) ***al**-awla:d-u* ***al**-kibaar*

the-boys-NOM the-old.PL-NOM

'The old boys'.

The f-structure and c-structure for the 'big boys' noun phrase are outlined below:

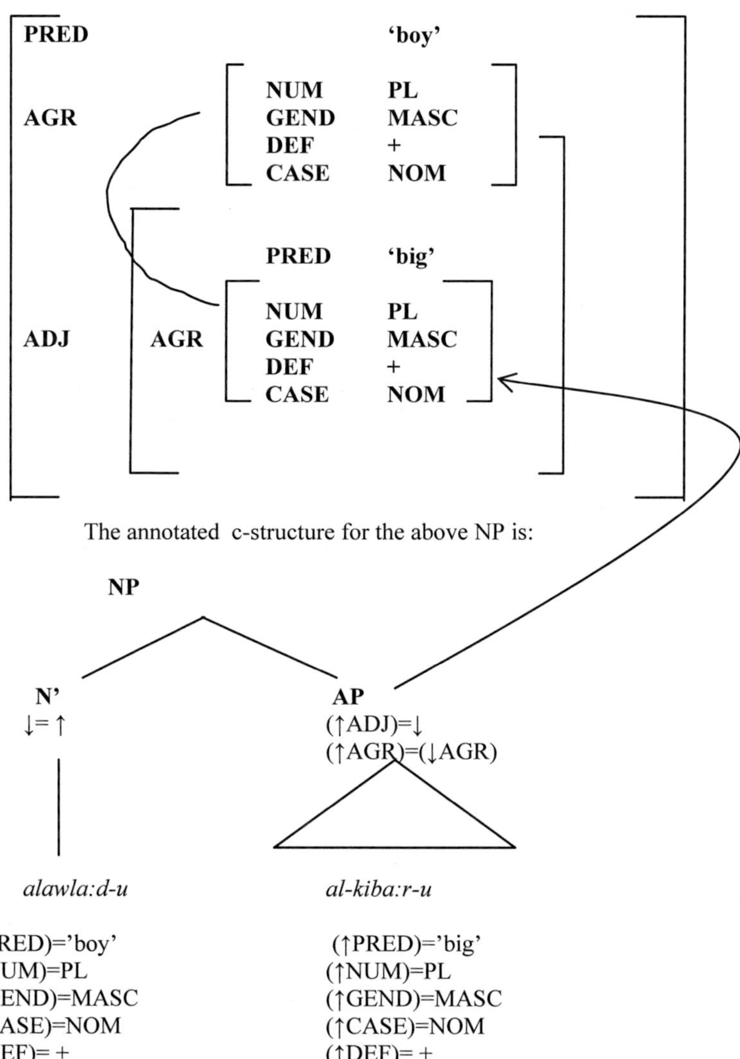

(b) [Noun-Pron =====➔Det-Adj]

(2) *bayt-**i** :* ***al-**qadi:m*
house-my the-old
'My old house'.

Example (2) above is an illustration on how definiteness can be marked by means of a possessive pronoun in Arabic. It is, therefore, similar to example (1) in the extent to which definiteness is expresses though the realisatio0n of this definiteness is achieved by different linguistic means.

(c) [Noun ===➔ Noun.Gen] *Idafa* structure (Possessive Construction)

darra:j-at-u	*al-'usta:dh* ***-i***	*al-jadi:d-at-u*	*gha:liyat-un*
bicycle-F.Nom	the-teacher-Gen	the-new-F.NOM	expensive-NOM

'The teacher's new bicycle (is) expensive.'

Because nouns in Arabic agree obligatorily with their specifiers first before any other dependents (Malouf 1998:5), the following f-structure and annotated c-structure for the above example are represented below:

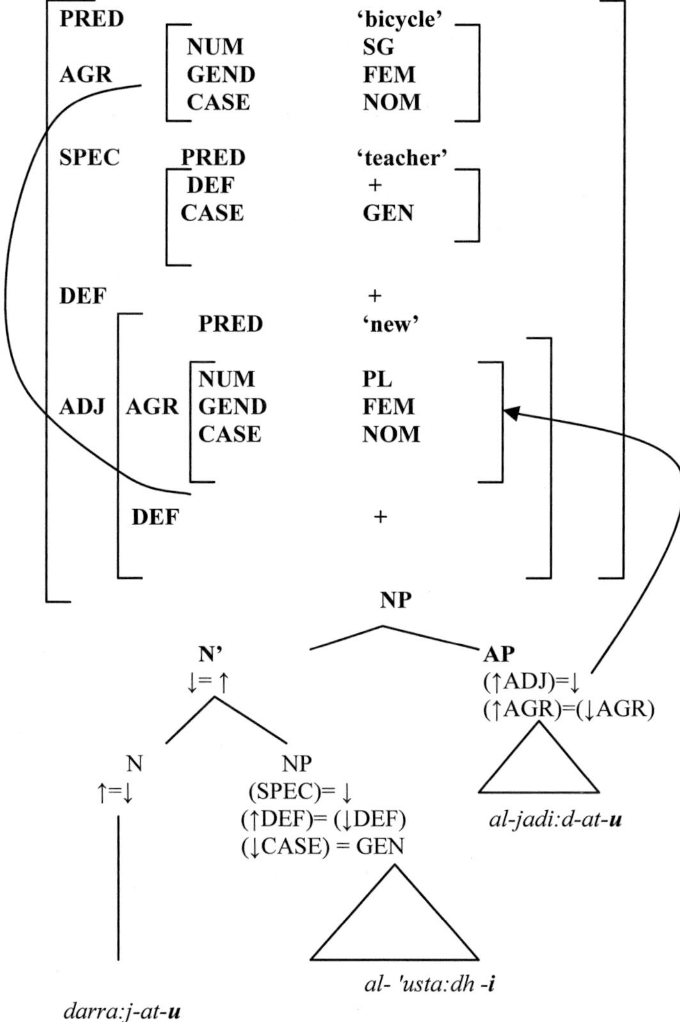

The formalised account of definiteness marking within Arabic NPs provides a clear hierarchy of structures underpinned by the amount of morphological marking shared between the head Noun and its modifier (adjective/complement). The following table summarises this typological hierarchy and identifies the specific linguistic features for each structure.

	Head N	Adj	Example	Typological issue
1	Def	Def	***al**-kita:b **al**-jadi:d* the-book the-new 'The new book'	Feature unification: Full marking of DEF marker on N and on ADJ
2	∅	Def	*∅-kita:b-i:* ***al**-qadi:m-u* book-my the-old-NOM 'My old book'	Partial Cancel of DEF marker (∅ marking head N)
3	∅	∅	*Madi:nat-u tu:nis* City-NOM Tunis 'The city of Tunis'.	Total Cancel of DEF marker (∅ on N and ∅ Complement)

Table 3. Typological hierarchy for definiteness marking in Arabic NP structures

The order of the structures above reflects the linguistic complexity of signalling 'definiteness' by means of either partial marking as in structure 2 [∅-N=➔Def -ADJ] or zero marking [∅-N=➔∅ -ADJ] as illustrated in structure 3.

Predictions for the Acquisition of Arabic NP

Because this chapter deals with intra-stage developmental issues, the following table focuses on stage 3 (Phrasal morphology) and zooms in on the internal linguistic and processing dynamics of structural hypotheses at the stage level. The directionality and amount of morphological marking are the key factors underlying the sequencing order within stage 3 as outlined in table (4) below for Arabic L2:

	Intra-Stage order	**Processing Prerequisites**	**Pattern of Information exchange**	**ASL Morphology Structure**	**Linguistic and processing features**
STAGE 3:	**3.1**	Phrasal procedure	Phrasal	DEF-N ==➔ DEF- Adj	Feature unification: Full marking of DEF marker on N and on ADJ
Phrasal Procedure	**3.2**	Phrasal procedure	Phrasal	∅ N.pro ==➔ DEF-Adj	Partial Cancel of DEF marker (∅ marking on head N)
	3.3	Phrasal procedure	Phrasal	∅N==➔∅ N.COMP 'Idafa structure' (Comp.)	Total Cancel of DEF marker (∅ on N and ∅ Complement)

Table 4. ASL predictions for DEF marking as a stage 3 structure

As far as research on the acquisition of Arabic as a second language is concerned, the few studies carried out in the past two decades are either too narrow in focus and, therefore, cannot claim to establish acquisition stages for Arabic grammar, or essentially descriptive studies (e.g., Bakalla 1980, Kuntz, 1996) that focus mainly on the major difficulties facing learners of Arabic as a second language. These studies are typically undertaken from a traditional error analysis approach where certain types of the learner's errors are analysed, accounted for and classified into various lexical, phonological and grammatical categories. Much of this research including morer recent efforts to work within a more developmental framework (e.g., Nielsen, 1997) ignores the key developmental issues in Arabic second language acquisition and as such will not be pursued any further in this paper.

This is exactly why a conceptual analysis of what motivates intra-stage developmental order in SLA is all the more crucial. Not only does this allow us to account for linguistic hierarchies of structures within stages, but more importantly it helps to identify the optimal test structures for a given developmental stage. This overcomes the assumption that all structures within a lower stage must be acquired before structures from the higher stage can emerge.

Phrasal morphology in Swedish

Swedish is a Germanic language with both agglutinating and synthetic features. Instead of person marking on verbs and/or case markings on nouns word order is used as the major signal of grammatical functions. The Swedish noun phrase have pre-nominal modifiers and may consist of the following basic constituents:

(Det)-(Adj)-N

There is extensive morphology at the phrase level in Swedish. Expanded noun phrases involve full agreement between modifiers and head nouns. The article and adjective agree with the head noun in gender (neuter or uter), definiteness (definite or indefinite) and number (singular or plural). In other words, there is exchange/merging of grammatical information between article, adjective and noun. The table below illustrates the basic morphological pattern involved in Swedish indefinite and definite noun phrases.

	Indefiniteness	Definiteness
Uter	En ny bok ('a new book')	Den ny-a bok-en ('the new book')
Neuter	Ett ny-tt hus ('a new house')	Det ny-a hus-et ('the new house')
Plural	Ny-a böck-er (new books')	De nya böck-er-na ('the new books')

Table 5: Swedish noun phrase morphology

In this paper, the discussion focuses on definiteness and we will therefore give a more detailed analysis of the definite noun phrases. For definiteness, there are three different patterns. 1) the noun is marked with a suffix –(e)n, or –(e)t, depending on the gender of the noun. 2) when there is an adjective modifying the noun definiteness is also expressed by a definite article and 3) when there is a possessor (possessive pronoun or a full noun in the genitive) the definite suffix on the noun is cancelled. The first structure, which only requires an addition by a suffix to a noun, belongs to the lexical level of Processability Theory and will therefore not be dealt with further. The tree diagram below illustrates how the feature definiteness is unified between article and noun suffix in the full agreement marking pattern, (structure 2).

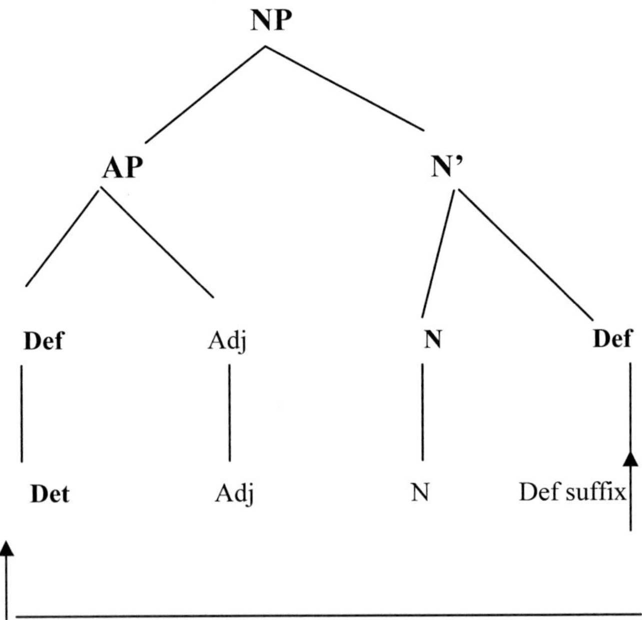

A Typological hierarchy for definiteness marking in Swedish NP structures:

As in Arabic, Swedish noun phrases exhibit different markings dependent on whether the context is a definite noun phrase with an article, or a definite noun phrase in a possessive construction. These two types are illustrated in the hierarchy below, as well as in the examples, that give both uter gender and neuter gender markings.

	Adj	Head N	Example	Typological issue
1	Def	Def	den nya boken the new-def book-the	Feature unification art-adj- - definite form
2	Def	Ø	lärarens nya bok teacher-the new-def book-Ø min nya bok my new-def book-Ø	Cancel of definiteness marker on the noun

Table 6: Typology of definiteness marking in Swedish NPs

Uter gender Neuter gender

(3) den nya boken ('the new book') det nya huset ('the new house')
DEF new-DEF book-DEF DEF new-DEF house-DEF

(4) lärarens nya bok Ø lärarens nya hus Ø
teacher-DEF-G new-DEF book teacher-DEF-G new-DEF house
(the teacher's new book') ('the teacher's new house')

Earlier studies of the L2 acquisition of Swedish noun phrase morphology

There has been a considerable amount of studies of the L2 acquisition of Swedish noun phrase morphology; e.g. Andersson (1992), Latomaa (1993), Axelsson (1994) Salameh, Håkansson & Nettelbladt (1996) and Glahn, Håkansson, Hammarberg, Holmen, Hvenekilde, & Lund, K. (2001). The results from these studies show that some NP structures emerge early, whereas other structures take a considerable time to be acquired.

Two of the studies will be presented in more detail. Axelsson (1994) investigated development of Swedish noun phrase morphology in a cross-sectional study of 60 adult L2 learners, who had received formal instruction in Swedish. Three stages were proposed, based on accuracy percentages. The NP types at stage 1 were names, bare nouns, and nouns with a single modifier, illustrated by the examples Johanna (name), bok (book), and tre flickor (three girls). These NP types were used very frequently and accurately (90%). The NP types at stage 2 displayed definite suffix and indefinite article, illustrated by the examples flickan (girlDEF), and en flicka (a girl). The accuracy rate was around

60%. Stage 3 contained complex NPs with adjective agreement in gender, number, and definiteness, illustrated by the example det gula huset (DEF ART yellow house.DEF). For this structure, both frequency and accuracy were rather low, 20-30%. Less than half of the learners managed to produce definite NPs with both a definite article and a definite suffix. Interestingly, no learner produced what we have called 'cancel definiteness marker', i.e. the form where the definiteness marker is cancelled on the noun, despite the fact that there were plenty of obligatory contexts for this structure to occur. Thus, it can be assumed that this structure belongs to a later level that the other noun phrase agreement structures.

Another investigation into the acquisition of NP agreement is the study by Salameh et al (1996). The data consists of oral production in a group of 18 Arabic-speaking children, five and six years old, acquiring Swedish as a second language. Of a total of 299 examples of noun phrases containing adjective and noun, only approximately 25 % had the target language form. The analysis of the data suggests the following implicational sequence:

No agreement (only lexical affixes)
Agreement between two constituents (adjective + noun)
Agreement between three constituents (article + adjective + noun)

As in the Axelsson study, the learners in Salameh et al failed to produce the 'cancel definiteness markers' that are the focus of this paper.

Summarizing earlier studies of L2 Swedish, there is a consensus that indefinite NP structures emerge early, but that the full agreement in definite noun phrase is a structure that develops during a long period and with much variation within the learner language. However, none of the above-mentioned studies has had an external point of reference with which one can compare the different morphological markings. In the present work, we take a different approach and test hypotheses based on the predictions from Processability Theory.

Predictions for SSL definiteness marking within phrasal agreement:

In the following, we will explore the possibilities of intra-stage development within the PT-stage of phrasal procedure (stage 3). The Swedish agreement patterns in full noun phrases are illustrated in table 8. Our hypothesis is that the full agreement markings will emerge before partial agreement, leading to a period of overgeneralization in the learner language, when the learner uses the same set of markings in all noun phrases (intra-stage 3.1). Later, the learner will be able to define the different constraints of markers in different contexts (intra-stage 3.2).

	Intra-Stage order	**Processing Prerequisites**	**SSL Morphology Structure**	**Linguistic and processing features**
Stage3: Phrasal Proce-dure	3.1	Phrasal procedures	Adj-DEF ===>Noun-DEF	Feature unification art-adj- - definite form
	3.2	Phrasal procedures	Adj-DEF ===> Noun Ø	Cancel of definiteness marker on the noun

Table 7: Predictions for SSL phrasal agreement

Empirical evidence for the PT-generated predictions:

Before dealing with the empirical findings for ASL and SSL separately an important issue across the two languages needs to be highlighted. This relates to the directional ordering of the partial cancel definiteness rule in Arabic [Ø---DEF] and its mirror image equivalent in Swedish [DEF- Ø]. This mirror image ordering is theoretically important because it will allow us to verify whether opposite directionality of this rule within the noun phrase structure would constrain learning in a different manner. If the learnability implications of this mirror image rule are similar in across ASL and SSL, then this will represent a further empirical evidence for the universal nature of PT claims. Let us first look at the data-generated acquisition sequences for the key structures in ASL as predicted within the PT framework and using the emergence criterion.

Results for ASL data

The data for this study was collected from learners of Arabic L2 in a classroom environment. Only oral data elicited through conversational interviews was used to ensure that the key feature of time-constrained production is maintained. The data sample consists of a stratified sample of individual learner data gathered from two learners studying Arabic in a formal classroom environment. The two English-speaking background (ESB) learners (one female, Louise and one male, George) were learning Arabic in a classroom environment. The main data eliciting procedures were eight spontaneous oral interviews conducted over four semesters of classroom language learning which consisted of a total of 52 instruction weeks.

Individual interviews were conducted four times over a two semester period and each lasted about 30 minutes. Each interview was organised around thematic discussions centred on familiar topics such as family and friends, holidays and tourism, study, the Middle East and personal hobbies. The interviews were structured with a view of eliciting narratives from the learners without explicit focus on grammatical forms. The following tables (5 and 6) report the learners' individual data with regard to definiteness marking within Arabic noun phrases (figures indicate occurrences in obligatory contexts).

	Structures	T1	T2	T3	T4
1	DEF-Noun ==➔ DEF- Adj	6/6 1.	7/7 1.	9/9 1.	8/8 1
2	DEF-Noun ==➔ DEF- Adj	2/4 0.5	2/3 0.66	4/4 1.	5/5 1.
3	∅Noun ====➔∅ Noun.COMP 'Idafa structure' (Comp.)	0	1/3 0.33	2/2 1.	2/2 1.

Table 8. The acquisition of Phrasal Agreement Morphology in ASL (Louise's data)

	Structures	T1	T2	T3	T4
1	DEF-Noun ==➔ DEF- Adj	5/5 1.	6/7 0.85	6/6 1.	7/8 0.87
2	∅ Noun.pro ==➔ DEF-Adj	1/3 0.33	2/4 0.5	2/3 0.66	3/3 1.
3	∅Noun ====➔∅ Noun.COMP 'Idafa structure' (Comp.)	0	1 /2 0.5	2/2 1.	2/2 1.

Table 9. The acquisition of Phrasal Agreement Morphology in ASL (George's data)

From a statistical analysis of these findings, it seems that at the first time of data collection neither learner was able to produce the *Idafa* structure (structure 3 on the sequence) characterised by a total cancel of the definite markers [∅-N==➔∅ -ADJ]. This is in contrast to structure 1 on the sequence [DEF-N===➔ DEF-ADJ] which has been produced by both learners in all instances of obligatory linguistic context. Structure 2 [∅-N ==➔ DEF-Adj] which exhibits partial cancel definite marker, and as predicted, emerges at Time 1 but with less frequency (0.3 and 0.5 ratios respectively) than structure 1 (1.0 for both learners). The following is a list of illustrative examples from both learners:

(a) [Def-Noun ====➔ Def-Adj]

(5) al-walad al-kabi:r huna:
the-boy the-big here

(6) *al-bint-u al-kabi:r-**at**-u huna:*
the-girl-Nom the-big-**F**.Nom here

(b) [Noun (pro.) =====➔Def-Adj.]
(7) * *askunu f:i shaqqat-**i:** saghi:ra*
live.1S in flat-**my** small

(c) [Poss.Noun ===➔ Noun] *Idafa* structure (Possessive Construction)
(8) * *a-skun fi: al-madi:nat melbourne*
I-live in the-city Melbourne

(9) **ya' mal abi: fi al-ja:mi'at Melbourne*
works my father in the-university Melbourne

The quantitative findings reported in tables 5 and 6 above are best illustrated in the samples of the learner language exhibited in examples 7 and 8 which show the consistent marking of definiteness with Arabic NP on both the head noun and its modifier. Both learners seem to have automated the sharing of this feature [+DEF] within the two elements of this syntactic structure. In example 9 where the partial cancel definiteness rule [∅ Noun.pro ==➔ DEF-Adj] applies, the learner in does not recognise the role of the possessive pronoun as a definiteness marker and, consequently, does not mark definiteness on the modifier. Similarly, in example 11 where the *Idafa* structure is used, the definite marker /al--/ can not be attached to either the head noun or its complement. This is because definiteness here can only be marked by means of the possessive linking relationship between the headnoun and its complement.

Results for SSL data

The corpus for the Swedish analysis consists of two learners with Swedish as a second language, one adult learner and one child learner. In contrast to the Arabic learners, the Swedish learners are naturalistic learners acquiring the target language outside the classroom. The data from the adult learner comes from the longitudinal corpus collected in the EALA project (Perdue 1993). Mari has Finnish as her first language. The child learner is a six-year-old boy with Karamanji as his first language (Håkansson & Nettelbladt 1993). In the analyses, all instances of noun phrases in a definite context were counted.

	Structures	T1	T2	T3	T4
1	Adj-DEF ==→ Noun -DEF	0/3	3/4	11/12	6/6
2	Poss Adj-DEF ==➔ Noun-∅	0/2	0/3	1/3	1/2

Table (10): The acquisition of Noun Agreement in SSL (Mari's data)

	Structures	T1	T2	T3	T4
	Adj-DEF ==→ Noun -DEF	4/5 0.80	6/8 0.75	8/9 0.89	7/7 1.
	Poss Adj-DEF ==➔ Noun-∅	0/3 .0	0/2 .0	3/3 1.	2/2 1.

Table (11): The acquisition of Noun Agreement in SSL (Ali's data)

(a) [Def.Art ====→ Adj-Def ====→Noun-Def]

(10) *den fattig flicka (Mari 1)
the poor-∅ girl-∅

(11) *den stora skillnad (Mari 1)
the big-the difference-∅

(12) det gamla huset (Mari 2)
the old-Def house-Def

(b) [Noun-Gen/Poss.Pro =====➔ Def-Adj ====→ Noun-∅.]
(13) * min gamla sängen (Mari 4)
my old-Def bed-Def

(14) hans fina ballong (Ali 3)
his fine-Def balloon-∅

The first two examples on definiteness (set a) are ungrammatical, in different ways. In number (10) there is no definiteness markers at all, except for the definite article. In example (11) both article and adjective signals definiteness, but not the noun. Finally, example (12) illustrates the target structure. In set b, the first example shows full definiteness marking in a possessive contexts, example 13 both on adjective and noun.. Example 14 illustrates the target use of definiteness markings in a possessive construction, with definiteness marked on the adjective but cancelled on the noun.

Discussion

Phrasal morphological processes involve feature unification/merging between constituents within a phrase. An important issue, however, is the form/function relationship. Some morphemes have a one-to-one relationship between form and function, while others may express a one to many form function relationship as is the case with the English morpheme –s which is used both for genitive, plural and verbal agreement. In the case of definiteness in Arabic and Swedish, we find several forms for the same function:

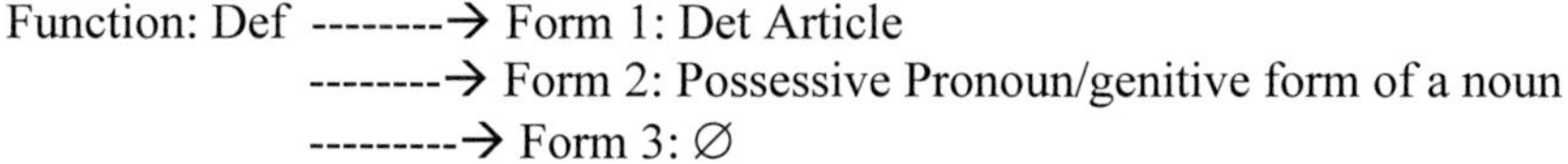
Function: Def --------→ Form 1: Det Article
--------→ Form 2: Possessive Pronoun/genitive form of a noun
---------→ Form 3: ∅

In Arabic all three forms are used, in Swedish only the first two. As has been pointed out by Pienemann (1998:113) this is an additional task. Even when the information exchange between constituents in a phrase is processable, the question of different forms remain to be acquired. Our empirical data point to a tendency for L2 learners who have acquired the first form to overuse it also in contexts where it is not applicable. In order to acquire new forms for old functions, they seem have to 'unlearn' the earlier form. We argue that this is done through a gradual development that is similar to the 'cancel inversion' in the L2 acquisition of English.

Distinguishing between different forms for the same function represents an additional processing and learning task. Cancel definite marker (i.e., zero realisation of DEF) is in many ways similar to the ESL's 'cancel inversion' in at least two areas: 1) it emerges later than the full definiteness/full inversion in the L2 development, and 2) it is gradual and can be assumed to be lexically driven. In his account of 'cancel inversion' in ESL, Pienemann states that it 'describes the fact that the word order phenomena observed in direct questions do not apply in the context of indirect questions' (Pienemann 1998:170). Pienemann suggests that the acquisition of cancel inversion is driven by the lexicon. The learner has to be able to differentiate between question words and complementizers in order for indirect questions to be processable. The cancel inversion phenomenon belongs to the level of subordinate clause procedures and represents a pattern of processability that is higher in the hierarchy than 'inversion'.

The intra-stage sequences for definiteness marking highlights the importance of articulating clearly the methodological and linguistic criteria for selecting the optimal structure for empirical testing. This also highlights the need to 'construct the distributional analysis in such a way that predictions can be tested on the emergence of forms, i.e. without functional accuracy' (Pienemann, 1998:11).

The findings of the study reported in this chapter show that second language learners who have acquired the first form to overuse it also in contexts where it is not applicable. In order to acquire forms for old functions, learners have to 'unlearn' the earlier form. This is an additional third task to (1) information transfer and (2) morphological affixation. It is argued that this is done through a gradual development that is similar to the 'cancel inversion' in the acquisition of English syntax. Hypothesis Space, within PT, already offers an ideal framework for dealing with developmental and variational issues in the learner language. What is proposed in this paper is extending the 'space' to incorporate sequences of multiple structures within specific stages.

Intra-stage sequencing is different from typical interlanguage variation in that predictable structures produced within a stage are not simplified versions of the same structure. Moreover, the learner need not access all structural options before moving the next developmental stage.

As already established in the SLA literature and in particular in PT-related research, 'developmental trailers' are a common feature in the learner language because there is a temporal gap between producing the linguistic context for a structure X and its actual rule application. This gradual development in the learner language can be captured in the intra-stage phenomenon where a formalised differentiation between optimal and no-optimal L2 structures can be the source of additional explanatory modules. As far as the choice of the optimal structure is concerned, the deciding factors relate to form-function mappings and their developmental implications. In other words and from a psycholinguistic perspective, those structures in the L2 that exhibit a one-to-one correspondence between form and function are most likely to be the most plausible candidate for the optimal structure status.

Variation within developmental stages in the learner language is systematic, rule-governed and can be explained within PT's 'Hypothesis Space' using linguistic descriptions as additional explanatory modules. The cross-linguistic evidence presented in this paper for ASL and SSL shows that even when the structure in question exhibits language-specific typological features (i.e. the mirror image ordering of NP structures: ∅-DEF in ASL as opposed DEF-∅ in SSL) this has not constrained processability across the two IL systems in different manners. In fact, the similar findings in ASL and SSL suggest that form-function relationships and the related realisation (or lack of) forms can be formalised in such a way that predictions are generalisable irrespective of the target L2.

PT's Hypothesis Space has been extended along both the variational and developmental axes to reflect stage-specific developmental issues. The following graph has been adapted from Pienemann's (1998:232) discussion on Hypothesis Space and illustrates the additional conceptual dimension (intra-stage sequencing) proposed in this paper.

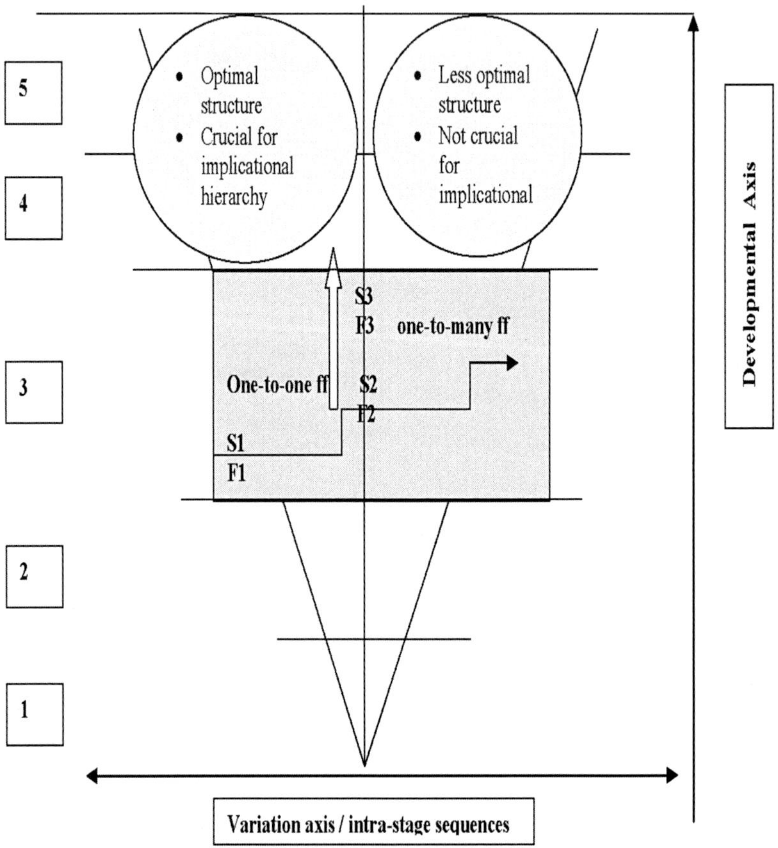

What the expanded Hypothesis space model indicates is that the implicational nature of second language development needs to be viewed as a two-tiered process that evolves in a step-like manner. The upward movement towards a higher acquisition stage is premised on the emergence of the optimal structure (S1) which linguistically would exhibit less complex form-function relationships (preferably one to one correspondence). This is indicated in the extended Hypothesis Space model through a discontinuing line that represents the vertical arrow. Yet, since most languages exhibit multiple structure at any given developmental stage, the horizontal movement (typically represented by the variational axis) acquires an internal predictable order or sequence with structures (S2, S3 etc…) being indicative of more complex linguistic and functional phenomena that have implications for language processing. From a methodological point of view, the optimal structure (S1) is also an ideal structure for empirical testing of the PT predictions whilst the more complex ones (S2, S3 etc…) are not the best candidates for testing theoretical predictions. In fact, this may help explain the sometimes contradictory research findings that claim to falsify implicational predictions generated through PT.

Conclusion

The empirical evidence presented in this paper for ASL and SSL shows those form-function mappings and the related morphological realisation (or lack) of forms can be formalised in such a way that predictions are generalisable irrespective of the target L2. The implications of this study's findings for PT pertain specifically to methodology and theory extension. In terms of methodology the potential contribution of this paper lies in formalising the criteria for selecting the optimal test structures in PT-related research. This methodological issue leads to the proposed extension of Hypothesis Space where an additional stage-internal dimension has been incorporated. This dimension reflects the multiplicity of interlanguage structures (in this study with differing form-function mappings but can relate to other typological phenomena) within a developmental stage.

References

Anderson, R.W. (1984). 'The one to one principle of interlanguage construction'. *Language Learning*. 34: 77-95.

Bresnan, J. (2001). *Lexical Functional Syntax.* Blackwell Publishers.

DiBiase, B. & Kawaguchi, S. (2002). 'Exploring the typological plausibility of Processability Theory: language development in Italian second language and Japanese second language'. *Second Language Research.* 18: 274-302.

Dik, S. (1978). *Functional Grammar.* Amsterdam: North Holland.

Ellis, R. (1994). *The Study of Second Language Acquisition.* Oxford: Oxford University Press.

Fassi Fehri, A. (1988). 'Agreement in Arabic, Binding and Coherence'. In M. Barlow & Ferguson, C. (eds.), *Agreement in Natural Languages.* USA: (CSLI) Center for the Study of Language and Information.

Glahn, E., Håkansson, G., Hammarberg, B., Holmen, A., Hvenekilde, A,. & Lund, K. (2001). 'Processability in Scandinavian Second language acquisition'. *Studies in Second Language Acquisition.* 23, 389-416.

Håkansson, G. (2001). 'Tense morphology and verb-second in Swedish L1 children, L2 children and children with SLI'. *Bilingualism: Language and Cognition.* 4, 85-99.

Håkansson, G. & Nettelbladt, U. (1993). 'Developmental sequences in L1 (normal and impaired) and L2 acquisition of Swedish'. *International Journal of Applied Linguistics.* 3: 131-157.

Håkansson, G., Pienemann, M. & Sayehli, S. (2002). T'ransfer and typological proximity in the context of L2 processing'. *Second Language Research.* 18: 250-273.

Källström, R. (1990). *Kongruens i svenskan [Agreement in Swedish].* Dissertation. University of Gothenburg.

Kihm, A. (2001). *Agreement in Noun Phrases in Semitic Languages: Its Nature and Some Consequences for Morphosyntactic Representations.* CNRS: Laboratoire de Linguistique Formelle.

Kremens, J. (2000). 'A recursive linearization approach to Arabic noun phrases'. The Netherlands: University of Nijmegen.

Kuntz, P. (1996). 'Students of Arabic: beliefs about foreign language learning'. *Al-Arabiyya.* 29: 153-177.

Mansouri, F. (2000) *Grammatical Markedness and Information Processing in the Acquisition of Arabic as a Second Language.* Munchen, Germany: LINCOM EUROPA Academic Publishers.

—. (1999). *The Acquisition of Arabic as a Second Language: From Theory to Practice.* Language Australia: The National Language and Literacy Institute of Australia (NLLIA) & the Language Acquisition Research Center (LARC), Sydney: University of Western Sydney (Macarthur).

Nielsen, H.L. (1997). 'On acquisition order of agreement procedures in Arabic learner language'. *Al-Arabiyya.* 30: 49-95.

Moutaouakil, A. (1985). 'Topics in Arabic: towards a functional analysis'. In A.M. Bokstein, C. deGroot & Mackenzie, J.L. (eds.), *Syntax and Pragmatics in Functional Grammar.* Dordrecht-Holland/Cinnamison, USA: Foris Publications.

Perdue, C. (1993) (ed.) *Adult language acquisition: Cross-linguistic perspectives.* Vol I & II Cambridge University Press

Pienemann, M. (1998). *Language Processing and Second Language Development: Processability Theory.* Amsterdam/Philadelphia: John Benjamins.

Pienemann, M. & Håkansson, G. (1999). 'A unified approach towards the development of Swedish as L2: a processability account'. *Studies in*

Second Language Acquisition. 21: 383-420.

Salameh, E.-K., Håkansson, G. & Nettelbladt, U. (1996). 'The acquisition of Swedish as a second language in a group of Arabic-speaking pre-school children: word order patterns and phrasal morphology'. *Logopedics Phoniatrics Vocology*. 21: 163-170.

Young, R. (1996). 'Form-Function Relations in English Interlanguage', In R. Bayley & Preston, D.R. (eds.), *Second Language Acquisition and Linguistic Variation.* Amsterdam/Philadelphia: John Benjamins Publishing.

CHAPTER 6

ASSESSING EFL-DEVELOPMENT ONLINE: A FEASIBILITY STUDY OF RAPID PROFILE

Jörg-U Keßler[1]

Rapid Profile is a computer-assisted procedure for screening speech samples collected from language learners to assess their level of language development as compared to standard patterns in the acquisition of the target language. This tool was developed from standard Profile Analysis (Crystal, Garman & Fletcher 1976) which was based on an interview, a full transcription of the interview and a detailed analysis of the transcript. *Rapid Profile* is a shorthand version of the original procedure developed by Pienemann within the LARC research projects (Pienemann 1990 and 1992) from the suggestions made by Clahsen (1985) and by Pienemann, Johnston & Brindley (1988). Since then, a lot of research has been conducted to make *Rapid Profile* a strong and applicable tool for online-assessment of learner language and the diagnosis of English as a Foreign Language (EFL) development.

Rapid Profile limits itself to the analysis of a number of well established morpho-syntactic features to be found in EFL learners' interlanguage (cf. Pienemann 1998). The linguistic features being focused on may not immediately resemble the full picture of human language, but they do in fact reflect far more of what we know of learner language development, as a whole, than is immediately apparent. This developmental path of learner language has been substantiated by many empirical findings (e.g. Pienemann, 1984 and 1998; DiBiase 2002; Mansouri & Duffy 2005; Keßler 2006a and 2006b).

One of the aims of our research group on *Rapid Profile* is to provide teachers with a diagnostic tool that can be applied in formal EFL settings. As one cannot expect teachers to be fully trained (psycho)linguists it is important to develop a training scenario that enables teachers with only limited background in linguistic theory to learn to manage *Rapid Profile* in in-service teacher training sessions that should last no longer than just a few afternoons.

Therefore a training environment was created that allows undergraduate students to learn about the underlying theory and to practice online-screenings with *Rapid Profile* in a condensed programme. None of the analysts trained in this programme and reported in this study had more than an introductory linguistics background before they commenced the training.

Linguistic Profiling using *Rapid Profile*

The principle behind linguistic profiling is rather straight-forward. Language development (first or second) follows a standard schedule. The standard schedule for any second language is described and explained in Processability Theory (Pienemann 1998 and 2005) as an incremental development of processing strategies by the learner:

> The logic underlying Processability Theory (=PT) (Pienemann 1998; 2005) is the following: at any stage of development the learner can produce and comprehend only those L2 linguistic forms which the current state of the language processor can handle. It is therefore crucial to understand the architecture of the language processor and the way in which it handles a second language. This enables one to predict the course of development of L2 linguistic forms in language production and comprehension across languages (Pienemann forthcoming).

Developmental patterns have been established for a number of languages both as L1 and L2. Linguistic profiling utilises these developmental schedules and compares the structures found in speech samples collected from (bilingual) learners in the language(s) involved. The analyst then has to locate the patterns found in the sample within the overall regularities of the standard developmental schedule. This approach is applied to the development of English as a Second Language (ESL) in the current version of *Rapid Profile*. It will then very quickly reveal the current state of interlanguage of individual learners.

This procedure is based on extensive second language acquisition research in formal and natural environments yielding a specific developmental schedule (see figure 1). Since *Rapid Profile* is criterion-referenced, it considers both what the learners can do, as well as what they cannot do at a given point in the EFL learning process.

Stage	Phenomena/criteria	Examples
6	Cancel Aux-2nd	I wonder *what he wants.*
5	Neg/Aux-2nd-? Aux-2nd -? 3sg-s -	Why *didn't* you tell me? Why *can't* she come? Why *did* she eat that? What *will* you do? Peter *likes* bananas.
4	Copula S (x) Wh-copula S (x) V-Particle	*Is* she at home? *Where* is she? Turn it *off*!
3	Do-SV(O)-? Aux SV(O)-? Wh-SV(O)-? Adverb-First Poss (Pronoun) Object (Pronoun)	*Do* he live here? *Can* I go home? *Where* she went? *What* you want? *Today* he stay here. I show you *my* garden. This is *your* pencil. Mary called *him.*
2	S neg V(O) SVO SVO-Question -ed -ing Plural –s (Noun) Poss –s (Noun)	*Me no* live here. / I don't live here. Me live here. You live here*?* John play*ed.* Jane go*ing.* I like cat*s.* Pat*'s* cat is fat.
1	Words Formulae	Hello, Five Dock, Central How are you? Where is X? What's your name?

Figure 1: Developmental Features for English as L2 (based on Pienemann 1998; cf. Pienemann 2006)

Some readers may think that the table presented in Figure 1 misrepresents Processability Theory because in Pienemann (1998:171) the areas of morphology and syntax were treated as separate modules.

Indeed, the interlocking of morphology and syntax is an important issue in the debate on L1-L2 differences. For instance, Clahsen (1990) showed that in L1 acquisition aspects of syntactic and morphological development do interlock, whereas in L2 acquisition they do not.

However, Figure 1 does not in any way suggest that all structures listed in the morphology and syntax domains need to develop in tandem. Instead, Pienemann (1998:244ff) introduces the concept of 'developmental trailers' for L2 acquisition which constitutes an aspect of the variational dimension in interlanguage development. Pienemann (1998:248) demonstrates that there is no 'guarantee that the learner will indeed produce a linguistic rule as soon as s/he is able to do so'.

The developmental schedules listed in Figure 1 constitute the descriptive background of the *Rapid Profile* procedure which yields a detailed description of the specific interlanguage rules present in a given speech sample, including developmental trailers. In this context it is crucial to consider the impact of teaching intervention, because experimental studies have shown that developmental trailers can be brought in line with the rest of the interlanguage through formal instruction (cf. Pienemann 1998; Mansouri & Duffy 2005). In other words, the *Rapid Profile* procedure is indeed based on the modular status of morphology and syntax in L2 acquisition, and it provides detailed information on each of these modules for every profile. When an overall stage is assigned to a sample in this procedure, this is done for reasons of feasibility. The overall stage represents the most developed structure found in the sample, and comparing the overall stage with the detailed profile will specify developmental trailers which can demonstrably be attacked through formal teaching.

To use *Rapid Profile* in practice, one first needs to collect a speech sample from the informant. For this purpose a communicative task is administered to elicit data that will serve as linguistic indicators of second language development (see also section 3.2 of this paper). The speech sample is coded online with the *Rapid Profile* software. In order to do this, the analyst simply checks the boxes on the computer interface that mark the developmental feature found in the speech sample. Figure 2 shows the user interface of the *Rapid Profile* online feedback as produced during the screening procedure. The software stores the information entered by the analyst (including some lexical information) and calculates – on this basis – the developmental level of the learner. The information is displayed on the feedback screen (cf. Figure 3). This online feedback permits the analyst to select appropriate communicative tasks that elicit further developmental features that may be underdetermined in the sample – providing a rich and diverse speech sample.

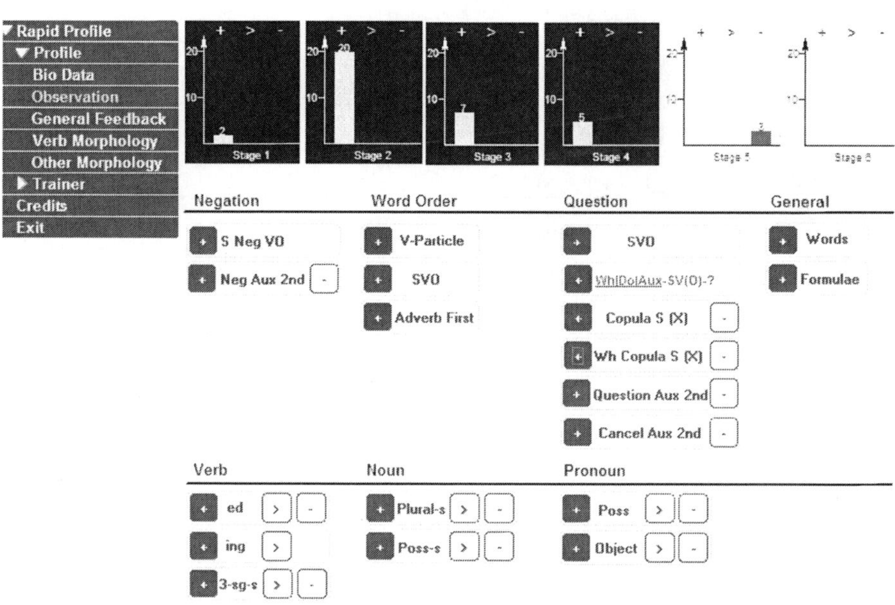

Figure 2: *Rapid Profile*: online feedback – observation

The 'General Feedback' (Figure 3) allows a more detailed insight into the current state of the learner language. This feedback also distinguishes between syntactic and morphological structures produced by the learner and fed into the programme by the analyst.

Additionally to the two feedback screens featured in Figures 2 and 3 *Rapid Profile* provides two more screens completing the online feedback. These two screens feature the morphological development of the learner language screened by the analyst in more detail. This is particularly important to get a better understanding of the underlying emergence criterion (Pienemann 1998:144ff) for morphology.

Within a short span of about 15 minutes, the sample collected and analysed using *Rapid Profile* renders a reliable conclusion about the learner's level of acquisition. The analysis provided by the system also allows the user to assess aspects of the lexicon and of variational features.

Rapid Profile II - Observation

- Rapid Profile
  - Profile
    - Bio Data
    - Observation
    - General Feedback
    - Verb Morphology
    - Other Morphology
  - Trainer
- Credits
- Exit

General Feedback

	Syntax	+	-	%	Acq	Morphology	+	>	-	%	Acq
6	Cancel Aux 2nd	0	0	0							
5	Neg Aux-2nd	0	0	0		3-sg-s	1	0	0	100	
	Aux 2nd-?	0	0	0							
4	Copula S (x)	2	0	100		Poss-Pro	0	0	0	0	
	Wh Copula S (x)	7	0	100	✓	Object	0	0	0	0	
	V-Particle	0		0		ed	0	0	0	0	
3	WH|Do|Aux SV(O)-?	4		100	✓	ing	8	0		100	
	Adverb-First	1		100		Plural-s	2	0	0	100	
	S Neg VO	0		0		Poss-s	0	0	0	0	
2	SVO (Word Order)	3		100	✓						
	SVO?	0		0							
1	Single Words	6		100	✓	Print	Save				
	Formulae	0		0							

Stage Gaps:

Figure 3: *Rapid Profile*: general feedback (learner profile)

The developmental profile yielded by this procedure permits the teacher in the EFL classroom to identify developmental features that are learnable at the given point in time. Thus, the teacher is enabled to decide which underlying structures can beneficially be focused on next in what I would like to refer to as a *developmentally moderated syllabus*. This is a concept I shall return to later in this paper.

Rapid Profile – A feasibility study for the EFL classroom

Underlying Hypotheses

Rapid Profile is based on the assumption that a speech sample of approximately 15 minutes of the interlanguage of an individual learner will be sufficient for an online-screening of a learner's profile using *Rapid Profile*. The study[2] reported in this paper aimed at answering two main research questions in order to find out whether this claim is valid: (1) Can sufficient speech data be collected to screen the development of learner language in about 15 minutes? and (2) Can analysts be trained to use *Rapid Profile* to conduct reliable online-screenings of learner language development, thus dispensing with the need for transcripts of the learners' (recorded) interlanguage?

In order to answer these research questions, a number of hypotheses were developed. Using Processabilty Theory (Pienemann 1998 and 2005) as a theoretical framework, the following hypotheses were tested in the study:

1. Speech samples of learner language with high data-density can be collected online by administering a variety of well-defined communicative tasks (cf. Pienemann 1998:280) in approximately 15 minutes.
2. *Rapid Profile* can be used to assess the current state of learner language development *online* in about 15 minutes.
3. *Rapid Profile* achieves a high degree of inter-rater-reliability in online-screenings when applied by trained analysts.
4. Analysts can be taught to use *Rapid Profile* reliably in 16 hours of workshops.
5. Due to the training in the workshop, analysts will not overrate developmental stages reached by any learner.

Eliciting the speech samples

The feasibility study was set up as two independent sub-studies. The first sub-study was designed to test whether an online-speech sample of approximately 15 minutes really can elicit sufficient relevant data to be able to screen the current state of interlanguage of an EFL learner (cf. Hypothesis 1) and whether such speech samples can be used to conduct *Rapid Profile* online screenings to assess the current state of learner language development (cf. Hypothesis 2). Therefore speech samples of four EFL learners from four different EFL classrooms from three different schools were collected. Two of the learners were about to finish an early start programme at primary school. They had started learning English in formal classroom settings at the age of eight. Their total EFL input was 145 lessons with two lessons per week. The other two learners started learning English at the age of ten and did not have any EFL instruction in primary school. They attended different secondary schools which both followed a more traditional EFL programme. Their total EFL input also was 145 lessons but it had been provided in a more intensive programme of 5 lessons a week. All four learners were taught English by a different teacher. The L1 of all four learners was German.

To test the first and the second hypothesis two undergraduate students collected speech samples from these four learners. For this purpose, one of them administered a range of communicative task especially designed to elicit linguistic indicators of the current EFL interlanguage of the learners[3] (cf. Keßler & Kohli 2006). Taking turns, one of the students elicited two speech samples while the other conducted the *Rapid Profile* online-screening. The interviews for the data elicitation took an average of 12.5 minutes and ranged between seven and 17 minutes. All interviews were video and audio-recorded. Each of the interviews was fully transcribed from the recordings. These transcripts were then checked according to the underlying structures needed for the online assessment using *Rapid Profile* (cf. section 2, especially figure 1). The data density[4] (Pienemann 1998) in all the interviews proved to be sufficiently high as each interview contained a large variety of underlying structures for each of the stages reached by the individual learners. Having a full transcript for each of the four learners the traditional linguistic profiling confirmed the current profile of L2-development for all the learners involved[5]. The elicited stages of acquisition attained by the learners ranged between stage 1 and stage 2 (primary school learners) and stage 4 and an early stage 5 by the learners who had started learning English at secondary school[6].

In section 3.1 I listed a number of hypotheses to be tested in this study. The data elicitation described in this section was set up to test the first two hypotheses:

1. Speech samples of learner language with high data-density can be collected online by administering a variety of well-defined communicative tasks (cf. Pienemann 1998:280) in approximately 15 minutes.
2. *Rapid Profile* can be used to assess the current state of learner language development *online* in about 15 minutes.

The speech samples collected and recorded during the data elicitation do not only prove those hypotheses to be correct. These speech samples also form the foundation for the second sub-study which is designed to test hypotheses 3 to 5 (cf. 3.1). As these hypotheses refer to the degree of inter-rater-reliability of trained analysts, let me briefly explain the training of the analysts before reporting on the test of the hypotheses.

Training the analysts

In order to optimise the training environment, two pilot-studies were launched at the universities of Paderborn/Germany and Newcastle upon Tyne/England. The actual training with fresh analysts was conducted during a compact seminar at the University of Paderborn comprising four afternoon sessions, each lasting four hours. During the first session the future analysts were provided with the theoretical background of linguistic profiling (e.g.

Crystal, Garman & Fletcher 1976), the evaluation of oral L2 speech production (e.g. Clahsen 1985; Pienemann, Johnston & Brindley 1988), the origin of *Rapid Profile* (e.g. Pienemann 1990, 1992), Processability Theory as the underlying theory (Pienemann 1998, 2005), and its impact on the EFL classroom (Keßler 2005). To ensure that all screening results obtained by the future analysts were based on a sound understanding of the theoretical background participants had to take part in a knowledge test, an off-line evaluation to show that they could identify underlying morpho-syntactic structures in transcribed interlanguage samples.

1. The Knowledge Test

The Knowledge Test was developed as an instrument to test whether future analysts are familiar with the morpho-syntactic structures underlying the *Rapid Profile* online-screening procedure (cf. Figure 1 and Section 2). In this test, the future analysts were confronted with written samples of leaner language taken from authentic transcripts. Each of these samples contained a predefined number of underlying structures to be traced by the test taker. As *Rapid Profile* is a diagnostic tool that does not only assess which structures learners already produce at their current state of interlanguage, but also records what these learners are not yet able to produce, the samples contained both positive as well as negative evidence for the underlying structures[7].

The user interface of the Knowledge Test resembles the *Rapid Profile* training software. This ensures that future analysts do not only prove their background knowledge of the underlying theory for online assessment but are also made familiar with the user interface for the training sessions. The similar user interfaces allow for a quicker training in the 16 hours of workshops as the analysts only have to manage one user interface that looks the same for the knowledge test, the training and the online-assessment.

After the completion of the knowledge test the analysts automatically receive feedback on their test results. This feedback includes a detailed printed list of all the sample sentences generated by the Knowledge Test. The feedback sheet contrasts the underlying target structures with the ones fed into the computer by the analysts. Thus, this detailed feedback provides insight into possible sources for errors and on what to focus on in the following training sessions.

To ensure founded screening results in the training sessions and in the online screenings, all analysts had to go through the Knowledge Test twice during the workshop. It was first applied after the introductory training session in order to establish further need for the training of particular underlying structures on an individual basis. The second application of the Knowledge Test was conducted at the end of the theoretical sessions just before the analysts moved to the hands-on interactive training with the pre-recorded audio speech samples. Only those analysts who had test results of at least 75 per cent were accepted for the interactive training. Even though the average result of the first application of the Knowledge Test was only 54.6 per cent, all analysts achieved at least 78.1 per cent in the second application. The average result of the second application was 86.8 per cent.

2. Interactive Training Sessions

During the hands-on computer-aided interactive training sessions each of the future analysts listened to pre-recorded and annotated authentic interlanguage speech samples. While listening to those speech samples the analysts used the training interface of the Rapid Profile software and fed the identified structures into the computer. The software then compares the structures found by the analysts to the annotations in its database. Thus, after each sample interview the analyst is provided with a feedback screen which gives detailed insight into both successful training as well as information about which structures will need to be covered in further training sessions. Figure 4 shows the interactive training on the computer.

Figure 4: Interactive Training Session with individual feedback on training results

Before being accepted for the online-screenings (feasibility study) all analysts had to pass a skills test. In this test they had to demonstrate their ability to identify a sufficient number of the morpho-syntactic structures relevant for a reliable learner language assessment with *Rapid Profile*. As one can see in Figure 5, it is not essential to identify all the underlying structures the sample contains. It is, however, very important to focus on identifying as many structures correctly as possible.

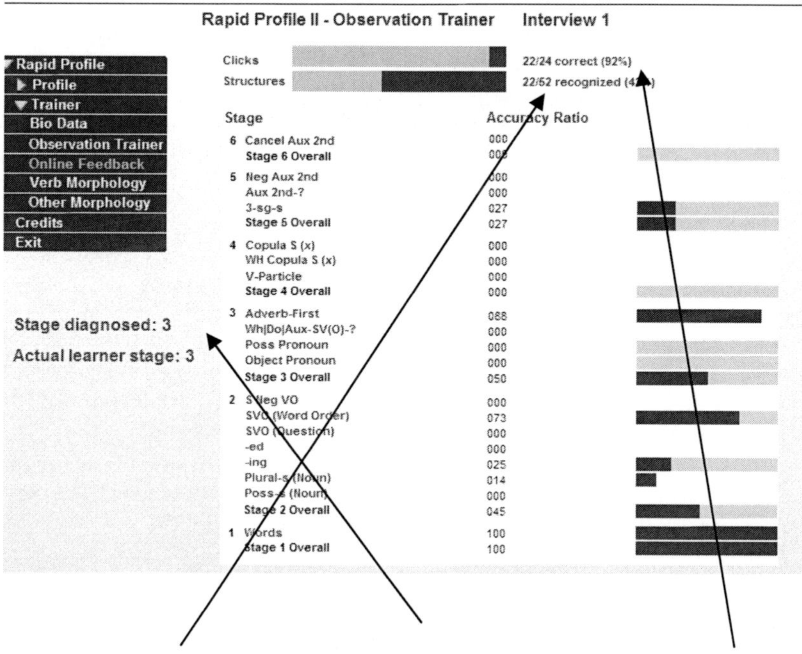

Figure 5: Feedback screen of the skills test (passed)

The lower bar indicates the number of correctly identified structures in relation to the total number of underlying structures. In this example the analyst has correctly identified 22/52 structures (42%).

The actual learner stage is set by default according to the underlying structures. This is compared against the assessment by the analyst during the training. In this example the analyst

The upper bar indicates the total number of clicks by the analysts. The light grey colour shows correct clicks.

Figure 5 shows that a rather low correct identification of the underlying structures can be sufficient to assess the actual learner stage correctly. This is important to keep in mind because it would not be realistic to expect any analyst to be able to screen all the relevant structures produced by a learner in online speech samples. Therefore the training session within the workshop focused very much on enabling the analysts to identify fewer numbers of structures but to do this as precisely as possible, rather than trying to click multiple structures even when not 100 per cent certain about a particular structure in the sample. The application of the emergence criterion (Pienemann 1998; see Section 2) caters for valid assessment on the basis of the correct identification of only a few of the underlying structures per stage produced by the learners in the online-screening procedure.

For further details, especially on the results of the knowledge test and the training of the analysts, see Keßler (2006b).

Overview of the main results of the study

After the interactive training the analysts were asked to take part in the feasibility study. The complete study comprised the intensive analysis of 84 interviews screened by the 21 analysts who had taken part in the workshop. Each analyst had to screen the learner language in four audio-recordings each of a learner from different EFL classrooms. The current state of the learners' interlanguage in this study ranged from stage 1 to (early) stage 5 (cf. Section 3.2). Figure 6 left gives an overview of the results of this study.

Figure 6: Feasibility Study – Results

	0	**-1**	**all**
T01	4	0	4
T02	3	1	4
T03	3	1	4
T04	3	1	4
T05	4	0	4
T06	3	1	4
T07	3	1	4
T08	3	1	4
T09	4	0	4
T10	3	1	4
T11	4	0	4
T12	3	1	4
T13	4	0	4
T14	4	0	4
T15	4	0	4
T16	3	1	4
T17	4	0	4
T18	3	1	4
T19	3	1	4
T20	4	0	4
T21	3	1	4
all	72	12	84
in %	**85.7**	**14.3**	**100**

The first column of the table in Figure 6 lists the analysts; in the next column (0) the number of correctly assessed interviews per analyst is listed. '0' characterises the number of stages the particular analyst neither over nor underrated during the online-screenings. A '4' means that this analyst did not over or underrate any of the learners during the online assessment. A '3' indicates three correct screenings by the analyst. The third column (-1) shows the number of interviews underrated by the analyst by one stage. The last column (all) summarises the total number of interviews by each of the analysts.

The bottom row of the table indicates the percentage of all the interviews screened by all the analysts in this study. As one can see, the 21 analysts diagnosed the correct developmental stage of the learners in 72 out of 84 interviews. In other words: The inter-rater-reliability of *Rapid Profile* ascertained by this study is 85.7 per cent.

An average of 85.7% of all interviews was screened correctly which means that the analysts concerned had assessed the current state of learner language correctly. These results reflect a very strict application of the emergence criterion. To avoid any formulaic language use (stage 1) being misinterpreted as a productive structure, *Rapid Profile* is designed in such a way, that three different evidences of any of the underlying syntactic structures are required before the software considers this very structure to be acquired. In morphology the case becomes even more complex as the software calculates both morphological as well as lexical variation in an integrated distributional analysis. I will discuss the impact of this very strict application of the emergence criterion in section 3.5 in more detail.

Nine analysts screened all interviews correctly and found enough evidence for the underlying structures; this showed that there were no *diagnostic gaps* at all. Those analysts are marked by a grey bar in Figure 6. All analysts screened at least 75% of their interviews correctly. The training in the 16 hour of workshops put a lot of emphasis on alerting the analysts not to overrate the state of interlanguage produced by a learner. We trained the analysts to feed only those structures into *Rapid Profile* which they were certain to have found in the speech sample and to be very careful. When in doubt about a particular structure in the sample they were encouraged to neglect it in the screening as the speech samples contained sufficient evidence of the underlying structures (cf. Hypothesis 1). As can be seen in Figure 6 none of the analysts ever overrated any of the learners. This special emphasis on not to overrate a learner is of great importance in terms of the application of *Rapid Profile* for online-screenings in the EFL classroom. Had a learner's stage of interlanguage development been overrated by the analyst, s/he would have, at the teaching stage, been given input which would not have met their developmental readiness (cf. Pienemann 1985; Di Biase 2002; Mansouri & Duffy 2005). In other words: overrating the current state of interlanguage of an individual learner would not contribute to teaching this learner along the *developmentally moderated syllabus*. I will come back to this in Sections 4 and 5 of this paper.

Let me conclude by referring again to Hypotheses 3 to 5 (cf. Section 3.1):

3. *Rapid Profile* achieves a high degree of inter-rater-reliability in online-screenings when applied by trained analysts.
4. Analysts can be taught to use *Rapid Profile* reliably in 16 hours of workshops.
5. Due to the training in the workshop analysts will not overrate developmental stages reached by any learner.

The results of second sub-study reported in this section clearly show, that these hypotheses also proved to be correct. We can establish that *Rapid Profile* provides a valid tool for online-assessment of learner language offering a very high degree on inter-rater-reliability and can be taught successfully to analysts (and teachers) with not more than basic pre-knowledge in a 16 hours workshop.

Discussing the results

As shown in the previous section of this paper using *Rapid Profile* for online screenings of leaner language is a quick and valid way of assessing the current state of interlanguage of individual EFL learners. Yet, there may remain some questions when relying merely on the online-screening results without taking the recorded speech data of the learner into account. All these issues revealed in this study derive from the very strict application of the emergence criterion (Pienemann 1998) within the software. Although the emergence criterion does not require more than one productive occurrence to count a syntactic structure to be acquired, *Rapid Profile* requires three different productive occurrences of any one syntactic structure in order to indicate the underlying stage to be acquired by the learner.

This strict application of the emergence criterion in *Rapid Profile* is meant to contribute to a more valid online diagnosis of the current state of interlanguage of the learners. In order to exclude a possible formulaic use of any of the underlying structures by the learner from being misinterpreted as an example of productive interlanguage (beyond stage 1) by the analyst, the software requires any syntactic structure to be entered into the programme at least three times before being accepted as productive.

The general idea underlying this strict application of the emergence criterion will not be questioned in this paper. We might, however, say that it may require more effort in the online screening process when assessing the interlanguage of more advanced EFL learners. For example, those learners with a more advanced interlangage (beyond stage 3) do not necessarily produce a lot of (syntactic) interlanguage features of stage three any more. As Figure 1 shows, all the syntactic structures characterising stage 3 follow an XP + SVO pattern, either in questions or by the fronting of an adverb. Additionally, of course, there are some morphological structures characterising stage 3, namely the possessive and the object pronouns. Once the learner has passed stage 3 in his interlanguage development, he does not necessarily have to produce a lot of questions following the stage 3 pattern of XP + SVO but can already ask questions according to stage 4 using inversion as in Copula S (X) or Wh-Copula S (X).

As the learners performing the elicitation tasks produce an enormous amount of speech data, clearly, no analyst will ever be able to enter all the structures produced by the learner into the *Rapid Profile* software when conducting an online screening of the learner producing learner language in real time. If the interlanguage samples provided by the learner do not contain many 'Adverb-first' structures and the learner already produces the questions beyond the XP + SVO pattern, the analyst might not be able to screen the amount of evidence for stage 3 required by the software because of the strict application of the emergence criterion. This may then lead to what I would refer to as a *diagnostic gap*. In contrast to a stage gap which would violate the implicational scale of incremental (learner) language development a diagnostic gap implies that the learner indeed produces a sufficient amount of interlanguage structures indicating the acquisition of a certain stage within the speech sample, but the analyst has missed entering at least three evidences of this very structure into the *Rapid Profile* software. Consequently a diagnostic gap does not question or falsify the processability hierarchy outlined by Pienemann (1998 and 2006). Figure 7 shows an example of the online feedback including such a diagnostic gap.

As *diagnostic gaps* in the online feedback (Figure 7) may occur and do not mean a violation of the implicational order of the developmental path of interlanguage development, *Rapid Profile* provides the analyst with an additional user interface to complement the online feedback. Using the online feedback (cf. Figure 3) as explained in Section 2 of this paper, the analyst can see whether the learner has produced a minimum of varying syntactic structures within stage 3 of the acquisition hierarchy.

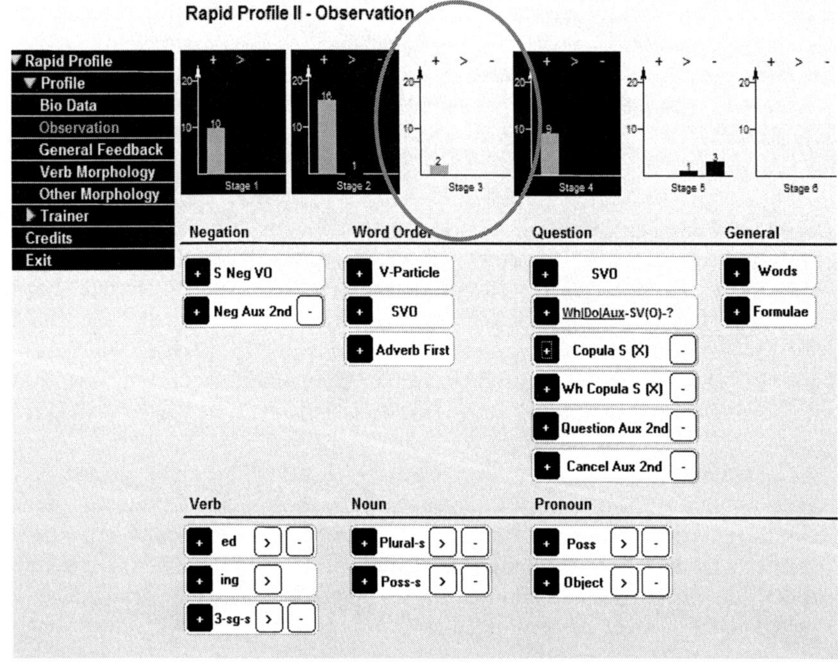

Figure 7: Rapid Profile: online feedback – observation (diagnostic gap at stage 3)

Referring to this feedback screen the analyst can then see whether the learner has already produced at least two evidences of the syntactic structure of 'wh/do/aux-SV (O)-?'. This structure is one way of expressing the XP + SVO pattern typical for stage 3. Of course the learner may as well have produced some more examples of this structure and/or of other structures characterizing stage 3. Yet, if the analyst has entered at least two individual productive occurrences of the very structure one can consider this structure to be diagnosed despite the *diagnostic gap*. Applying Pienemann's emergence criterion it would not be premature in this case to assess that this particular learner has acquired stage 3 of the processing hierarchy even though not all the possible structures for this stage have yet been screened. The strict application of the emergence criterion by the software however requires the analyst to find one more example of the structure in question before *Rapid Profile* would indicate this stage as being acquired in the online feedback screen (cf. Figure 2).

In other words, the 'General Feedback' screen (cf. Figure 3) helps the analyst decide whether his online screening has produced a diagnostic gap. If this feedback screen does not give a satisfying image of stage 3 interlanguage development, the analyst will have to administer another task, thus prompting the learner to produce some more linguistic evidence for this stage.

Implications for the EFL classroom

Teachers need to know about both the underlying theory of learner language development and the current state of their learners' interlanguage to make instructed second language acquisition more successful. A tool for quick L2 assessment is essential especially in heterogeneous classrooms (Keßler 2005; Pienemann 2006), for it is only when teachers know about each learners' state of interlanguage development that they can exploit the developmental readiness principle to support individual learning (e.g. Pienemann 1985; Mansouri & Duffy 2005). Di Biase (2002) stresses the importance of the developmental readiness principle when pursuing a form-focused instruction in the classroom.

As the current state of interlanguage development may change during a period of instruction it is important to repeat the assessment of the learner language regularly. This again stresses the necessity of an instrument that allows for quick assessment in the EFL classroom setting. This study[8] has shown that *Rapid Profile*, based on a strong foundation of theory, and valid in construct, provides a reliable means of such measurement.

Rapid Profile also ensures that the valid and very precise profiles of learner language which it can help us to generate, can be produced quickly in the EFL classroom (cf. Hypotheses 1 and 2). Training analysts to operate the software does not require more than a basic understanding of general linguistics and can be carried out in a few afternoon sessions. Thus, *Rapid Profile* offers a practicable alternative to any other standard means of L2 assessment as proficiency (e.g. Bachman & Palmer 1996; Bachman 1997; McNamara 2000) or the Portfolio (e.g. Council of Europe, 2000) in the EFL classroom.

Understanding underlying SLA theory in formal EFL instruction is the basis of effective second language learning in the classroom. *Rapid Profile* at this stage of its development can already successfully be applied to trace interlanguage development of individual learners across the EFL classrooms and across school boundaries. Many countries include early start EFL programmes in their curriculum for primary school education. In Germany, English has been part of the compulsory curriculum at primary schools since 2003. German EFL learners at beginners' level are now eight years of age and typically they receive input of two 45-minutes sessions per week. This should lead to a restructuring of the ESL-programme that already exists at the secondary school level but no one is quite sure about how to go about it. The main problem is: How are we to reliably assess what the learners at primary school have actually learned? How can we successfully continue the path of acquisition in secondary schools? In order to provide a successful transition from Primary school to Secondary school teachers of both types of school need to be aware of what they can gain from research in both SLA and English Language Teaching (ELT) (Keßler, 2006a). Linguistic profiling using *Rapid Profile* provides the teacher with exactly the kind of knowledge most relevant to them. In other words, learner language profiles as diagnosed by this instrument will support a smooth transition from primary schools to secondary schools. Thus, *Rapid Profile* contributes to a more beneficial continuity of ELT from the early start to a more target language like final state of the acquisition of English as a second language in classroom settings.

Another implication of linguistic profiling for the EFL classroom also derives from the clearer understanding we now have of learner language development and how it can be fostered by teaching the foreign language in formal settings. If the teacher is familiar with SLA theory and is able to conduct online-screenings of his learners' interlanguage he will most precisely know what his learners are developmentally ready to acquire next (cf. Pienemann 1985; Di Biase 2002; Mansouri & Duffy 2005). This does not, of course, imply a return to the grammar-translation syllabus without meaningful input. On the contrary, effective ELT relies on an interactive approach to the language classroom. Learners need to negotiate for meaning (cf. Long 1996). Task-based approaches to ELT are widely seen as one way of allowing for as much interaction in the EFL classroom as possible. If teachers know about the current state of interlanguage of their learners they can much more precisely and carefully choose tasks for their learners in classroom activities that address the actual L2-profile of *all* learners. By arranging the tasks along those profiles diagnosed by *Rapid Profile* the teacher can select the tasks according to a *developmentally moderated syllabus*.

For the future such a syllabus ought to be implemented into a new generation of textbooks and resource books which will have to sequence the underlying grammatical structures according to the developmental sequence for English as a second language. Before such textbooks are created, *Rapid Profile* can support the teacher by diagnosing current interlanguage stages of his learners. Once these stages have been identified for the individual learners, teacher will be able to reorganise the given structure of any textbook into a sequence which their learners are developmentally ready to acquire. Focusing on these very structures when correcting learner mistakes will then support the individual learner and thus foster interlanguage development towards a more target language like state[9].

Unfortunately it would be premature to introduce a valid *developmentally moderated syllabus* in this paper. Before this can be done, we will have to conduct a number of follow-up studies to establish an empirically valid basis for such a syllabus. Apart from the need for more empirical research on the effects of a *developmentally moderated syllabus*, there are many more open research questions to be answered to make the EFL classroom more successful. The following section of this paper will address some of those open research questions.

Further Research required

The study described in this paper has shown the validity and the reliability of *Rapid Profile*. It has also demonstrated the feasibility of online-screening procedures of learner language in EFL settings. Yet, as discussed in Section 3, there are some open questions that require further research in order to be answered. In this section I will sketch out three main areas for further research concerning the application of *Rapid Profile* in the EFL classroom in a more institutionalised way. These areas for further research include:

- the application of the emergence criterion during online-screening sessions;
- development of tasks for the efficient elicitation of dense interlanguage data during the screening; in particular for stage 3 and its integration into a practice oriented database for tasks within the software;
- the inclusion of interlanguage variation into the online-screening procedure.

To prevent too many *diagnostic gaps* on the one hand and a premature rating of a formulae as a productive structure on the other, it is essential to find out in another study how strictly the emergence criterion (Pienemann 1998) has to be applied in online-screenings. It would definitely be too superficial to apply the emergence criterion for syntax in a one-to-one relationship in *Rapid Profile*. Any such application might very easily lead to possible misinterpretations of formulae as more advanced structures. Yet, the very strict application of the emergence criterion as it is applied in the current version of *Rapid Profile* may also lead to ambiguous results, especially when the *diagnostic gap* is not to be found at stage 3 for a learner whose interlanguage has reached stage 4. A more problematic case of *diagnostic gaps* would be a scenario where a learner whose interlanguage development has just moved to an early state of stage 5. This early stage 5 might then actually not be diagnosed by an analyst who misses out just some of the underlying stage 5 structures produced by such a learner[10]. Underrating those learners would then prevent the teacher from arranging for the input that would be most beneficial to those learners (cf. Section 4 of this paper).

The second area of open research questions has to do with the need to find a range of tasks that enables learners with a more advanced interlanguage than stage 3 to produce more stage 3 structures. Here, tasks that help to elicit 'adverb-first' (for syntax) and the different pronouns (for morphology) are urgently required. Research should contribute to finding such tasks and to empirically showing that they can provide the expected, and necessary, data density.

Once we are able to set up task types which meet these requirements the next step should then be to integrate a whole range of successful elicitation tasks for all stages of learner language development into the software. This would enable the analyst to choose appropriate tasks from a larger database which might then lead to a more precise online screening procedure minimizing the amount of *diagnostic gaps*.

The current version of *Rapid Profile* allows for a valid and reliable screening of interlanguage development. Of course interlanguage development does not reveal the full picture of learner language. There are of course many more aspects to language, such as phonology, the mental lexicon, pragmatics, variation, and many more.

Rapid Profile provides a very precise instrument for the assessment of learner language development. Processability Theory (Pienemann 1998 and 2005) provides a theoretical framework that allows the widening of the current scope of *Rapid Profile*. This framework does not only explain and predict interlanguage *development* due to a growing processing capacity built up by the learner, Processability Theory also explains and predicts interlanguage *variation* in a neat, empirically founded falsifiable framework. In other words: using traditional methods of linguistic profiling including transcripts already offers a valid approach to study learner language variation (Liebner 2006; Pienemann 1998 and 2006) and to use insight into this kind of variation to predict interlanguage development. The next step would now be to include the concept of variation into the software to allow a quick and valid way of tracing interlanguage variation in the online screening procedure when using *Rapid Profile*. This would allow us to widen the scope of the instrument without compromising its precision.

First attempts to include interlanguage variation into the *Rapid Profile* procedure have already been made by the Paderborn Research Group directed by Manfred Pienemann[11].

Conclusion

The study confirmed the validity and reliability of *Rapid Profile*. It also proved its feasibility for the use in ELT settings. *Rapid Profile* is a precise diagnostic tool for leaner language development. It provides teachers with important insight into the developmental path of their learners'. This knowledge is very important because it provides teachers with a very concise idea of what they can teach successfully according to their learners' developmental readiness (Pienemann 1985; Mansouri & Duffy 2005).

Knowing about learner language development and interlanguage variation and being able to elicit valid profiles of attainment with *Rapid Profile* is one very important milestone in the assessment of L2 learners in formal classroom settings. Yet, this cannot be sufficient for the language teachers who want to support their students' EFL development in the most effective way. It is therefore crucial to develop a theory-based methodology for the EFL classroom that takes the SLA insights into account and applies them in the classroom. Unfortunately we are not yet in a position to provide a sound and empirically tested *developmentally moderated syllabus* which enables both learners and teachers to get the best out of current SLA theory. Further research and a joint effort of SLA specialists, applied linguists and practitioners in the EFL classroom is needed to transfer the great insight into learner language development into a framework that provides beneficial backwash for the EFL classroom. Besides a more sensible grading of the underlying grammatical features of the target language both in text books as well as the classroom discourse (cf. *developmentally moderated syllabus*) the task-based approach (e.g. Candlin 1987; Long 1985 and 1996; Bygate, Skehan & Swain 2001; Carless 2002; Ellis 2003; Pienemann 2006; Keßler in press) seems to offer a promising way of combining the application of SLA theory with pedagogically sound practices in the EFL classroom.

Notes

[1] I would like to thank the following people for their input and comments on this paper: Manfred Pienemann (Paderborn and Newcastle upon Tyne), Bruno Di Biase (Western Sydney), Fethi Mansouri (Deakin) and two anonymous reviewers.

[2] This study is part of my research for receiving a Ph.D. in the field of Applied English Linguistics supervised by Manfred Pienemann at the University of Paderborn. It has been submitted in full length in Keßler (2006b).

[3] For more details, especially on task variation and the steadiness hypothesis see Pienemann (1998).

[4] For the definition of 'data density' see Pienemann (1998).

[5] For more details, especially the transcripts and the results of the traditional linguistic profiling see Keßler (2006b)

[6] Though each of the learners had received an EFL input of approximately 145 lessons, the different elicited stages of acquisition must not be considered a comparison of achievement between two totally different types of schools, as the learning conditions vary considerably among different schools.

Yet, the results very clearly show that *Rapid Profile* offers a diagnostic tool that can provide insight into current learner language levels for individual learners. This insight can help the teacher to foster a learner's interlanguage development by taking his current stage of acquisition as the basis for further teaching (cf. section 4 of this paper).

[7] An example for positive evidence of a structure would be 'We are going.' (+ ing; + SVO); an example for negative evidence of a structure would be 'He go home.' (- 3-sg-s); a question at stage 3 might be considered an example of both positive and negative evidence 'What you want.' (+ Wh-SVO-?; - Aux-2nd-?). Also see Figure 1 in Section 2 of this paper.

[8] For further proof of the inter-rater-reliability as well as the practicability of Rapid Profile in EFL settings see for example Pienemann (1992 and 2006) and Keßler (2006b).

[9] Di Biase (2005 and personal communication) refers to this special kind of focus-on-form as developmentally moderated focus-on-form.

[10] In fact this is another result of the study discussed in Section 3. Actually all the analysts who underrated one interview did this in the interview with Sarah, a learner whose interlanguage proved to be at an early stage 5. Yet, all but one analyst rather produced a *diagnostic gap* for stage 5 as they diagnosed at least one stage 5 syntactic structure plus a whole range of stage 5 morphological structures ('3-sg-s'). As those analysts did not meet the strict application of the emergence criterion, *Rapid Profile* did not indicate stage 5 as being acquired when referring to the 'online feedback – observation' (cf. Figure 2). A closer look at the 'online feedback – General Feedback' (Figure 3) showed very clearly that the analysts had traced some evidence for both syntactic as well as morphological features for stage 5.

[11] For futhter details see Keßler (2006b). The Paderborn Research Group is also preparing a publication which will include a unified PT-based approach to explain and predict interlanguage development and variation as well as its application in the EFL classroom.

References

Bachman, L. F. (1997). Fundamental Considerations in Language Testing. Oxford: Oxford University Press.

Bachman, L. F. & Palmer, A. S. (1996). Language Testing in Practice. Oxford: Oxford Univeristy Press.

Bygate, M., Skehan, P. & Swain, M. (2001). Researching Pedagogic Tasks. London: Pearson Education.

Candlin, C. (1987). 'Towards task-based language learning.' In C. Candlin & D.F. Murphy (eds.), Language Learning Tasks. Englewood Cliffs: 5-22.

Carless, D. (2002). 'Implementing task-based learning with young learners.' ELT Journal. 56, 4: 389-396.

Clahsen, H. (1985). 'Profiling second language development: A procedure for assessing L2 proficiency.' In K. Hyltenstam and M. Pienemann (eds.), Modelling and Assessing Second Language Acquisition. Clevedon: Multilingual Matters: 283-331.

—. (1990). 'The comparative study of first and second language development.' Studies in Second Language Acquisition. 12: 135-153.

Council of Europe (2000). European Language Portfolio. Strasbourg: Language Policy Divison. (http://culture2.coe.int/portfolio/inc.asp?L=E&M=$t/208-1-0-1/main_pages/../&L=E&M=$t/208-1-0-1/main_pages/introduction.html, 24.11.2005).

Crystal, D., Fletcher, P. & Garman, M. (1976). The Grammatical Analysis of Language Disability. London: Arnold.

Di Biase, B. (2002). 'Focusing strategies in second language development: a classroom-based study of Italian L2 in primary school.' In B. Di Biase (ed.), *Developing a Second Language: acquisition, processing and pedagogy issues in Arabic, Chinese, English, Italian, Japanese, and Swedish*. Melbourne: Language Australia, 95-120.

—. (2005). *A comparative study of second language teaching program outcomes under different implementation conditions in upper primary school.* ARC Final Report - Strategic Partnerships with Industry - Research and Training - (SPIRT) Project C59906982 (Administering organization: University of Western Sydney).

Ellis, R. (2003). *Task-based Language Learning and Teaching*. Oxford: Oxford University Press.

Keßler, J.-U. (2005). `Fachdidaktik *meets* Psycholinguistik – Heterogenität im Englischunterricht erkennen, verstehen und als Chance nutzen.' In K. Bräu & Schwerdt, U. (eds.), *Heterogenität als Chance. Vom produktiven Umgang mit Gleichheit und Differenz in der Schule.* Münster: LIT, 263-284.

—. (2006a). 'Englischerwerb im Anfangsunterricht der Primarstufe und der Sekundarstufe: Plädoyer für ein empirisch fundiertes Übergangsprofil.' In M. Pienemann, J.-U. Keßler & Roos, E. (eds.), *Englischerwerb in der Grundschule. Ein Studien- und Arbeitsbuch*. Paderborn: Schöningh/UTB, 159-184.

—. (2006b). *Englischerwerb im Anfangsunterricht diagnostizieren. Linguistische Profilanalysen und deren didaktische Konsequenzen für den Übergang von der* nt.

—. (in press). 'Negotiation for intercultural meaning in secondary school EFL classrooms: Australia – a project.' In W. Delanoy & L. Volkmann (eds.), *Cultural Studies in the EFL classroom*. Heidelberg: Winter.

Keßler, J.-U. & Kohli, V. (2006). 'Erhebung von Sprachprofilen im frühen Englischerwerb: kommunikative tasks in Forschung und Unterricht.' In M. Pienemann, J.-U. Keßler & Roos, E. (eds), *Englischerwerb in der*

Grundschule. Ein Studien- und Arbeitsbuch. Paderborn: Schöningh/UTB, 89-96.

Liebner, M. (2006). 'Variationsverhalten in verschiedenen Lernergruppen.' In M. Pienemann, J.-U. Keßler & Roos, E. (eds.), *Englischerwerb in der Grundschule. Ein Studien- und Arbeitsbuch*. Paderborn: Schöningh/UTB, 141-156.

Littlewood, W. (2004). 'The task-based approach: some questions and suggestions.' *ELT Journal*. 58, 4: 319-326.

Long, M.H. (1985). 'A role for instruction in second language acquisition: Task-based language teaching.' In M. Pienemann & Hyltenstam, K. (eds.) *Modelling and Assessing Second Language Acquisition*. Clevedon: Multilingual Matters: 77-99.

—. (1996). 'The role of linguistic environment in second language acquisition.' In W. Ritchie & T. Bhatia, T. (eds.), *Handbook of Research on Second Language Acquisition*. New York: Academic, 413-468.

Mansouri, F. & Duffy, L. (2005). 'The pedagogic effectiveness of developmental readiness in ESL grammar instruction.' *Australian Review of Applied Linguistics*. 28, 1: 81-99.

McNamara, T. (2000). *Language Testing*. Oxford: Oxford University Press.

Pienemann, M. (1984). 'Psychological constraints on the teachability of languages'. *Studies in Second Language Acquisition*. 6, 2, 84: 186-214.

—. (1985). 'Learnability and Syllabus Construction.' In Keneth Hyltenstam & Pienemann, M. (eds.), *Modelling and Assessing Second Language Acquisition*. Clevedon: Multilingual Matters, 23-75.

—. (1989). 'Is language teachable? Psycholinguistic Experiments and Hypotheses.' *Applied Linguistics*. 10, 1: 52-79.

—. (1990). *LARC Research Projects 1990*. Sydney: NLIA/LARC.

—. (1992). *Assessing Second Language Acquisition Through Rapid Profile*. Ms. Sydney.

—. (1998). *Language Processing and Second Language Development: Processability Theory*. Amsterdam: John Benjamins.

—. (ed.) (2005). *Cross-linguistic Aspects of Processability Theory*. Amsterdam: John Benjamins.

—. (2006). 'Spracherwerb in der Schule: Was in den Köpfen der Kinder vorgeht.' In M. Pienemann, J.-U. Keßler & Roos, E. (eds.), *Englischerwerb in der Grundschule. Ein Studien- und Arbeitsbuch*. Paderborn: Schöningh/UTB: 33-63.

—. (forthcoming): 'Processability Theory'. In B.VanPatten & Williams, J. (eds.), *Theories in Second Language Acquisition: an Introduction*. Blackwell.

Pienemann, M., Johnston, M. & Brindley, G. (1988). 'Constructing an acquisition-based procedure for second language assessment.' *Studies in Second Language Acquisition*. 10, 2: 217-243.

Pienemann, M. & Keßler, J.-U. (forthcoming): 'Measuring bilingualism.' In P. Auer & Wei, L. (eds.) Vol. 5: Multilingualism. *Handbook of Applied Linguistics*. Berlin/New: York: Muton/de Gruyter.

CHAPTER 7

TESTING THE TOPIC OF HYPOTHESIS: THE L2 ACQUISITION OF CHINESE SYNTAX [1]

Yanyin Zhang

The SLA research paradigm focusing on the developmental aspect of the L2 linguistic system is characterised by approaches to the way IL grammars are processed by the learner during the actual speech production and comprehension event (for an overview, see Pienemann 2003). Processability Theory (PT) proposed that given the limited processing capacity of L2 learners at various stages of the learning, 'only those L2 linguistic forms which the current state of the language processor can manage' (Pienemann 2003, p.686) can be acquired by the learner. This means language acquisition is constrained by the development of processing capacities, and that the processing capacity of a learner at a particular point limits the kind of L2 forms he/she is able to produce.

Within the PT framework, the processing capacity is articulated in a number of linguistic and psycholinguistic models and theories including Levelt's (1989) model of language production, the Lexical-Functional Grammar (Bresnan1982), and the concept of 'feature unification' or 'information exchange' between constituents (for details, see Pienemann 1998, 2003). These form the basis for the universal hierarchy of IL development in which language processing procedures define stages of L2 development and give concrete shapes to L2 linguistic forms at each stage. Table 1 (Pienemann 2003, p.695) is the processing hierarchy of L2 English. Cross-linguistic studies have shown an overwhelming support for the PT prediction that second language acquisition follows a universal path constrained by the development of processing skills (e.g., Pienemann 2005, Pienemann and Håkansson 1999, Håkansson, Pienemann and Sayehli 2002, Glahn, Håkansson, Hammarberg, Holmen, Hvenekilde, and Lund, K. 2001, Di Biase and Kawaguchi 2002, Kawaguchi 2005a, Jansen 1991, 2005, Zhang 2001, 2005).

Processing procedure	L2 process	Morphology	Syntax
5 subordinate clause procedure	Main and subordinate clause		Cancel INV
4 S-procedure	Interphrasal information	*SV agreement* (=3sg-s)	Do 2nd, INVERSION
3 Phrasal procedure	Phrasal information	*NP agreement*	ADV, Do-Front, Topi Neg+V
2 Category procedure	Lexical morpheme	*Plural, past -ed* Possessive pronoun	Canonical order
1 Word/lemma	'words'	Invariant forms	Single constituent

Table 1. Processing procedures applied to English (Pienemann, Table 20.6 2003, p.695)

Recently, Pienemann, Di Biase and Kawaguchi (2005) have extended PT, adding to it a new dimension, namely, 'the speaker-induced discourse-pragmatic choices and their markings in syntactic and morphological structure' (Di Biase 2005). They pointed out that this interface between syntax and discourse pragmatics helps to account for a number of syntactic phenomena such as the 'ADV rule' (verb in the second position following the initial adverb) in V/2 languages (Swedish, German), the pro-drop phenomenon (Italian, Spanish, Japanese, Chinese), the topicalization and passivization (Japanese, Italian, Chinese), etc. The new dimension also contributes to a more robust account of the acquisition of the type of languages which 'relies more on syntax than agreement morphology' such as Japanese and Chinese (Di Biase 2005). This new dimension is formalized as the Topic Hypothesis (Pienemann, Di Biase and Kawaguchi 2005).

The present study takes into account the recent advance in PT by applying the Topic Hypothesis to the analysis of the syntactic development in the L2 Chinese of three adult learners. In the following, the Topic Hypothesis is presented first, followed by a brief description of some of the relevant typological features of Chinese, in particular, the syntactic manifestation of topic, subject, and word order. Next, a PT-based synthesis is proposed, relating syntactic structures of Chinese to the Topic Hypothesis. The resulting processing hierarchy of the Chinese IL syntax will be tested in this study. At the outset, a word of caution: the Topic Hypothesis is not to be taken as the theoretical solution to the second language acquisition of syntax, hence, the syntactic structures being investigated in this study are by no means exhaustive, neither in terms of teaching and learning objectives, nor in terms of Chinese grammar as a whole. Nevertheless, they do represent the basic structures which feature prominently in Chinese language and pedagogy.

The Topic Hypothesis of L2 syntax

The Topic Hypothesis (Pienemann, Di Biase and Kawaguchi, 2005) takes the 'sentence topic' as the crux in its conceptualization of IL syntactic development, drawing in particular on the notion of 'prominence' at sentence, discourse and semantic levels. At the discourse-pragmatic level, Levelt (1989) pointed out that when expressing a conceptual structure, the speaker takes a certain perspective. Through the choice of the topic which embodies the central message, the speaker distinguishes it from the comment that is made about the topic. Linguistically, the speaker 'can choose between affirmative and question forms, between active and passive' to encode the topic information (Di Biase 2005). At the sentence level, the speaker can manipulate this central information by placing it in sentence initial position, giving it 'prominence,' thus guiding the hearer's attention and effecting his/her representation of meaning in the hearer.

Semantically and grammatically, the initial or the Topic position of a canonical structure[1] is frequently the grammatical SUBJ(ect) of the sentence encoding the thematic role of AGENT, both of which occupy the most prominent position in the discourse and grammatical function hierarchies (Bresnan 2001, Choi 2001, Pienemann, Di Biase and Kawaguchi 2005,). However, the different perspective of a speaker or a particular choice made by a speaker may instigate in the initial position an element other than the grammatical SUBJ or the AGENT argument, as in the passive structure, the OBJ(ect)-topicalization, and the English *wh*-question. The key feature of these structures is non-canonicity manifested in the disruption of the default mapping between thematic roles and their corresponding grammatical function such as shown in Figure 1. According to Di Biase (2005, p.19, also Pienemann, Di Biase and Kawaguchi, 2005),

> Non-canonical choices lead to linguistic non-linearity, and they come at a cost in terms of processing. This means that the production of the structures which are necessary to achieve those discourse-pragmatic choices are constrained by their processability.

Incorporating the above discourse-pragmatics, the Topic Hypothesis predicts that learners go through three stages in their acquisition of L2 syntax, beginning with a canonical order and progressing toward a non-linear order of sentence structures. The process is characterized by the exploration of the initial position of the sentence as follows:

Stage 1. TOP equals SUBJ: TOPsubj V (O)
Stage 2. TOP equals ADJ(unct): TOPadj SV(O)
Stage 3. TOP equals OBJ: TOPobj SV

These three patterns of assigning the Topic role to different grammatical functions or constituents represent three developmental stages of L2 syntax. In the following, each stage is discussed in detail.

A. TOP = SUBJ (TOPsubj V(O))

When the TOP is SUBJ, the IL is characterized by canonical word order. This is the initial stage of IL syntax where the grammatical SUBJ and sentence TOP are not differentiated. The SUBJ is identified as default TOP of the sentence, and both are aligned with the thematic role of AGENT. In other words, the initial IL syntax is organized through direct mapping between semantic function (argument structure), the word order (constituent-structure) and the grammatical function (functional-structure) as Figure 1 shows (Pienemann, Di Biase and Kawaguchi 2005, Di Biase 2005, also Choi 2001).[2] Sentence (1) is an example from English.

1) John loves Mary.
   TOPsubj V O

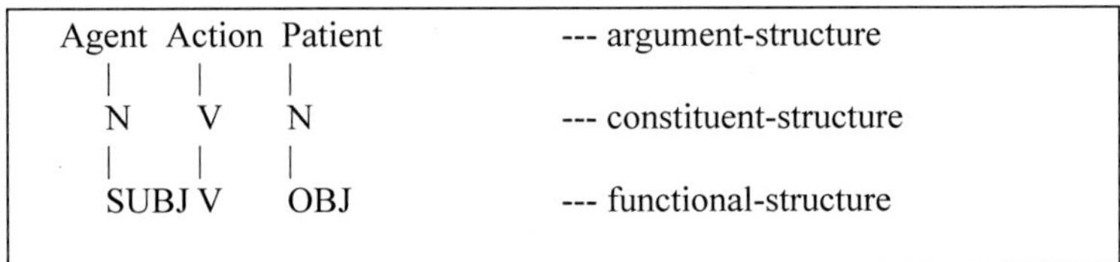

Figure 1. Unmarked alignment of a-, c-, and f-structures

In terms of processing, this unmarked linear alignment of the three levels of representation is computationally the least costly means of organizing syntax (Pinker 1984, 1989, cited in Di Biase 2005) because no information exchange between constituents is involved (Pienemann 1998, Pienemann, Di Biase and Kawaguchi 2005). The structure can be processed by the Category Procedure at PT Stage 2 which requires the skill to analyze the category information of lexical items as N, V, A, etc. (See Pienemann 1998 for a discussion of processing procedures). Language acquisition literature over the last 40 years has produced ample evidence to support the direct canonical mapping as the processing strategy in the early language development of L1 and L2 alike (for a brief review, see Pienemann, Di Biase and Kawaguchi 2005).

B. TOP = ADJ (TOPadj SV(O))

The differentiation between TOP and SUBJ takes place when an element (XP) other than SUBJ is adjoined to the canonical string, occupying the TOP position in the c-structure. The presence of XP causes the separation of TOP and SUBJ such that the SUBJ is no longer the default TOP of a sentence. Depending on the syntactic constraints of a language, the TOP position being assigned to a non-SUBJ element may in turn lead to structural modifications that disrupt the canonical order (as in German, Swedish), or which call for differential morphological markings of TOP and SUBJ constituents (as in Japanese). The XP element is either ADJ(unct) such as adverbial phrase expressing contextual information, or a *wh*-word bearing a grammaticized discourse function--the FOCUS function--in the f-structure (Bresnan 2001). In any case, the Topic Hypothesis proposes that while the XP permits constituents to be marked for the discourse function TOP, the rest of the sentence preserves canonical mapping, resulting in the following IL rule:

S --> XPtop SV(O)

Examples (2), (3) and (4) may be produced by the learner at this stage. In all three examples, the TOP function (underlined) is assigned to an element other than grammatical SUBJ, and the rest of the sentence is canonically structured. In (2) and (4), the TOP is assigned to ADJ *yesterday* and *da* 'there,' whereas in (3), it is assigned to a *wh*-word. In English, the XP adjunction of a non-SUBJ element leads to the collapse of the canonical order of *wh*-questions only, whereas in German, the disruption of the canonical order affects all structures. In German, sentence (4) should have the verb *spielen* 'play' in the second position, after *da* 'there' (*Da spielen Kinder*). Despite syntactic constraints in the target language, learners of various L1 backgrounds have been shown to go through this stage in their progression toward acquiring target language grammar (See Clahsen, Meisel and Pienemann 1983, Pienemann and Håkansson 1999, Håkansson, Pienemann and Sayehli 2002, Pienemann 1998).

2) Yesterday, John saw a movie.

3) *What he want?

4) *Da Kinder spielen.[3]
There children play
There children are playing.

C. TOP = OBJ (TOPobj SV)

When the TOP function is assigned to a core argument other than SUBJ, radical structural modifications occur. A frequently observed phenomenon is 'object topicalization' or 'object fronting' in which the grammatical OBJ occupies the sentence-initial position. In (5), the topicalized *pingguo* 'apple' is the OBJ and PATIENT argument of the verb *chi* 'eat.' Unlike the XP rule at the previous stage, the TOP element *pingguo* 'apple' bears the grammatical function of OBJ in the sentence and it binds the PATIENT argument, as illustrated in the f-structure (5a) in which the OBJ is linked with the discourse function of TOP.

5) Pingguo wo chi le.
Apple I ate PEFF
I ate the/that apple.

5a) f: [TOP ['*pingguo* (apple)']
SUB ['*wo* (I)']
PRED '*chi-le'* (ate)<(f SUBJ) (f OBJ)>
OBJ]

From a discourse-pragmatics point of view, the speaker gives prominence to the message encoded in the OBJ of the sentence. In languages such as Chinese, the positional prominence is also associated with such information as definiteness and specificity (see detailed discussion in the next section). In terms of sentence processing, the grammatical functions must be identified syntactically rather than positionally because the mapping process between the semantic function and the grammatical function of the OBJ-topicalization sentence is non-linear. One can no longer rely on one-to-one mapping without functional analysis. According to PT, S-Procedure is required to carry out the mapping processes.

In summary, the Topic Hypothesis posits the following three incremental stages of IL syntax:

Stage 1. TOP and SUBJ are undifferentiated; this gives rise to canonical word order;
Stage 2. XP-adjunction in which TOP is assigned to non-core arguments leading to differentiation between TOP and SUBJ and giving rise to pragmatic word order;
Stage 3. TOP is assigned to core arguments such as OBJ resulting in OBJ topicalization, a deviation from canonical word order.

The Topic Hypothesis states:

> In second language acquisition learners will initially not differentiate between SUBJ and TOP. The addition of an XP to a canonical string will trigger a differentiation of TOP and SUBJ which first extends to non-arguments and successively to arguments thus causing further structural consequences (Pienemann, Di Biase and Kawaguchi, 2005, p.239).

In the next section, the notion of Topic and Subject in Chinese and the associated word order issue is discussed to provide a wider context for the application of Topic Hypothesis to the present study of L2 Chinese syntax.

Topic, subject and word order in Chinese syntax

According to Li and Thompson (1981, p.19), 'the notion of subject is not a structurally well-defined one in the grammar of Mandarin.' They pointed out that a very common sentence type in Mandarin Chinese (henceforth Chinese), such as 6), consists of the scheme NP + NP + Verb + NP where the first NP cannot occur after the verb although they may be in a verb-object relation (Li and Thompson 1981, p.19)

6) Nei -kuai tian women jia -fei.
That-piece field we add-fertilizer
That field, we fertilize.

Li and Thompson (1981, p.19) stated that the structure of sentences such as 6) 'can be more insightfully described in terms of the topic-comment relation rather than in terms of the subject-predicate relation' and that the first NP *nei-kuai tian*, 'that field' is more appropriately described as the topic of the rest of the sentence (see also Li and Thompson,1976). Fang (1992, p.9) concurred with Li and Thompson by stating that 'In Chinese… [t]he topic occurs first, and the comment follows.' He cited sentence (7) to show that the first NP (which he called 'Subject') *ta* 'he/she' does not have any argument relation with the verb *si* 'die':

7) Ta si le die.
He die PERF *father* (PERF = Perfective aspect marker)
His father died. / He lost his father.

Li and Thompson (1976) listed seven discourse and grammatical features / criteria with which the topic-comment structure such as (6) can be differentiated from a subject-predicate structure such as (8). Among them were non-argument relation between the topic and the verb, the positional requirement of the topic being always sentence initial, the definiteness of the topic element, the non-involvement of the topic in such grammatical processes as passivization, verb-serialization, etc. Li and Thompson (1976) pointed out that the topic-comment structure exhibiting these features were so common and so basic in Chinese that it was best to describe Chinese as a 'topic-prominent' language.

8) Xiao Li xihuan shuxue.
Little Li like math
Little Li likes math.

Of the characteristics common to topic-prominent languages discussed in Li and Thompson (1976), the surface coding of the topic element is especially relevant to the present discussion. Unlike languages such as Japanese and Korean in which the surface coding for grammatical functions, including the Topic, is formalized through morphological marking, the Topic in a Chinese sentence is recognized solely by its initial position. In speech, there may be a slight pause (Li and Thompson 1981), or a modal particle such as *a, ne, y,a* after the topic (or subject) constituent (Chao 1968). However, these are by no means obligatory devices for topic marking and are not recognized or formally described as such in Chinese grammar.

Furthermore, the topic in Chinese may be any element as long as it is the focus of the discourse. According to Fang (1992:9), 'In Chinese, the most important word or phrase is always placed at the sentence initial position…, and the rest of the elements are produced as the predicate.' The 'most important word or phrase' refers to the discourse information which may be grammatically realized as SUBJ, OBJ, ADJ, etc. While the SUBJ is held to be the default topic (Li and Thompson 1976, Bresnan 2001) in line with the Topic Hypothesis, topicalization of non-subject constituents is permitted and in fact frequently occurs (See DeFrancis 1967). Example (9) consists of two clauses. In both clauses, the initial constituent is not the subject but the object argument of the verb. Also in both sentences, the subject is optional and is frequently omitted in discourse as long as it is recoverable from the context.

9) Yao chi le, zhen ye da le.
Medicine eat PERF. *Needle also jab* PERF.
I took the medicine, and also had the needle.

On the issue of word order, Li and Thompson (1981) pointed out that it was difficult to establish the 'basic' word order of Mandarin Chinese. On the basis of Greenberg's (1963) language universals, Li and Thompson claimed that

Mandarin 'has many SVO features as well as many SOV features' (p.26).[4] However, a sample text count by Li and Thompson (1981) yielded more SVO than SOV sentences. Most of the simple declarative sentences, sentences which do not bias in favor of any discourse information have the SVO order.

Li and Thompson (1981) further pointed out that in Chinese, the order of the major constituents with respect to the verb is governed primarily by semantic factors rather than by grammatical functions. Semantic information such as definiteness and specificity, old and new information, known and unknown information, all play a role in the syntactic structure (or word order) of a sentence. In Chinese, the preverbal positions, including sentence initial, signals definiteness and specificity of the referent, or old and known information, whereas the postverbal position indicates indefiniteness, non-specificity or new information. This contrast between discourse information vis-à-vis positional alignment is shown in (10a/b/c). The postverbal *pingguo* 'apple' in (10a) is indefinite and non-specific, whereas the preverbal *pingguo* 'apple' in (10b) and (10c) refers to a particular and specific 'apple' known to the interlocutors. This discourse meaning-based word order is sometimes grammaticalized such that a particular meaning involving the grammatical object being definite and specific can only be expressed with a particular sentence structure in which the object occurs in the preverbal position, as shown in what is often called the *ba*-structure in (10c). The passive sentence of (10d) is another case in point. The argument *pingguo* 'apple' occurs in a preverbal position because it is definite and known to the interlocutors, and is the focus of the discourse. (10c) and (10d) are related semantically as they both express what has happened to THE 'apple,' a known, definite and specific referent in the discourse event.[5]

10a) Wo <u>chi</u> pinguo le.
I <u>*eat*</u> *apple* PERF
I ate an apple.

10b) Pingguo wo <u>chi</u> le.
Apple *I* <u>*eat*</u> PEFF
I ate the/that apple.

10c) Wo ba pinguo <u>chi</u> le.
I BA *apple* <u>*eat*</u> PERF
I ate the/that apple.

10d) Pinguo bei/gei (wo) <u>chi</u> le.
Apple PASS *(I)* <u>*eat*</u> PERF (PASS=Passive voice marker)
The/That apple was eaten (by me)

In summary, the typological features of Chinese topic, subject and word order outlined above show that (a) Chinese is a topic prominent language, with a basic SVO word order; and (b) the word order interacts with information structure in discourse.

The Topic Hypothesis and Chinese L2 syntax

Given the Chinese typological features associated with topic, subject and word order, what can we say about the L2 acquisition process of Chinese syntax? Table 2 is a processing hierarchy proposed for Chinese, based on the Topic Hypothesis and PT.

Processing procedures	L2 processes	Topic Hypothesis	Chinese syntax
4. S-procedure / WO Rules	Inter-phrasal information	TOP = OBJ (TOPobj VO)	OSV, SOV
3. Phrasal procedure	Phrasal information	TOP = ADJ (TOPadj SVO)	XP SV(O): adverbial subordinate clause *wh-* adverbial
2. Category procedure	None	TOP = SUBJ (TOPsubjVO)	Canonical SV(O): declarative interrogative (*y/n, wh-*, intonation)
1. Word/Lemma	None		words, single constituents formulaic expressions

Table 2. Processing Hierarchy of L2 Chinese syntax

Following the initial stage of words and single constituents, the learner moves to acquire the Category Procedure which enables him/her to analyze the lexical categories of words. Equiped with this skill, the learner can carry out direct mapping between the conceptual structure, the core grammatical function, and the surface structure of a sentence. The structural outcome is canonical SV(O) in which the TOP and the SUBJ are assigned to the same constituent (TOP=SUBJ). At this stage simple SV(O) declarative and interrogative sentences, including *y/n*, *wh-* and intonation questions are all processable.[6] Note that unlike English and German, the Chinese interrogative structure follows the same word order as its declarative counterpart. The *yes-no* question in (11) is formed with a sentence-final particle *ma*, while in (12), the *wh*-question has the unknown information expressed by the *wh*-word *in-situ*. Unlike Japanese, there is no morphological marking for grammatical or semantic relations. In both (11) and (12), the basic canonical order is preserved, so is the relationship between TOP and SUBJ.

11) *y/n question*
Wang chi pingguo ma?
Wang eat apple Qpar (Qpar = Question particle)
Does Wang eat apples?

12) *Wh-question*
Wang chi shenme?
Wang eat what
What does Wang eat?

When XP is adjoined to the sentence, such adverbials as time and locative phrases, subordinate clauses, and other topic-like elements can be expressed sentence initially. When that happens, the SUBJ is no longer the default TOP, as the TOP function is assigned to XP. In (13), (14) and (15), the XP (underlined) is a locative adverbial phrase, a subordinate clause of time, and an NP respectively. Chinese grammar does not constrain the word order alteration as the result of XP adjunction.

13) Zai Aodaliya, wo kandao hen duo daishu.
In Australia, I saw very many kangaroo.
In Australia, I saw many kangaroos.

14) Shangke yihou, wo hui sushe.
Go-class after, I return dormitory
After class, I go back to the dormitory.

15) Na zhang hua, Gupo chuan lan de chenshan. (D.T2.5, #3)
that CL *picture, Gupo wear blue* ATT *shirt* (CL = Classifier)
In that picture, Gupo wears a blue shirt.

However, there is one catch: the default position of adverbial XP such as time and location in Chinese grammar is preverbal, between the SUBJ and the verb (Li and Thompson 1981), as shown in (16) and (17). While this order is not strictly maintained in a declarative structure by the speaker due to discourse-pragmatic consideration, it is fairly well preserved when the XP is a *wh-* word as (18) and (18a) show. The fact that in Chinese, almost any element can be TOP does not apply to *wh-* questions.

16) S → SUBJ TIME LOCATION V…

17) Wo 5 dian zai tushuguan xuexi.
I 5 o'clock in library study.
I study /studied in the library at 5 o'clock.

18) Ni zai nar xuexi?
You in where study
Where do you study?

18a) *Zai nar ni xuexi?
In where you study?
*You study where?

Finally, at the last stage in the Topic Hypothesis where the OBJ is assigned the TOP function and occupies the initial position of a sentence, a range of non-canonical structures are hypothesized to occur. They include relative clause, passive, *ba*-structure and OBJ topicalization. Examples (19) and (20) are both OBJ topicalization structures. In (19), the OBJ (underlined) of *xiewan* 'finish-writing' is topicalized to the initial position while in (20), it is to the preverbal position. Both deviate from the linear alignment of a canonical structure at Stage 1.

19) Zhe ge lianxi nimen xiewang le ma? (K, T7.1, #7)
This CL *exercise you write-finish* PERF Qpar
Have you finished this exercise? / This exercise, have you finished?

20) Wo luyinji bu yong. (S, T9.4, #29)
I tape-recorder not use.
I don't use the tape recorder.

In the following, the Topic Hypothesis is tested in a longitudinal study investigating the acquisition process of L2 Chinese syntax. The test structures are those listed in Table 2 and discussed above. They are common sentence structures which are produced and heard frequently by Chinese people in their daily communication, and were among the structures taught in the Chinese language program where the data was collected.

Within this general investigative framework, what is of particular interest is the question whether learners, especially those from an English language background, would assign *wh*-words to the TOP position. Both Chinese and English grammar constrain the syntactic position of *wh*-words: in English, they are constrained to be in the initial position, whereas in Chinese, they are constrained to remain *in situ*. From a PT perspective, this means the Chinese *wh-* interrogative structure requires lower level processing procedures than the English *wh*-interrogative structure because in Chinese, the *wh*-structure employs the same canonicalmapping strategy as the declarative structure. Both belong to PT stage 2 (Category Procedure). Therefore the interrogative structure should emerge simultaneously as the declarative structure in the L2 Chinese of the learner. The question remains as to whether learners actually do produce *wh-*questions when required, and if they do, would they place *wh*-constituent sentence initially? Secondly, when TOP and SUBJ are differentiated through the appearance of the topicalized XP element, would the Chinese IL grammar be constrained by the target language grammar, with the *wh*-ADJ(unct) *in situ*, or would it give way to processing constraints, topicalizing the *wh*-ADJ?

The study

Informants and data collection

The study was longitudinal and non-interventional. The informants of the study, Kate, Sharon, and Dave,[7] were English native speakers in their late teens and early 20's at an Australian university. They were absolute beginners of Chinese when being selected although each had learned a foreign language before.[8] They attended the same lectures (5 hours per week) during the entire data collection period. Kate and Dave were in the same tutorial group (5 hours per week).

Their Chinese speech data was collected regularly throughout the first year of the Chinese course. The first data collection session was held five weeks after the course started. Subsequent sessions took place every three weeks except during three class-free periods.[9] Each session lasted between 15 to 50 minutes, with later sessions considerably longer than the early ones. A total of nine data sets were obtained from Kate and Dave, and eight from Sharon (who missed session 6 due to a time clash).

The data collection session was structured. Except for the last group session, the informants and the researcher met individually, working on tasks which required the informants to respond to different situations or scenarios spontaneously. The tasks were communicative, consisting of problem-solving, role-play, picture-based oral composition, story-retelling, and various descriptive activities. Many of the tasks were trialled on native speakers of Chinese to ensure their effectiveness. Each session ended with a conversation in which some of the linguistic forms were elicited again in a casual and implicit manner (for details, see Zhang 2001).

Data analysis

The interview sessions were audio-taped and later transcribed. Grammatical features were tagged. The analysis focused on structurally valid instances defined as sentences whose argument structure was complete. Sentences involving subject / object ellipsis were not considered even though they were well-formed because a pro-drop sentence in which the SUBJ argument is not overtly represented cannot be used to test against the Topic Hypothesis. Example (21), a pro-drop sentence, is an example of invalid evidence.

21) Meitian ji dian qichuang? (Dave, T4.9, #63)
everyday when get up
When do you get up everyday?

Findings

A. TOPsubjVO

Table 3 presents the findings of four simple SV(O) structures in which the TOP is the SUBJ of the sentence. The structures are canonical statements (Statement), *yes/no* questions (*Y/N*), *wh*-questions (*Wh*-), and intonation questions (Qinto) (questions formed through rising intonation). The slash sign (/) indicates the ratio between well-formed sentences and total number of relevant evidence found in the data corpus. Structurally ill-formed sentences usually lacked a verb or had double marking for the interrogative (i.e., co-occurrence of *wh*-word and *y/n* question marker *ma*). The plus sign (+) is used to indicate the presence of the structure in the data. The empty cell indicates no structural evidence in the data (e.g., the informants did not ask any questions in a particular observation session). The top row 'T1, T2…T9' refers to each of the data collection sessions.

The findings showed clearly that at T1, after five weeks or 50 hours of study, all three informants were able to produce canonical structures. Both affirmative and interrogative sentences of the SVO type were produced in abundance. *Wh*-questions typically focused on the OBJ argument, with the *wh*-word placed *in-situ*, as illustrated in (22) and (23). All but one were simple canonical sentences,[10] and the canonical structure was in the data corpus throughout the entire one-year observation period.

22) Mama jiao shenme? (D T1.1, #18)
Mom call what?
What's mom's name?

23) Ta zai nar? (S T1.3, #26)
he be-at where
where is he?

A close examination of the data in T1 further revealed the connection between the sentence structure (SV(O)) produced by the informants, the verb types, and the communicative content. A total of 8 verb types were used by the informants to inquire about the identity of people in a photo session (see Table 4). The majority of the verbs were transitive, which were sufficient for the expressive needs of the informants to explore such information as the name (family and given name), occupation, nationality, place of residence, relationship between people in the photos. It is of course conceivable that a relatively mature L2 grammar might motivate more structural variations than those found at T1. However, the informants were constrained by their L2 lexical stock and processing skills. Consequently, anything beyond the canonical structure did not appear to be an option at the TOPsubjV(O) stage.

Informant	Structure	T1	T2	T3	T4	T5	T6	T7	T8	T9
Dave	statement	9/13	+	+	+	+	+	+	+	+
	Y/N?	9/21	4/4	2/2	2/2					1/1
	Wh-?	9/14	5/5	8/8					3/3	
	Qinto?	7/10	4/4	+	+			+	+	
Kate	Statement	17/17	+	+	+	+	+	+	+	+
	Y/N?	15/15	15/15	5/5	5/5			3/3		1/1
	Wh-?	37/37	15/15	9/9	3/3		2/2		2/2	4/4
	Qinto?	2/2			+					
Sharon	Statement	26/27	+	+	+	+	N/A	+	+	+
	Y/N?	20/25	4/5			1/1		5/5	1/1	
	Wh-?	18/18	12/12		*1/1				2/2	
	Qinto?	2/2				1		-	1	

Table 3. TOP = SUBJ (TOPsubjVO)

Verb	Dave	Kate	Sharon
Shi 'be'	+	+	+
Jiao 'call (given name)'	+	+	+
Xing 'call (surname)'	+	+	+
Zhu(zai) 'live (in)'	+	+	
Zai 'be in/at'	+		+
Chang 'sing'			+
Xuexi 'study'			+
Jiao 'teach'			+

Table 4. Verbs at T1

**Jiao* 'to call (given name)' and *jiao* 'to teach' differ in tones.

Although the L2 Chinese of the informants was structurally restricted at T1, it was communicatively effective. Thanks to the canonical order of both declarative and interrogative structures in Chinese grammar, the informants were able to not only make descriptive statements but also to seek information through questions, thus fully utilizing the canonical mapping procedure. The evidence was clear that at T1, the informants produced the structure in which the SUBJ and the TOP functions were assigned to one and the same constituent in the sentence initial position, as predicted by the Topic Hypothesis.

B. TOPadj SVO

Table 5 tabulates the sentences in the data which contained an XP adjunct (ADJ). This included time and locative adverbials (Adv), *wh*-time and locative phrases (*Wh*-), subordinate clauses of time (Sub-cl),[11] and other types of non-core argument constituents (otherADJ). The initial, the medium, and the final position in which these ADJs occurred in a sentence is separated by a slash (/). Thus, 0/2/1 means that of the three sentences with ADJs, none had ADJ initially, two ADJs were placed preverbally, and one was in sentence final position. Where a slash is not present, as in the 'otherADJ' category, the positional contrast was not present; only the initial position was occupied (see (27)). Examples (24), (25), (26) and (27) from the data illustrate typical ADJ distributions (the ADJs are underlined).

The distribution of the ADJ as displayed in Table 5 tended to be complementary: the 'otherADJ' and the vast majority of the 'sub-clause' occurred sentence initially (except for four cases in Dave T4 and T5). The *wh*-ADJ, on the other hand, appeared overwhelmingly preverbal, between the SUBJ and the verb.[12] The distribution of the adverbial ADJ (ADV) seemed mixed: Dave and Sharon had more preverbal ADVs than Kate, who tended to place such ADJs initially.

24) *ADJ initial*
Mingtian ni zuo shenme? (Kate, T2.8, #34)
tomorrow you do what?
What do you do tomorrow?

25) *ADJ preverbal*
Wo de baba zai yinhang gongzuo. (Sharon, T.2.6, #6)
I POSS *dad in bank work*
My dad works at the bank.

26) *wh- ADJ preverbal*
Ta zai nar gongzuo? (Dave, T2.7.2, #12)
he in where work
Where does he work?

27) *Other ADJ initial*
Na zhang hua Gupo chuan lan de chenshan. (D T2.5, #3)
that CL picture Gupo wear blue ATT shirt
In that picture Gupo is wearing a blue shirt.

Further distributional analysis of the ADV category of time and location shown in Table 6 pointed to the tendency of all three informants to place locative adjuncts preverbally, in contrast to time adjuncts, which appeared to favor the sentence-initial TOP position. Here learner variations were observed: Kate explored the TOP position more extensively than Dave and Sharon. The overall picture of T2 and hereafter was that the informants were able to produce ADJs of various types in two sentential positions: initial (or TOP) and preverbal, both of which are permitted by Chinese grammar.

Informant	Structure	T1	T2	T3	T4	T5	T6	T7	T8	T9
Dave	otherADJ		2	1			4	1	1	1
	Sub-cl		3/0/0	2/0/0	9/3/0	2/1/0	3/0/0	17/0/0	3/0/0	3/0/0
	Adv		9/28/0	5/17/0	14/21/0	7/17/1	9/10/0	23/21/8	7/12/0	4/6/0
	Wh-		0/3/0	0/4/0					0/4/0	
Kate	otherADJ									
	Sub-cl				3/0/0	2/0/0	1/0/0	5/0/0	2/0/0	
	Adv		14/8/0	3/3/0	21/8/0	13/2/0	16/5/0	23/16/0	5/5/0	6/1/0
	Wh-		0/0/1*	-	0/1/0				0/5/0	
Sharon	otherADJ		8	1	7		N/A		1	
	Sub-cl		4/0/0	5/0/0		2/0/0			3/0/0	1/0/0
	ADV		19/21/2	10/15/0	23/17/4	15/23/4		12/14/5	13/25/1	1/2/0
	Wh-	0/1/0	0/2/0	0/1/0	0/1/0				0/3/0	

Table 5. TOPadj SV(O)

Informant	ADV	T1	T2	T3	T4	T5	T6	T7	T8	T9
Dave	Location		5/16/0	1/5/0	1/6/0	1/3/0	3/4/0	1/6/1	0/6/0	1/0/0
	Time		4/14/0	4/12/0	13/15/0	6/14/1	6/6/0	22/15/7	7/6/0	3/6/0
Kate	Location		0/8/0	0/3/0	1/5/0	1/2/0	1/5/0	3/5/0	0/5/0	
	Time		14/0/0	3/0/0	20/3/0	12/0/0	15/0/0	20/11/0	5/0/0	6/1/0
Sharon	Location		4/17/1	0/8/0	0/2/1	4/12/2	N/A	4/9/0	7/19/1	0/1/0
	Time		15/4/1	10/7/0	23/15/3	11/11/2		8/5/5	6/5/0	1/1/0

Table 6. Distribution of Adverbial phrases

C. TOPobj SV

Finally, OBJ topicalization emerged in T6 and T7 respectively (see Table 7). Produced in small quantities by the informants toward the end of their first year study, most of the sentences had the core argument, the OBJ, in the TOP position while a few had it in the preverbal position, between the SUBJ and the verb. This was indicated by a lower case 'v' in Table 7. In the following examples (28 to 32), the OBJ constituent is underlined. Clearly, these examples showed evidence of non-canonical alignment in that the SVO order is being disrupted by the dislocation of the OBJ argument. The processing skill required to manage such an operation lies in successful mapping of the c-structure to f-structure at the sentence level (S-procedure in PT) so that the constituents in a non-canonical sentence nevertheless retain their functional categories (as SUBJ, OBJ).

28) Zhege lianxi nimen xiewanle ma? (K, T7.1, #7)
this CL exercise you write-finish-PERF Qpar
This exercise, have you finished? / Have you finished this exercise?

29) Na ge lao nan shuo de Gupo ting de dong. (D, T8.2, #20)
that CL old man say RC Guop listen DE understand

What that old man said, Gupo could understand. /
Gupo could understand what that old man said.
(RC = Relative clause marker)

30) *Biede ke wo bu shangke. (S, T7.1, #4)
other class I not take-class
Other classes, I don't go. / I don't go to other classes.

31) Wo luyinji bu yong. (S, T9.4, #29)
I tape-recorder not use.
I don't use the tape recorder.

32) Wo xiang laoshi zheyang dianying bu xihuan. (D, T7.1, #9)
I think teacher this kind movie not like
I think teacher doesn't like this kind of movie.

Informant	T1	T2	T3	T4	T5	T6	T7	T8	T9
Dave						1	2 1v	2	1
Kate							3		
Sharon							1		1v

Table 7. TOPobj SV

In Table 8, the developmental profile of the informants is summarized. The plus sign '+' indicates the presence of the structure in the data, which can also be interpreted as acquisition of the structure. The minus sign '-' means the relevant structure was not found in the data although the structural context was present (e.g., no topicalized *wh*-ADJ although *wh*-ADJ was present). The empty cell means neither the structure in question nor its context was found in the data (e.g., no sentence containing a *wh*-ADJ was produced). D, K, and S are the initials of the informants. The result shows quite clearly that the developmental profile of the TOP function in the data supports the Topic Hypothesis. A three-tier progression was consistently observed in the data. The informants reached the canonical stage (TOPsubjVO) at T1, the TOP-SUBJ disassociation stage (TOPadj SVO) at T2, and the OBJ topicalization stage (TOPobjSV) at T6 and T7 respectively.

Topic Hypothesis	Structure	T1	T2	T3	T4	T5	T6	T7	T8	T9
3. TOP = OBJ	OSV	-	-	-	-	-	D+	K+ S+	+	+
2. TOP = ADJ	ADJ *Wh*-ADJ		+ -	+ -	+ -	+ -	+ -	+ -	+ -	+ -
1. TOP = SUBJ	SV(O) Declarative Interrogative	+	+	+	+	+	+	+	+	+

Table 8. Development of L2 Chinese syntax

Discussion

As an explanation of the development of IL syntax, the Topic Hypothesis offers a theoretical explanation for a number of widely observed IL phenomena. For example, in IL German and Swedish, the requirement of verb 2nd (V/2) is not fulfilled when the topic position is occupied by an element other than grammatical SUBJ (Pienemann, Di Biase and Kawaguchi 2005). This phenomenon is even observed in the IL of learners whose native language is also V/2, e.g., Swedish learners of German (Håkansson, Pienemann and Sayehli, 2002). In the English IL, it is also frequently observed that if the TOP position is occupied by a non-SUBJ *wh*-word, an auxiliary verb does not always occur in the second position. That is, learners go through a stage where the *wh*-question is formed as 'Wh-SVO' (Cazden, Caancino, Rosansky, and Schumann, 1975, cited in Larsen-Freeman and Long, 1991, pp. 92-93). All this demonstrates that XP adjunction constitutes a distinctive IL developmental stage.

This stage is also observed in Japanese L2 which exhibits TOP-SUBJ disassociation through differential morphological marking (Kawaguchi, 2005a, 2005b). At the TOP=SUBJ stage, the TOPsubj is marked by either *-ga* (NOMinative) or *-wa* (TOP) without differentiation, showing formulaic patterns. At the TOP=ADJ stage, the learner is able to mark the SUBJ with *-ga*, because the first position is already occupied by *-wa* marked element (i.e., the TOPadj). Kawaguchi (2005b) observed that learners of Japanese initially produced only canonical SOV structures in which the SUBJ was consistently marked by *-ga.* Once they started marking the TOP constituent in the first position which was clearly not SUBJ, the *-wa/-ga* distinction became clearer and -ga became more firmly established as a subject marker.

Although Chinese grammar has neither structural nor morphological requirements on the presence of XP adjunction as those displayed in Japanese and German, it does have one restriction on the *wh*-element, that is, the *wh-*

element cannot be assigned to the TOP position unless it is a grammatical SUBJ. The informants in the present study did comply with both grammatical constraints and discourse principles: the XPadj was placed in both TOP position and preverbally, but only preverbally when it was a *wh*-element.

The developmental pattern shown in the present study raises the issue of cross-linguistic transfer so widely discussed in the SLA literature. Of the various models and hypotheses pertaining to transfer, the Developmentally Moderated Transfer Hypothesis (Pienemann, Di Biase, Kawaguchi and Håkansson, 2005) seems to account for the findings of Chinese L2 *wh*-structures best. The DMT states that the influence of L1 on L2 is constrained by the learner's current processing capacity. Regardless of the 'typological constellation,' a learner whose IL processing skill is at PT stage 2 would not be able to transfer L1 material that requires Stage 4 processing procedure. Conversely, a structure which is high up in the developmental hierarchy is never transferred at the initial stage. Therefore, one's L1 cannot serve as the entire base for the initial state of L2 acquisition. On the other hand, the learner would be able to acquire L2 forms and structures vastly different from his/her L1 once the necessary processing skills are developed. In Kawaguchi's (2005a) longitudinal and cross-sectional study of L2 Japanese by speakers of English, French and Portuguese, for example, no word order transfer was observed from the learners' respective L1s to Japanese L2. All informants produced Japanese canonical order SOV at a stage at which the canonical mapping skill was developed. Similarly, Håkansson, Pienemann and Sayehli's (2002) study of Swedish school children learning German as L2 demonstrated that those children whose current processing skill was at the ADV(erb) fronting stage (i.e., TOPadj SVO) did not transfer the V/2 rule from their L1 despite the fact that the same rule existed in both Swedish and German. Rather, they produced sentences (ADV SVO) which conform to neither the grammar of L1, nor the grammar of L2 both of which have ADV VSO.

In the present study, the informants were native speakers of English. In the English grammar, the *wh*-constituent of an interrogative sentence is invariably in the most prominent position, the TOP (or FOCUS) position. This is a salient feature of English (and indeed of many Indo-European languages) that contrasts sharply with Chinese *wh*-structures which have the *wh*-constituent *in situ*. Anecdotal stories often attribute such word-for-word renditions of a Chinese sentence to Chinese learners of English 'You ask me, me ask who?' meaning 'You ask me this question, but who do I ask for an answer?' Following the Topic Hypothesis and processability hierarchy, the Chinese *wh*-structure is clearly lower on the developmental hierarchy than that of English (see Table 8). As a result, no transfer was observed in the L2 Chinese of the English-speaking informants at all. Indeed, '[s]tructures higher up the processability hierarchy are never transferred at the initial state, regardless of typological constellation' (Pienemann, Di Biase, Kawaguchi and Håkansson, 2005, p.111).

Topic Hypothesis	Structure	Chinese	English
Stage 3 TOP = OBJ	OSV		Owh aux SV
Stage 2 TOP = ADJ	XP SVO	S ADJwh VO	*ADJwh SVO
Stage 1 TOP = SUBJ	SVO	Swh VO SV Owh	Swh VO

Table 9. Processing hierarchy of Chinese and English *wh*-questions

Conclusion

The Topic Hypothesis offers a new perspective in which the L2 syntactic development and the discourse and pragmatic dimensions of language production become closely associated in the step-by-step progression of language acquisition. The developmental pattern of the L2 Chinese sentence structures investigated in this study supports the principle of the Topic Hypothesis. The data show the successive disassociation between TOP and SUBJ elements, and between grammatical functions and sequential positions in a sentence. The progression from linear alignment between arguments, grammatical functions and word order to non-linear alignment was motivated by and regulated through a set of discourse-pragmatic as well as grammatical principles. Furthermore, as evidenced by the present study, the dynamics of cross-linguistic transfer exhibit itself through developmentally moderated constraints (Pienemann, Di Biase, Kawaguchi and Håkansson 2005) which not only regulate what learners are not able to transfer, but also what they would not transfer.

Notes

[1] A canonical structure, according to Pienemann, Di Biase and Kawaguchi (2005), is an active sentence in which the Agent and Patient arguments are linked to Subject and Object in a default fashion.

[2] The regular relationship between thematic roles and grammatical relationship has been supported by a number of on-line experiments on child and adult comprehension (e.g., Bever 1970, Hayashibe 1975, Sano 1977, Otsu 1994, Sasaki 1998, cited in Di Biase 2005 and Pienemann, Di Biase and Kawaguchi 2005).

[3] Cf. Larsen-Freeman and Long, 1991. p.271.

[4] Features of SVO languages included SVO sentences, prepositions, auxiliaries preceding the verb. Features of SOV languages included SOV sentences, prepositional phrases preceding the verb, postpositions, aspect markers following the verb, relative clauses and genitive phrases preceding the head noun (Li and Thompson 1976).

[5] The meaning-based word order in Chinese also extends to certain adverbial expressions (Li and Thompson 1981). For example, the preverbal position signals the time and location of an event shown in (1a) and (2a), whereas the postverbal position indicates the duration and destination of an action as illustrated in (1b) and (2b). (The verb is underlined)

(1a) Preverbal: Time
Wo 12 dian shuijiao.
I 12 o'clock sleep
I sleep at 12 o'clock.

(1b) Postverbal: Duration
Wo shui le 12 ge xiaoshi
I sleep PERF *12* CL *hour*
I slept for 12 hours.

(2a) Preverbal: Location
Ta zai zhuozi shang pa.
He/She at table on crawl
He/She is crawling on the table.

(2b) Postverbal: Destination/Goal
Ta pa shang zhuozi.
He/She crawl up table
He/She crawls onto the table.

[6] Negative and pro-drop structures also belong here (Di Biase 2005).These structures are not examined in this paper.

[7] These are fictitious names.

[8] Kate had learned German, Sharon Indonesian and Dave Korean.

[9] Two weeks within each semester and five weeks between two semesters.

[10] This was an interesting case of self-correction through self-monitoring. The locative phrase was initially placed at the end of the sentence, which was then self-corrected in a recast in which it was placed preverbally.

Ta jiao Hanyu nar no (pause) Ta zai nar jiao Hanyu?(S T1.3, #12, #13)
He teach Chinese where no (pause) He at where teach Chinese?

Where he teaches Chinese no (pause) Where does he teach Chinese?

[11] Cause-effect, conditional, and transitional sub-clauses were not considered. The durative adverbial (e.g., *san tian* 'three days') was not included in the ADJ analysis and it never occurred initial position in the data.

[12] There was one case where the *wh*-ADJ was placed postverbally: *Ni gongzuo nar?* You work where? (Kate, T2.8, #28)

Acknowledgements

I wish to thank Manfred Pienemann, Bruno Di Biase, Satomi Kawaguchi and an anonymous reviewer for their suggestions and comments on the study. I value the discussions I had with the participants of the 5th International Symposium on Processability, Second Language Acquisition and Bilingualism (Deakin University September 2005). I am grateful, as always, to the informants whose L2 speech was used as the data for this study. I thank Karl Rensch for his help with editing. The mistakes that remain are mine.

References

Bever, T. G. (1970). 'The cognitive basis for linguistic structures'. In J. Hayes (ed.), *Cognition and the Development of Language*. NY: John Wiley, 279-362.

Bresnan, J. (ed.), (1982). *The Mental Representation of Grammatical Relations*. Cambridge, MA.: MIT Press.

—. (2001). *Lexical-functional Syntax.* Malden, MA.: Blackwell.

Bresnan, J. & Kanerva, J. M. (1989). 'Locative inversion in Chichewa: a case study of factorization in grammar'. *Linguistic Inquiry*. 20, 1: 1-50.

Cazden, C., Caancino, E., Rosansky, E., & Schumann, J. (1975). *Second Language Acquisition Sequences in Children, Adolescents and Adults.* Final report submitted to the National Institute of Education, Washington, D.C.

Chao, Yuen-ren. (1968). *A Grammar of Spoken Chinese.* Berkeley and Los Angeles: University of California Press.

Choi, Hye-Won. (2001). 'Phrase structure, information structure and resolution of mismatch'. In P. Sells (ed.)., *Formal and Empirical Issues in Optimality Theoretic Syntax*. Stanford, Cal.: CSLI Publications, 17-62.

Clahsen, H., J. Meisel & Pienemann, M. (1983). *Deutsch als Zweitsprache. Der Spracherwerb ausländischer Arbeiter*. Tübingen: Narr.

Dalrymple, M. (2001). *Syntax and Semantics. Lexical Functional Grammar.* Vol. 34. San Diego, CA: Academic Press.

DeFrancis, J. (1967). 'Syntactic permutability in Chinese'. In W. Austin (ed.), *Papers in Linguistics in Honour of Leon Dostert*. Mouton.

Di Biase, B. (2005). *The Topic Hypothesis in Processability Theory: The Syntax-pragmatics Interface in L2 Development*. Paper presented at the 5th International Symposium on Processability, Second Language Acquisition and Bilingualism. Melbourne: Deakin University, 26-28 September.

Di Biase, B. and Kawaguchi, S. (2002).' Exploring the typological plausibility of Processability Theory: Language development in Italian second language and Japanese second language'. *Second Language Research,* 18, 3: 274-302.

Fang, Y. (1992). *Shiyong Hanyu Yufa*. Beijing: Beijing Yuyan Xueyuan Chubanshe. [*Practical Chinese Grammar*. Beijing: Beijing Language Institute Press].

Glahn, E., Håkansson, G., Hammarberg, B., Holmen, A., Hvenekilde, A., & Lund, K. (2001). 'Processability in Scandinavian second language acquisition'. *Studies in Second Language Acquisition*. 23, 389-416.

Greenberg, J. (1963). 'Some universals of grammar with particular reference to the order of meaningful elements'. In J. Greenberg (ed.), *Universals of Language*. Cambridge, MA.: MIT Press, 73-113..

Håkansson, G., Pienemann, M., & Sayehli, S. (2002). 'Transfer and typological proximity in the context of L2 Processing'. *Second Language Research*, 18, 3: 350-273.

Hayashibe, H. (1975). 'Word order and particles: a developmental study in Japanese'. *Descriptive and Applied Linguistics*. 8: 1-18.

Jansen, L. (1991). 'The development of word order in natural and formal German second language acquisition'. *Australian Working Papers in Language Development*. 5, 1-42.

—. (2005). *The Acquisition of Word Order in Anglophone Formal Learners of German: Further Empirical Evidence*. Paper presented at the 5th International Symposium on Processability, Second Language Acquisition and Bilingualism. Melbourne: Deakin University, 26-28 September.

Kawaguchi, S. (2005a). *Acquisition of Japanese as a Second Language: a Processability Perspective*. Unpublished Ph.D. dissertation. University of Western Sydney.

—. (2005b). 'Argument structure and syntactic development in Japanese as a second language'. In M. Pienemann (ed.), *Cross-linguistic Aspects of Processability Theory*. Amsterdam: Benjamins, 253-298.

Larsen-Freeman, D., & Long, M. (1991). *An Introduction to Second Language Acquisition Research.* London: Longman.

Levelt, W.J.M. (1989). *Speaking: From Intention to Articulation.* Cambridge, MA.: MIT Press.

Li, C., & Thompson, S. (1976). 'Subject and topic: a new typology of language'. In C. Li. (ed.), *Subject and Topic.* New York: Academic Press, 457-490.

Li, C., & Thompson, S. (1981). *Mandarin Chinese: a Functional Reference Grammar.* California: University of California Press.

Otsu, Y. (1994). 'Early acquisition of scrambling in Japanese'. In T. Hoekstra & Schwartz, B. D. (eds.), *Language Acquisition Studies in Generative Grammar.* Amsterdam: John Benjamins, 252-264.

Pienemann, M. (1998). *Language Processing and Second Language Development: Processability Theory.* Amsterdam: John Benjamins.

—. (2003). 'Language processing capacity'. In C. Doughty & Long, M. (eds.), *The Handbook of Second Language Acquisition.* Malden, MA.: Blackwell, 679-714.

—. (ed.) (2005). *Cross-linguistic Aspects of Processability Theory.* Amsterdam: John Benjamins.

Pienemann, M., Di Biase., & Kawaguchi, S. (2005). 'Extending Processability Theory'. In Pienemann, M. (ed.), *Cross-linguistic Aspects of Processability Theory.* Amsterdam: John Benjamins.

Pienemann, M., Di Biase, B., Kawaguchi, S. And Håkansson, G. (2005). 'Processability, typological distance and L1 transfer' In M. Pienemann (ed.), *Cross-linguistic Aspects of Processability Theory.* Amsterdam: John Benjamins.

Pienemann, M. & Hakansson, G. (1999). 'A unified approach towards the development of Swedish as L2: a processability account'. *Studies in Second Language Acquisition.* 21: 383-420.

Pinker, S. (1984). *Language Learnability and Language Development.* Cambridge, MA.: Harvard University Press.

—. (1989). *Learnability and Cognition: the Acquisition of Argument Structure.* Cambridge, MA.: MIT Press.

Sano, K. (1977). 'An experimental study on the acquisition of Japanese simple sentences and cleft sentences'. *Descriptive and Applied Linguistics.* 10: 213-233.

Sasaki, Y. (1998). 'English and Japanese interlanguage comprehension strategies: An analysis based on the competition model'. *Applied Psycholinguistics.* 6: 190-204.

Zhang, Y. (2001). *Second Language Acquisition of Chinese Grammatical Morphemes: A Processability Perspective*. Unpublished Ph.D. dissertation, Australian National University, Canberra.

—. (2005). 'Processing and formal instruction in the L2 acquisition of five Chinese grammatical morphemes'. In Pienemann, M. (ed.), *Cross-linguistic Aspects of Processability Theory*. Amsterdam: Benjamins, 233-273.

Zhu, Dexi. (1982). *Yufa Jiangyi*. Beijing: Shangwu Yinshuguan. [Lectures on Grammar. Beijing: Commercial Press].

CHAPTER 8

LEXICAL AND GRAMMATICAL DEVELOPMENT IN JAPANESE-ENGLISH BILINGUAL FIRST LANGUAGE ACQUISITION[1]

Yuki Itani-Adams

Children's language learning is characterised by their universal success and the ultimate attainment achieved. In other words, while some variation in the rate of development is documented, all normally developing children become a native speaker of the languages they are exposed to in their environment. There is a similarity in the way they learn their languages. For example, in first language (L1) acquisition studies, children are universally reported to acquire content words such as nouns and proper nouns earlier than verbs (Gentner and Boroditsky 2001). However, there is some evidence to show that children are sensitive to the language-specific features of the input languages. Verb learning is one such example. Japanese and Korean children[2] were found to acquire verbs at an earlier age than English children (Choi 1998; Gentner and Boroditsky 2001; Ogura 1998). This difference is thought to reflect the differences in the proportion of nouns and verbs in the input languages children receive. Japanese and Korean are categorised to be a verb-friendly language whereas English is noun-friendly. Therefore Japanese and Korean children receive more input of verbs than do English children. Such typological differences are also reflected in the learning of word order in L1 acquisition. The canonical word order for Japanese is SOV whereas for English it is SVO. Children of the respective languages are reported to use the language specific canonical word order from the time they put multiple words together.

Recent L1 acquisition studies posit a view that there is a link between the development of lexicon and the emergence of grammar. Critical mass hypothesis (Marchman and Bates 1994) proposes a strong relationship between vocabulary size and the complexity of grammar. Such a relationship between vocabulary size and the complexity of grammar was found cross-linguistically. Bates, Dale, and Thal (1995) observed this relationship for L1 English children. A similar relationship was found for L1 Italian children (Caselli, Casadio and Bates 1999) and for L1 Japanese children (Ogura 1998). Each of these studies used a large body of reported data obtained from the MacArthur Communicative Development Inventory (MCDI) (Fenson, Dale, Reznick, Thal, Bates, Hartung, Pethick and Reilly 1993). The cross-linguistic comparisons mentioned above are all based on monolingual children's data.

However not every child acquires only one language. Some children acquire two languages simultaneously. Those who are regularly exposed to two languages from birth receive two sets of linguistic input in their environment. Do such children develop the two languages as separate linguistic systems? This question is one of key issues debated in the field of bilingual first language acquisition. Bilingual first language acquisition is defined to be the acquisition of two languages by a child who has regular exposure to them from birth (De Houwer 1990). There are two hypothesises proposed on this issue. One proposed by Volterra and Taeschner (1978) is that bilingual children initially develop one linguistic system which is later differentiated into two linguistic systems. The other hypothesis is that from the start, bilingual children differentiate two linguistic systems. This is known as the Separate Development Hypothesis (De Houwer 1990). Recent empirical studies such as De Houwer (1990), Juan-Garau and Pérez-Vidal (2000), Meisel (1990), Mishina (1997), Paradis and Genesee (1996), and Yip and Matthews (2000) support the Separate Development Hypothesis. These studies focused on the development of morphosyntax of the two languages in a bilingual child. They found that the two languages of their bilingual informants developed in a language specific manner, resembling that of monolingual children of respective languages, thus concluding that the two languages develop separately.

This study forms part of a larger investigation into the bilingual first language acquisition of Japanese and English in one child, using Processability Theory (PT henceforth; Pienemann 1998a; Pienemann, Di Biase and Kawaguchi 2005) as its theoretical framework. This paper focuses on that part of the study addressing the lexical development and the emergence of morphosyntax (verbal morphology and word order) in the two languages of one bilingual child. It addresses the connection between lexical and morphosyntactic development. The specific issues addressed in this paper are: 1) if the lexicon of the two languages develops in a language-specific manner, 2) when and how verbal morphology in the two languages emerge, and 3) if the initial word order of each language reflects the canonical word order of the input language. If the lexicon and word order were found to develop differently between the two languages, especially if they developed in a language specific manner, then it would support the view that bilingual children develop their two languages separately. The typological difference between the languages in this study offers an ideal opportunity for cross-linguistic comparison.

PT adopts the concept of grammatical encoding procedural skills required for processing of language by a mature native speaker postulated by Levelt (1989) and the concept of "feature unification" from Lexical Functional Grammar (LFG; Bresnan 1982). PT proposes that each processing procedures allows the learners to exchange grammatical information processable by the specific procedural skills. Therefore the acquisition or the automatization of each procedural skill enables a learner to acquire the morphosyntactic feature processable by the skill. These skills are acquired in the following sequence.

(1) 1 Lemma access
2 Category procedure
3 Phrasal procedure
4 S-procedure
5 Subordinate clause procedure, if applicable
(Pienemann 1998a, p.7)

PT's typological plausibility has been supported by various empirical studies, including Japanese as second language (JSL) and English as second language (ESL) (see Di Biase and Kawaguchi 2002; Kawaguchi 2005 for adult JSL; Iwasaki 2004 for child JSL; Pienemann 1998a for adult and child ESL). PT has also been supported for first language (L1) acquisition (Pienemann 1998b for German as L1). This paper presents the first attempt to apply PT to the context of bilingual first language acquisition. While PT addresses the development of morphology and syntax, the development of lexicon has not yet been addressed by the theory. The present study can contribute to development of the theory of language acquisition in this area.

This paper commences with a brief description of PT followed by a description of the data used for this study. Then it presents a discussion of the investigation of the acquisition of different types of lexicon for Japanese and English. The paper then details the investigation of the relationship between the lexicon and grammar, focusing on the verb stem and verbal morphology, and verbs and the semantic function of the arguments. The last section summarizes the findings.

Processability Theory

Processability Theory (PT; Pienemann 1998a; Pienemann, Di Biase and Kawaguchi 2005) was developed to explain second language acquisition (SLA). PT adopts the concept of grammatical encoding procedural skills required for processing of language by a mature native speaker postulated by Levelt (1989). PT also adopts the concept of "feature unification" from Lexical Functional Grammar (LFG; Bresnan 1982). LFG posits that syntactic information, which together with semantic information necessary for the generation of sentences, is annotated within lexicon. The lexical entries of the words in a sentence, *Peter owns a dog,* are given in (2) as an example taken from Pienemann (1998a, p.94).

(2)	Peter:	N,	PRED	=	'Peter'
	owns:	V,	PRED	=	'own' (SUBJ, OBJ)
			TENSE	=	present
			SUBJ PERSON	=	3
			SUBJ NUM	=	SG
	a:	DET,	SPEC	=	'a'
			NUM	=	SG
	dog:	N,	PRED	=	'dog'
			NUM	=	SG (from Pienemann 1998a, 94)

Each processing procedural skill allows a specific type of information exchange between lexicons. PT posits that for a language learner, these processing procedural skills will be automatized in a sequence, thus forming a hierarchy. Each level of the hierarchy is a prerequisite for the next level. In PT, the acquisition of morphological features is defined by the emergence of the morphological feature in question. The emergence is determined by the evidence of productivity of the feature by having lexical as well as form variations.

The original version of PT (Pienemann 1998a) focuses on the acquisition of morphology while the extension of PT (Pienemann, Di Biase and Kawaguchi 2005) addresses the development of syntax. The hierarchy of procedural skills, the structural outcomes for each level in the two languages are tabulated in Table .

With respect to morphology, in Stage 1, "word/lemma access", a learner acquires *words* of the target language. In this stage, it is predicted that information in lexical entry is not yet annotated and the learner has not developed any language-specific procedure. There is no information exchange required at this stage. In Stage 2, "category procedure", information in lexical entry begins to be annotated. However no exchange of such information with any other parts of phrase or sentence is required yet. The acquisition of this stage is predicted to be realised by the suffixation of verbal morphemes for both Japanese and English, as well as the suffixation of the plural *–s* on the English nouns. The following stage, "phrasal procedure", a learner is able to exchange grammatical information across lexicon within a phrase, e.g., *V-te V* structure for Japanese and the number feature in *two* and *dogs* in a phrase *two dogs* for English. The next stage, "S-procedure", allows a leaner to exchange grammatical information across phrases. The unification between noun marking and the morphology in predicate for Japanese is predicted to appear in this stage. An example of such unification is the marking of the OBL(ique) argument with the dative marker *–ni* in passive, causative and benefactive structures. For English, the agreement between the singular third person SUBJ and the verbal morphology *–s*, SV-agreement (e.g., *he walks*), is predicted to appear. A detailed LFG account of Japanese morphosyntactic structures is found in Di Biase and Kawaguchi (2002) and that of English structures is found in Pienemann (1998a).

For syntax, PT predicts canonical word order to appear in Stage 2. Canonical word order occurs when conceptual semantic functions are directly mapped to the linguistic grammatical functions. According to Pinker (1984), agentive argument is directly mapped to subject (S), theme/patient to object (O) and goal/location to oblique object (OBL). English canonical word order is SVO, whereas that of Japanese is SOV. In English the grammatical functions are expressed strictly by the word order. In Japanese the grammatical functions are expressed by case marking particles. The nominative (NOM) marker *-ga* typically marks S by default. The accusative (ACC) marker *-o* marks O by default. The dative (DAT) marker *–ni* marks OBL. Another particle is the topic (TOP) marker *-wa*. This particle marks S by default (see Bresnan 2001) but can topicalise other arguments. Japanese allows ellipsis of argument and particles when the information is understood by the participants of the interaction. A verb alone can occur in an utterance when S and O and other information are understood. There are no person, number and gender features in Japanese.

Processing procedures	Type of information exchange for morphology	Japanese morphology	English morphology	Syntactic Structural outcome
4. S-procedure	Inter-phrasal	agreement of noun marking and the morphology in the predicate	SV agreement (e.g., he walks)	Topicalisation of core arguments (e.g., OBJ)
3. Phrasal procedure	Phrasal	V-*te* V	NP agreement (e.g., two dogs)	XP adjunction (XP + canonical)
2. Category procedure	none	Verbal inflection	Plural -*s*, Verbal inflection (-ed, -ing)	Canonical word order
1.Word/ lemma access	none	invariant forms	invariant forms	---

Table 1. Hierarchy of Processing Procedures and Hypothesised Linguistic Outcome in Japanese and English for Each Procedure (from Pienemann 1998a; Di Biase and Kawaguchi 2002; Pienemann, Di Biase and Kawaguchi 2005)

Data

The informant for this study, Hannah[3], is a first born female child of a family of an English-speaking father (coded as Father) and a Japanese-speaking mother (coded as Mother). Hannah was raised in a "one parent one language" home environment from birth. Father spoke English and Mother spoke Japanese to Hannah. Between Mother and Father, English was the language of communication. The data was recorded using simultaneous audio and video recorders. Each set of recordings consisted of two sessions—one of approximately 45 minutes of interaction with a Japanese-speaking adult and one of approximately 45 minutes of interaction with an English-speaking adult. The recordings were conducted to capture naturally occurring interaction between the participants. The recordings at monthly intervals were transcribed orthographically from ages 1; 11 (one year and eleven month old) to 4; 10. Altogether 38 sets of recordings consisting of 72 recording sessions, i.e., 38 Japanese sessions and 38 English sessions, were transcribed. Transcribed data sets were identified by the sequential number of the transcribed session (1 to 38) followed by the letter J or E for Japanese or English respectively. Monthly sets of sessions from 1; 11 to 2; 10, and at tri-monthly intervals from 2; 10 to 4; 10 were selected for analysis in the appropriate languages (sessions 1 to 13 followed by 16, 19, 22, 25, 28, 31, 34, and 38). Hannah's utterances from the selected transcribed sessions formed the data for the study. Data were analysed monthly during the first year of the investigation in order to obtain a detailed description of the language development during the period in which monolingual children are reported to show rapid linguistic development. The total duration of recording was 925 minutes for Japanese data and 1120 minutes for English data. The Appendix provides the coding for each recording session analysed and Hannah's age at each session.

The description of Hannah's language at the start of investigation (age 1; 11) in each language is shown in At the time her vocabulary size was 137 for Japanese and 105 for English. This figure does not indicate the exhaustive number of lexical items in Hannah's lexicon at the stage, but indicates the number of lexical items uttered by Hannah during the first recording session. Phonological variations of a lexical item were counted individually. At the age of 1; 11, no indication of lexical or form variation in terms of morphology, thus no productive use, was detected. For syntax, she was at the one-word stage. This was indicated by the mean length of utterance (MLU) at the time being 1.1.

	Lexical size	**Morphology development**	**Syntax**	**Age**
Japanese	137	No lexical form variation	1.1 MLU	1;11
English	105	No lexical form variation	1.1 MLU	1;11

Table 2. Hannah's lexical and grammatical development at 1; 11

Composition of Lexicon

Past research of L1 acquisition found that children universally learn content words earlier than relational words regardless of the language they were learning—the phenomenon is termed *noun-advantage* (Gentner and Boroditsky 2001). Content words are words whose referents are conceptually easier to grasp, such as names of objects (e.g., *ball, spoon*) and animate beings (e.g., *cat, dog*). On the other hand, relational words are the words that express the relation between entities. Such relations are expressed differently according to the language, so children need to learn the language specific ways to express them. Gentner and Boroditsky (2001) views this cognitive and linguistic dominance of lexicon to be a continuum. At one extreme end of the continuum lies the concrete nouns, while at the other end lies the relational words, i.e., language specific grammatical words. According to Gentner and Boroditsky (2001), nouns, proper nouns and kinship terms belong to the content word end of continuum, while verbs, conjunctions and determiners belong to the other end of the continuum. While noun-advantage was found cross linguistically, some variation in the timing of verb learning with different languages was detected. It was reported that children acquiring Korean or Japanese, which are more verb friendly than English, acquired verbs at an earlier age than English children (Gentner and Boroditsky 2001; Ogura, Naka, Yamashita, Murase and Mahieu 1997; Oshima-Takane, Naka and Miyata 1997).

I investigated the composition of Hannah's lexicon of two languages, one of which is more verb friendly than English. The data were grouped into six groups of six-monthly periods. In each group of data for each language I analysed the relative proportions of nominal and verb types. Different verb forms of the same verb stem were counted as different types. Both lexical verbs and auxiliary verbs are included in the verb category. The nominals include proper nouns, common nouns and kinship terms. Other relational terms in Japanese are nominal particles. This study investigated nine nominal particles: *ga* (NOM)*, o* (ACC)*, ni* (DAT)*, no* (GENITIVE)*, de* (instrumental)*, e* (goal)*, kara*(source)*, to* (comitative) and *wa* (TOPIC). Other relational terms in English investigated here are spatial prepositions, determiners, and conjunctions, as classified by Gentner and Boroditsky (2001).

The results are shown in Figure 1 and Figure 2. It was found that Hannah used more nominals than verbs in both English and Japanese at the beginning of the period of investigation. This result is consistent with universal noun-advantage of early languages. Despite the differences in the input languages, Hannah began the learning of both languages with nominals. In other words, Hannah bootstrapped into both languages through nominals, not through words that were frequent in the input languages, such as preposition and determiners for English, or verbs or particles for Japanese.

While the universality of noun-advantage was detected, a difference between English and Japanese was also detected in the use of verbs. In English, the use of nominals remained greater than that of verbs throughout the period of investigation. However in Japanese, while nominals were initially used more than verbs, usage of verbs progressively increased. During the final six months of the investigation, from the time Hannah was 4; 4, the proportion of verbs became greater than that of nominals. In other words, the dominant type of lexicon was reversed for Japanese. Hannah's Japanese and English lexicon followed separate developmental patterns, each resembling that of the respective L1. The two languages began to show separate usage patterns after the age of 3; 6.

These results suggest that the language learning mechanisms for both languages must be able to extract nouns from the input languages. At the same time, the different ways verbs are used by Hannah in the two languages suggest the lexical learning is a language-specific operation.

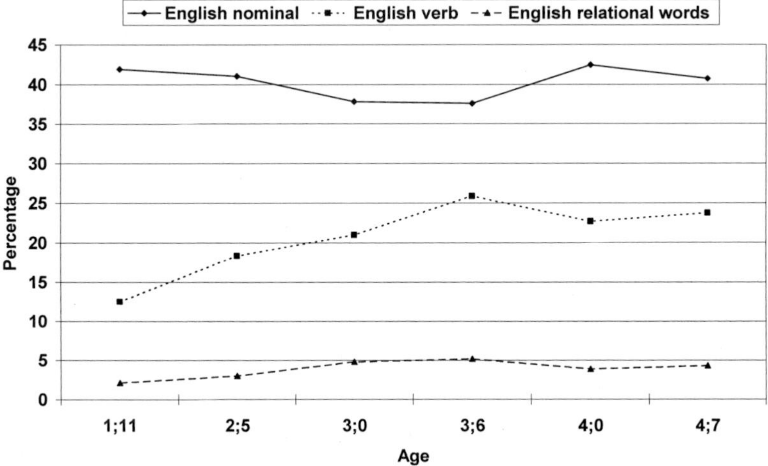

Figure 3. Percentage of different categories of English lexicon

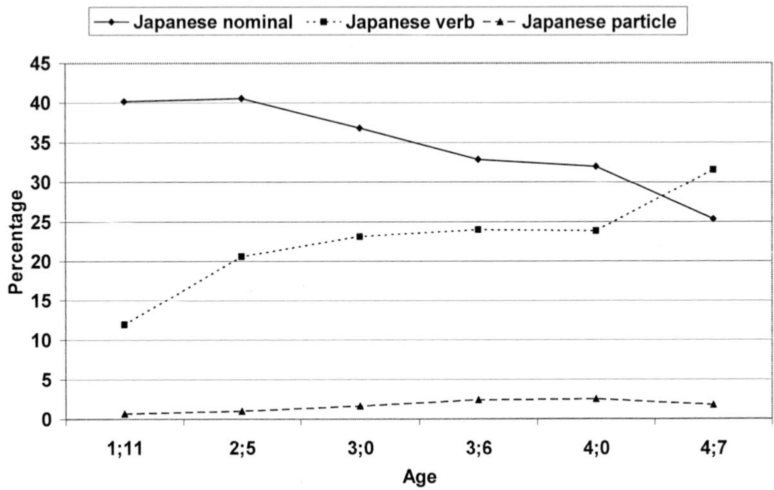

Figure 4. Percentage of different categories of Japanese lexicon

Relationship between Lexicon and Grammar

Bates, Dale and Thal (1995), Bates and Goodman (1999), Caselli, Bates, Casadio, Fenson, Sanderl and Weir (1995), and Caselli, Casadio and Bates (1999) reported a strong relationship between vocabulary size and the development of grammar. These studies based their analyses on the large body of reported data from 1001 EL1 children aged between 1; 6 to 2; 6, obtained using the MacArthur Communicative Development Inventory (MCDI). The MCDI is a checklist used for a parent or caregiver to record which words are known to children. The researchers' data showed a non-linear correlation between vocabulary size and sentence complexity. The relationship between vocabulary size and the onset of grammar was found to be as follows:

(3) 1 Word combination appears for a vocabulary range of 50 to 200.
2 Verbal morphology appears during a vocabulary range of 400 to 600.
3 Sentence complexity accelerates when vocabulary becomes more than 400.

Ogura (1998) reported results from 658 Japanese children using a Japanese version of the MCDI developed by a team she led. In her report, Ogura compared the results of Japanese and English children and concluded that some aspects of development are parallel in these two languages. Similarities were found in the timing of production of word combination and complex sentences.

Japanese children were reported to begin combining words (this includes a combination of a word and a particle) around the time their lexical size reached 50 to 100. An increase of sentence complexity was detected in the vocabulary range of 200 to 400.

For both English and Japanese, data from L1 acquisition showed a strong relationship between vocabulary size and grammar. Bates and Goodman (1999) argued this relationship shows that "grammar is an inherent part of the lexicon" (p. 53). Caselli, Casadio and Bates (1999) followed this view and argued that the relationship between lexicon and grammar "provides evidence in favour of lexicalist theories in which the development of vocabulary and grammar are based on common mechanisms" (p. 76). This supports the argument proposed in Lexical Functional Grammar (e.g., Bresnan 2001) that grammar is lexically driven. This finding of the relationship between vocabulary size and grammar also led to the proposal of a hypothesis known as the critical mass hypothesis (Marchman and Bates 1994). In this hypothesis, Marchman and Bates argue that acquisition of morphology is led by the "increase in the size of the lexicon beyond a particular level, i.e., the vocabulary had achieved a 'critical mass'" (p. 342).

The above mentioned cross-linguistic comparisons of the relationships between lexicon and grammar have been made on the basis of separate monolingual reported data. The current study investigated the relationship between verb stem and verbal morphology in the bilingual context using production data.

1. Relationship between Verb Stems and Verbal Morphemes

Before presenting the results, I present a brief description of English and Japanese verbal morphology. English has three verbal morphemes. They are –*ing* to express progressive aspect (e.g., Tom is reading a book), *-ed* to express the past tense (e.g., Mary walked to school yesterday) and *–s* to express the relation between the subject and verb in present indicative sentence when the subject is the third person singular (e.g., He walks to school everyday). Brown (1983) found, in his study of the acquisition English by three monolingual children, that the first morpheme to be acquired by them was *–ing,* followed by *–ed* and then by the third person singular *–s.*

Japanese verbal morphology is more complex. Japanese verbs inflect for tense, polarity, negation and other aspects. A verb stem is suffixed by one or more morphemes. A verb stem never occurs alone—it is always suffixed by at least one morpheme. In this paper I use the nonpast tense of a verb without the hyphenation between the stem and the nonpast morpheme to indicate the verb stem. For inflected verb forms, I hyphenate a verbal morpheme to the verb stem.

Examples of suffixation are given in (4) with a verb stem *miru* (= look). The five morphemes in (4) are the first ones to appear in Japanese L1 acquisition (Clancy 1985).

(4)

Morpheme	Function/Meaning	Example	
–te	request (REQ)	*mi-te* (look-REQ)	'look!'
–ta	past tense (PAST)	*mi-ta* (look-PAST)	'looked'
–u	non past tense (NONPAST)	*mi-ru* (look-NONPAST)	'(I'll) look'
–nai	negation (NEG)	*mi-nai* (look-NEG)	'(I) don't look'
–teru	present progressive (PROG)	*mi-teru* (look-PROG)	'(I'm) looking'

More than one verbal morpheme can agglutinate to one verb stem. When this happens they are suffixed in a certain order according to the information the morphemes carry. Shibatani (1990, p. 306) gives the order of verbal morphemes as follows:

(5) V stem-causative-passive-aspect-desiderative-negation-tense.

Next I present Hannah's development of verbal morphology in the two languages, from the analyses based on her utterances from 1; 11 to 2; 4, the first six months of the period of investigation. Only lexical verbs were considered. Furthermore, I did not include utterances that appeared immediately after an adult utterance in the identical form for the analysis on the basis that they may possibly be echoic. I discuss Hannah's development of Japanese verbal morphology first.

1.1 Japanese

Japanese agglutinative verbal morphology allows more than one morpheme to be suffixed to a verb stem. I use the term "single morpheme" to mean the suffixation of one morpheme to a verb stem and "double morpheme" to mean when more than one morpheme agglutinate and suffix to a verb stem. The analysis of the non-echoic utterances identified 26 verb stems which appeared with single or double morphemes. The combination of verb stem and morphemes was analysed. The results of the analysis are tabulated in Table 3. For each verb stem, the table shows the actual verb stem, English meaning, the number of different morphemes suffixed to the verb stem, and the actual forms in which the verb appeared in the data. Hannah's age when the actual item appeared for the first time in the data is indicated next to each item in ( ). The productivity of the morpheme is determined by a distributional analysis of lexical and form variations.

Hannah used five verbal morphemes during these six months: *-te* (REQ), *-ta* (PAST), *-u* (NONPSAT), *-teru* (PROG), *-nai* (NEG). Of these five morphemes, Hannah used the four, *-te* (REQ), *-ta* (PAST), *-u* (NONPAST) and *-nai* (NEG), productively with both lexical and form variations. This group of morphemes is also reported to be the first one to be acquired by monolingual Japanese children (Clancy 1985). The first evidence of the acquisition of verbal morpheme was with *-te* at the age of 2; 2. At 2; 2 Hannah's Japanese lexical size was 510. This figure agrees with the findings of studies on monolingual children that verbal morphology appears when vocabulary size reaches between 400 and 600 (e.g., Bates, Dale and Thal 1995). It is interesting to note that findings from studies using a large reported data of monolingual children collected using MCDI (e.g., Bates, Dale and Thal 1995; Ogura 1998) and from the present study using production data from one child agree with each other.

The verb that was most productive in terms of suffixation was *akeru* (= open), which occurred with three different morphemes: *ake-te* 'open-REQ', *ak-eta* 'open-PAST' and *ake-nai* 'open-NEG'. Two verbs, *taberu* (= eat) and *aru* (= exist[4]) occurred with two different single morphemes. *Taberu* appeared as *tabe-te* 'eat-REQ' and *tabe-ta* 'eat-PAST'. *Aru* appeared as *at-ta* 'exist -PAST' and *ar-u* 'exist-NONPAST'. The verb *iku* (= go) occurred with one single morpheme *it-ta* 'go-PAST' and one double morpheme. *Iku* was suffixed by the polite morpheme *-masu* which was agglutinated by the cohort morpheme *–shoo* forming *ik-ia-shoo* 'iku-POLITE-COHORT' (=let's go). The verb *naku* (= cry) also occurred in two different forms: *nai-te* 'cry-REQ' and *nai-te-nai* 'cry-PROG-NEG' (= (I'm) not crying). The remaining verbs appearing in the six sessions did not have form variation. Of the verbs Hannah used during these six months (not necessarily productively), she used the request form with *–te* most dominantly. The dominance of this form in Hannah's data may reflect the general behaviour of young children that they frequently ask for things.

The results indicate that a few verbs facilitate (or act as the model for) verbal feature markings for later morpheme acquisition. These few verbs are the first ones to have the feature annotated in their lexical entries. In Hannah's case, these verbs were *akeru* (= open), *taberu* (= eat), *aru* (= exist), *iku* (= go), and *naku* (= cry). These were the first verbs to carry morphological varieties of feature marking: request, tense and polarity. It is assumed that the verbs not yet showing form variation, such as *kika-nai* 'listen-NEG' and *nor-u* 'ride-NONPAST', would later follow the pattern of the model verbs. It was observed that acquisition of morphemes commenced with request

Verb stem		No of morph	Single morphology					double morph
			te (request)	ta (past)	u (nonpast)	teru (progressive)	nai (negative)	
akeru	open	3	ake-te (2;2)	ake-ta (2;2)			ake-nai (2;1)	
taberu	eat	2	tabe-te (2;3)	tabe-ta (2;4)				
aru	be(exist)	2		at-ta (2;1)	ar-u (2;1)			
naku	cry	2	nai-te (2;3)					nai-te-nai (2;3)
iku	go	2		it-ta (2;2)				ik-ia-shoo (2;4)
suwaru	sit	1	suwat-te (2;1)					
tatsu	stand	1	tat-te (2;1)					
miru	look	1	mi-te (2;2)					
kuru	come	1	ki-te (2;3)					
oku	place/put	1	oi-te (2;3)					
okiru	get up	1	oki-te (2;3)					
toru	take	1	tot-te (2;3)					
matsu	wait	1	mat-te (2;4)					
miseru	show	1	mise-te (2;4)					
iru	be (exist)	1	i-te (2;4)					
motsu	hold	1	yot-te (2;4)					
kowareru	be broken	1		koware-ta (2;3)				
okkochiru	fall	1		okkochi-ta (2;3)				
yogoreru	get dirty	1		yoware-ta (2;3)				
dekiru	can do	1		deki-ta (2;4)				
iru	need	1					ira-nai (2;1)	
shiru	know	1					shira-nai (2;1)	
kiku	hear	1					kika-nai (2;2)	
suru	do	1			shu-u (1;11)			
noru	ride	1			nor-u (2;3)			
oboeru	remember	1				oboe-teru (1;11)		

Table 3. Summary of Japanese Verbs and Their Suffixation

1.2 English

As with the Japanese data, I analysed the obvious non-echoic utterances including lexical verbs from the data between the ages of 1; 11 and 2; 4. Thirty-one verb stems were identified. These verbs appeared in the bare form (infinitive and present tense), progressive form (*-ing*), irregular past tense, and past participle. The progressive morpheme *-ing* was the only suffixation used during this period, and its usage was productive. Six verb stems *play, sleep, come*, *check, jump* and *cry* appeared with *–ing.* Of these six verb stems, four of them, *play, sleep, come*, and *check,* had form variation. The form variation in each case was the bare form and *–ing*. Table shows the verbs, the number of different forms, and the actual forms in which they appeared. For English, the five verbs *play, sleep, come*, and *check* facilitated the acquisition of verbal morphemes. It is interesting to see that the verbs *play, sleep,* and *check,* which can occur as nouns as well as verbs, are the items that initiated the feature marking for verbs.

Hannah's English verbal morphology emerged at the age of 2; 3. At 2; 3 her English lexical size was 584. Again this figure agrees with the findings from the studies using reported data collected by MCDI. Of the three different English verbal morphemes (*-ing*, *-ed*, *-s*), Hannah acquired *–ing* first. This agrees with the findings by Brown (1973). For English the first feature to be annotated in lexical entry was progressive.

Verb	No of forms	bare form	*-ing* form
play	**2**	**play (2;3)**	**play-ing (2;3)**
sleep	**2**	**sleep (2;3)**	**sleep-ing (2;4)**
come	**2**	**come (2;3)**	**com-ing (2;4)**
check	**2**	**check (2;4)**	**check-ing (2;3)**
jump	**1**		**jump-ing (2;1)**
cry	**1**		**cry-ing (2;4)**
see	**1**	**see (1;11)**	
catch	**1**	**catch (2; 0)**	
open	**1**	**open (2; 0)**	
know	**1**	**know (2;1)**	
look	**1**	**look (2;1)**	
shut	**1**	**shut (2;1)**	
do	**1**	**do (2;2)**	
go	**1**	**go (2;2)**	
hold	**1**	**hold (2;2)**	
say	**1**	**say (2;2)**	
try	**1**	**try (2;2)**	
get	**1**	**get (2;3)**	
help	**1**	**help (2;3)**	
like	**1**	**like (2;3)**	
make	**1**	**make (2;3)**	
press	**1**	**press (2;3)**	
put	**1**	**put (2;3)**	
ride	**1**	**ride (2;3)**	
set	**1**	**set (2;3)**	
show	**1**	**show (2;3)**	
sit	**1**	**sit (2;3)**	
wake	**1**	**wake (2;3)**	
want	**1**	**want (2;3)**	
eat	**1**	**eat (2;4)**	
wait	**1**	**wait (2;4)**	

Table 4. Summary of English Verbs and Their Suffixation

Hannah's development of verbal morphology in the two languages showed a similar pattern to each other. For both Japanese and English, Hannah began the feature marking with a few verbs. Although the pattern was similar, the actual lexical items and features acquired were language-specific. For Japanese, they were *akeru* (= open), *taberu* (= eat), *aru* (= exist), *iku* (= go), and *naku* (= cry), and for English they were *play, sleep, come*, and *check.* The first features to be annotated was *–te* (request) for Japanese and *–ing* (progressive) for English. These were also found to be the first to be acquired in L1 studies of the respective languages. In terms of PT stages, verbal morphology is predicted to emerge in Stage 2 (category procedure stage). Hannah reached Stage 2 in Japanese at the age of 2; 2 and in English at the age of 2; 3. These results suggest that Hannah's Japanese and English were developing separately, but in a parallel manner.

At the time of emergence of verb morphology, Hannah's vocabulary size was 510 for Japanese and 584 for English. Both were within the range of vocabulary size found to relate to the appearance of verbal morphemes in L1 studies, thus supporting the critical mass hypothesis. This means that, for Hannah, PT's Stage 2 was not reached until her vocabulary achieved the critical mass.

2. Relationship between Verbs and Semantic Function of Arguments

In order to characterise the development of Hannah's syntax, the semantic functions of the argument were examined. The expletive argument was not included in this analysis. Only utterances with lexical verbs which were clearly non-echoic were considered. This analysis was also conducted with the data from the ages 1; 11 to 2; 4 for both languages.

Studies of L1 acquisition found that children follow the language specific canonical word order. For English, Brown (1973, p. 156) concluded that children start with the SVO word order from an early age. This conclusion was drawn from Brown's own data and other studies of spontaneous speech. While there were few instances of non-SVO word order, the utterances in SVO word order predominated. For Japanese, Clancy (1985) summarised previous studies and said that children used the SOV word order from an early age. While post positioned word order (where O follows the V) was also found to be used by children in the data, it reflected the structure of adult speech of after thought and emphasis. The psychological test conducted by Lust and Wakayama (1981) found that children aged between 2; 5 and 2; 11 were sensitive to SOV word order. While both categories of children were found to use the non-canonical word order, they predominantly used the language specific canonical word order.

2.1 Japanese

Among the group of data analysed here, there were 17 utterances that had arguments with lexical verbs. For some instances of the noun *mama* (= mummy) used before a verb it was difficult to determine if it was used as an agent of the verb or a vocative for Hannah to draw the attention of Mother. An example is *mama suwat-te* (= mummy sit down) uttered by Hannah when she requested Mother to sit down. These unclear cases were not included in the analysis.

The semantic functions of the argument appearing in the data were agent, theme/patient, and goal/location. There was one sample in which the semantic function of the argument was agent. The example (6) occurred with *sur-u* (do-NONPAST), here pronounced as *shuu*. The order of the semantic functions here is "agent + action". In this example, H is the speaker code. The Japanese utterance is presented followed by its free English translation. Then Hannah's age of the time of producing the example (2; 2), the session number code (4J) and turn number of the particular utterance within the session (87) are shown in ( ). In this paper, all the example utterances are presented using this convention.

(6)	H	*hana shu-u*	(= I (will) do (it).)	(2;2, 4J, 87)

There were four samples in which the argument was the theme/patient. They all occurred with verbs with the *–te* morpheme, Hannah requesting her mother to do some action. Two examples are given in 7(a-b). In (7b) the verb for *hold* is *mot-te,* however, here it was pronounced as *yaat-te,* and *sai* is an incomplete form of *kudasai* (= please). The arguments of all the four samples were placed before the verbs, forming the pattern of "theme/patient + action".

(7)	a	H	*dore tot-te*	(= Take which one?)	(2;3, 5J, 888)
	b	H	*mama kotchi yaat-te-sai*	(= Mummy, please hold this.)	(2;4, 6J, 22)

There were two samples in which the argument was the goal/location. One of them is presented in (8). From the context, it was determined that a teddy bear was to get on the train. The nouns *denshan* (= train) was followed by the sound *ni*. Here the status of *ni* cannot be determined clearly. It may be the dative marker to mark the goal followed by a verb *noru* (= get on) pronounced as *or-u*. Prior to this instance there was no utterance with *ni* following a noun in the data. The *ni* may also be the verb *nor-u* pronounced as *nior-u*. Due to this uncertainly, *ni* is not claimed to be a dative marker here. Nonetheless it is clear that the noun *denshan* is the destination of the verb. The order of the semantic functions for both samples was "goal/location + action".

(8)	H	*denshan ni oru no*	(= (Teddy bear) gets on the train.)	(2;3, 5J, 470)

In Japanese, there were no instances of utterance where more than one argument appeared during the six months of the investigation. However in all the one-argument utterances, verbs were placed in the sentence final position. All the arguments preceded the verb (action) without case marking particles.

2.2. English

As they did for Japanese, some of Hannah's English utterances also presented difficulties in determining the agentive function of vocative when the word *daddy* was followed by a verb, e.g., *daddy hold this*. As for Japanese, these unclear cases were not categorised as agent. English data presented utterances with one argument and utterances with two arguments.

The semantic functions appearing during these six months were agent, theme/patient, and goal/location. There were seven samples with agentive argument. The verbs appearing with agentive argument were in the bare or *-ing* forms. The verb stems appearing in this condition were: *check, go, like, open, coming, jumping,* and *playing*. One example of each type of verb form is given in 9(a-b). In all samples, verbs followed the argument, forming the order of "agent + action".

(9)	a.	H	open. Hannah open	(2;1, 3E, 339)
	b.	H	daddy I coming too	(2;4, 6E, 1124)

There were 12 samples with theme/patient. For the utterances with theme/patient, two examples are given in 10(a-b). For (10b) Hannah said this when she and Father were going outside to check their hens. In all samples the argument appears after the verb, i.e., "action + theme/patient".

(10)	a.	H	catch ball . catch ball catch ball	(2;2, 4E, 206)
	b.	H	checking it . daddy. X XX mhm	(2;3, 5E, 1514)

There was one sample that had goal/location as shown in (11). In this instance Hannah indicated that she wanted to go outside. Here the order of the verb and argument was "action + goal/location".

(11)	H	come outside too	(2;3, 5E, 1382)

As can be seen with one argument English utterances, the position of the verb expressing the action differs depending upon the type of argument forming "agent + action", "action + theme/patient" and "action + goal/location".

There were 14 utterances with two arguments. All of them had the combination of agent and theme/patient. Two examples are presented in 12 (a-b). Of these, 13 had the bare form of the verb (e.g., *do, press, see, want, eat*), one occurred with the verb *done* (*I done that*), while no verbs occurred with *–ing*. This may indicate that there is a trade-off between the complexity of lexical forms and the complexity of sentence structure. That is, the more complex sentence structure becomes, the less complex lexical form becomes. The order of semantic functions for all these samples was "agent + action + theme/patient".

(12)	a.	H	me do it u:m h	(2;3, 5E, 276)
	b	H	daddy? somebody eat dat	(2;4, 6E, 488)

English data presented utterances with either one or two arguments. For both types of utterances the semantic functions of the argument were agent, theme/patient, and goal/location. The verb was placed after the agent, but before the theme/patient or goal/location. In the two argument utterances, the semantic function was the combination of agent and theme/patient. With two argument utterances, a trade-off between the lexical and the sentence complexity was found. When sentence structure became more complex the lexical complexity was not maintained.

Between 1:11 and 2:4, Hannah used arguments that express agent, theme/patient and goal/location in both Japanese and English. Hannah's English displayed more instances of utterances with arguments, including multiple arguments within an utterance, than her Japanese. This may reflect the input languages. Japanese allows nominal ellipsis while English does not.

In Japanese, verbs were consistently placed at the final position regardless of the semantic function of the argument. The Japanese data showed the following order patterns: "agent + action", "theme/patient + action" and "goal/location+ action". In English, however, the position of the verb changed depending upon the semantic function of the argument. The verbs were placed after agentive arguments, but before arguments when they were theme/patient or goal/location. Furthermore, with two arguments within an utterance, verbs were placed between them. The order patterns found in English data were: "agent + action", "action + theme/patient", "action + goal/location" and "agent + action + theme/patient".

Using the direct mapping between the semantic functions and grammatical functions (Pinker 1984), Hannah's Japanese showed the word order of SV and OV and her English SVO. In other words, Hannah's word order agreed with the canonical word order of the respective language. Hannah's Japanese did not use the case marking particle during these six months. It is assumed that she relied on word order to express the semantic functions at this stage. Hannah's word order in the two languages agrees with the findings of initial word order of L1 acquisition in the respective languages. From this it can be concluded that Hannah's two languages were developing in a separate, language-specific manner.

Lexical-Grammatical Development Connection

Hannah's lexical size and her word order in each language at the time of the emergence of verbal morphology are summarized in Table 5. For Japanese the first verbal morpheme *–te* (request) emerged when Hannah was 2; 2. At the time, her lexical size was 510 and her word order showed the "agent + action" combination. The first occurrences of the other combinations, "theme/patient + action" and "goal/location + action", were found at 2; 3, a month after the emergence of the verb morphology. For English, the first verbal morpheme *–ing* (progressive) emerged when Hannah was 2; 3. At the time, her lexical size was 584. At 2; 3 Hannah produced utterances with the pattern of "action + goal/location" and "agent + action + theme/patient" for the first time, however, she had produced utterances with the patterns of "agent + action", "action + theme/patient" prior to 2; 3.

In PT, the verbal morphology is predicted to emerge in Stage 2 (category procedure). PT predicts the canonical word order emerges during the same stage (Stage 2). From the emergence of verbal morphology, it can be considered that Hannah reached Stage 2 at 2; 2 in Japanese and 2; 3 in English. The results from the English data showed that two-argument utterances forming the canonical word order (SVO) indeed appeared at the same age as the verbal morphology. However, it needs to be noted that Hannah was already producing utterances that reflected the English input language prior to 2; 3. Furthermore, for Japanese, Hannah used word order rather than the case marker to show the relationship between the argument and the verb. These findings may suggest that syntax develops earlier than morphology.

	Lexical size	**Morphology development**	**Syntax**	**Age**
Japanese	**510**	***-te* (request)**	**Agent + action**	**2;2**
English	**584**	**-ing (progressive)**	**Agent + action Action + theme/patient Action + goal/location Agent + action + theme/patient**	**2;3**

Table 5. Hannah's Lexical and Grammatical Development at the Time of Emergence of Verbal Morphology

Summary

This paper presented the first attempt to explore the relationship between the lexicon and grammar within the framework of Processability Theory, using bilingual production data.

This study showed that in the case of lexical learning, nouns bootstrapped the child (Hannah) into her respective languages. This indicates that the language learning mechanism must be able to extract nouns from different input languages. The study also found that verbs show different patterns of development, resembling those of monolingual children. This indicates lexical learning is also a language specific operation.

The way Hannah moved into morphology from lexicon was similar in both languages. A few verbs were marked with features in both languages and they were thought to facilitate the feature markings of other verbs. However, the actual lexical items and features to be marked were different in each language. The results from the analysis confirmed Hannah reached PT's stage 2 after her vocabulary achieved the critical mass.

With respect to the semantic functions, use of arguments was more prevalent in English than Japanese between the age of 1; 11 and 2; 4. This reflects the characteristics of the input languages. Hannah expressed agent, theme/patient and goal/location in both languages. While Japanese utterances during this age contained only one argument, English had utterances that contained up to two arguments. In the two-argument utterances, no verbs had any suffixation of a morpheme. This suggests a possible trade-off between lexical complexity and sentence complexity.

Hannah's word order was found to be language-specific. While the position of the verb stayed in the final position for Japanese, it changed depending upon the semantic function of the argument for English. Hannah's Japanese showed the word order pattern of "agent + action", "theme/patient + action" and "goa/location+ action". Her English showed the pattern of "agent + action", "action + theme/patient", "action + goal/location" and "agent + action + theme/patient". Hannah's word order agreed with the canonical word order of the respective languages, and this supports the hypothesis proposed by PT. Hannah's word order also agreed with the findings of L1 studies of the respective languages.

For English, the SVO word order with two arguments and the verbal morphology emerged at the same time. However prior to this, the syntax had already appeared in the data in the form of SV and VO. For Japanese the grammatical functions were initially expressed by the word order rather than the case marker. These results may suggest that syntax emerges earlier than morphology.

The results from this study indicate that each of Hannah's two languages developed in a language specific way, with the two languages developing separately, but in a parallel manner. This is further evidence in support of the Separate Development Hypothesis for bilingual first language acquisition.

References

Bates, E., P. S. Dale, and D. Thal. 1995. Individual differences and their implications for theories of language development. In *Handbook of child language,* ed. P. Fletcher and B. MacWhinney, 96-151. Oxford: Blackwell.

Bates, E. and J. Goodman. 1999. On the emergence of grammar from the lexicon. In *The Emergence of Language*, ed. B. Macwhinney, 29-79. Mahwah, NJ: Lawrence Erlbaum.

Bresnan, J., ed. 1982. *The mental representation of grammatical relations.* Cambridge: The MIT press.

—. 2001. *Lexical-functional syntax.* Oxford: Blackwell.

Brown, R. 1973. *A first language: The early stages.* Cambridge, MA: Harvard University Press.

Caselli, M., E. Bates, P. Casadio, J. Fenson, L. Sanderl, and J. Weir. 1995. A cross-linguistic study of early lexical development. *Cognitive Development,* 10: 159-199.

Caselli, M., E. Bates, P. Casadio, J. Fenson, L. Sanderl, and J. Weir. 1999. A comparison of the transition from first words to grammar in English and Italian. *Journal of Child Language,* 26: 69-111.

Choi, S. 1998. Verbs in early lexical and syntactic development in Korean. *Linguistics,* 36: 755-780.

Clancy, P. 1985. The acquisition of Japanese. In *Crosslinguistic study of language acquisition, Vol. 1, Data,* ed. D. Slobin, 373-524. Hillsdale: Lawrence Erlbaum.

De Houwer, A. 1990. *The acquisition of two languages from birth: A case study.* Cambridge: Cambridge University Press.

Di Biase, B. and S, Kawaguchi. 2002. Exploring the typological plausibility of processability theory: Language development in Italian second language and Japanese second language. *Second Language Research*, 18: 274-302.

Fenson, L., P. Dale, J. S. Reznick, D. Thal, E. Bates, J. Hartung, S. Pethick, and J. Reilly. 1993. *The MacArthur Communicative Development Inventories: User's guide and technical manual.* San Diego, CA: Singular.

Gentner, D., and L. Boroditsky. 2001. Individuation, relativity, and early word learning. In *Language acquisition and conceptual development,* ed. M. Bowerman and S. Levinson, 215-256. Cambridge: Cambridge University Press.

Iwasaki, J. 2004. Child Acquisition of Japanese L2: a Processability Account. Paper presented at Processability and bilingualism seminar at the University of Western Sydney, October 2004.

Juan-Carau, M., and C. Pérez-Vidal. 2000. Subject realization in the syntactic development of a bilingual child. *Bilingualism: Language and Cognition,* 3: 173-191.

Kawaguchi, S. 2005. Argument structure and syntactic development in Japanese. In *Cross-linguistic aspects of processability theory,* ed. M. Pienemann, 254-298. Amsterdam: John Benjamins.

Levelt, W. J. 1989. *Speaking: From Intention to Articulation.* Cambridge: MIT Press.

Lust, B. and T. Wakayama. 1981. Word order in first language acquisition of Japanese. In *Child Language - An International Perspective,* ed. P. Dale & D. Ingram, 74-90. Baltimore: University Park Press.

Marchman, V. A., and E. Bates. 1994. Continuity in lexical and morphological development: A test of the critical mass hypothesis. *Journal of Child Language,* 21: 339-366.

Meisel, J., ed. 1990. Two first languages: Early grammatical development in bilingual children. Dordrecht: Foris.

Mishina, S. 1997. Language separation in early bilingual development: A longitudinal study of Japanese/English bilingual children. PhD diss., UCLA.

Oshima-Takane, Y., N. Naka, and S. Miyata. 1997. Early emergence of nouns and verbs: A crosslinguistic study of Japanese and English. Abstract for paper presented JCHAT/CHILDES Meeting 97. http://jchat.cyber.sccs.chukyo-u.ac.jp./JCHAT /tutorial/meeting97/onm.html (November 2nd 2005).

Ogura, T., N. Naka, Y. Yamashita, T. Murase, and A. Mahieu. 1997. Nihongo kakutokuji no goi to bunpoo no hattatsu: Clan puroguramu ni yoru bunseki. *Koobe daigaku hattatsu kagakubu kenkyuu kiyoo* l.4 (2): 31-57.

Ogura, T., N. Naka, Y. Yamashita, T. Murase, and A. Mahieu. 1998. Makkaasaa nyuuyouji gengo hattatsu shitsumonshi no kaihatsu to kenkyuu. Monbu shoo kagaku kenkyuuhi kiban kenkyuu (C) Kenkyuu seika hookoku sho. Kobe: Kobe University.

Paradis, J., and F. Genesee. 1996. Syntactic acquisition in bilingual children. *Studies in Second Language Acquisition,* 18: 1-25.

Pienemann, M. 1998a. *Language processing and second language development*: Processability Theory. Amsterdam: John Benjamins.

—. 1998b. Developmental dynamics in L1 and L2 acquisition: Processability Theory and generative entrenchment. *Bilingualism: Language and Cognition* 1: 1-20.

Pienemann, M, B. Di Biase., and S. Kawaguchi. 2005. Extending processability theory. In M. Pienemann (Ed.), *Cross-linguistic aspects of processability theory*, ed. M. Pienemann, 199-253. Amsterdam: John Benjamins.

Pinker, S. 1984. *Language learnability and language development*. Cambridge, MA: Harvard University Press.

Shibatani, M. 1990. *The Languages of Japan.* Cambridge: Cambridge University Press.

Volterra, V., and T. Taeschner. 1978. The acquisition and development of language by bilingual children. *Journal of Child Language,* 5: 311-326.

Yip, V., and S. Matthews. 2000. Syntactic transfer in a Cantonese-English bilingual child. *Bilingualism: Language and Cognition,* 3: 193-208.

Appendix

Sessions Selected for Analyses—Codes and Hannah's Age

Japanese session	Hannah's age (year;months,day)	English session	Hannah's age (year;months,day)
1J	1;11,12	1E	1;11,12
2J	1;11,27	2E	1;11,29
3J	2;1,12	3E	2;1,9
4J	2;2,13	4E	2;2,17
5J	2;3,16	5E	2;3,16
6J	2;4,14	6E	2;4,15
7J	2;5,11	7E	2;5,10
8J	2;6,18	8E	2;6,19
9J	2;6,26	9E	2;6,26
10J	2;7,6	10E	2;7,6
11J	2;7,24	11E	2;7,28
12J	2;9,15	12E	2;9,9
13J	2;10,5	13E	2;10,5
16J	3;0,22 & 3;0,24	16E	3;0,21
19J	3;3,3	19E	3;3,0
22J	3;6,14 & 3;6,15	22E	3;6,15 & 3;6,17
25J	3;9,15	25E	3;9,12
28J	4;0,21	28E	4;0,15 & 4;0,20
31J	4;3,23	31E	4;3,23
34J	4;7,26	34E	4;7,25
38J	4;10,26	38E	4;10,25 & 4;10,27

Notes

[1] This is a working paper presented at the 5th International Symposium on Processability, Bilingualism and Second Language Acquisition held at Deakin University, 26-28 September, 2005. I would like to thank Bruno Di Biase and Satomi Kawaguchi for their discussion and comment on my work. The paper in its present form may contain errors and the analysis was exploratory in nature.

[2] I use the term "Japanese children" to mean monolingual children who acquire Japanese as their first language. A similar convention is used for other languages.

[3] Hannah is a pseudonym .

[4] This verb is used for inanimate objects.

[5] This verb is used for animate objects.

CHAPTER 9

PHONOLOGICAL AND VISUAL SHORT-TERM MEMORY CODIFICATION IN ENGLISH-CHINESE BILINGUALS

Lidia Suárez and Winston D.Goh

Do English-Chinese bilinguals process their languages differently from monolinguals? What are the differences between balanced and non-balanced bilinguals?

Answering those questions is not irrelevant. In China nowadays, many children are exposed to English, which has become an asset for accessing higher education and promising jobs. In Singapore and Hong Kong, English plays an important role especially in education, official, and business matters, although Chinese is taught and used daily by a large part of the population. Furthermore, an increasing number of colleges and secondary schools in the U.K. offer Chinese as an elective or compulsory subject, and Chinese nannies are in steep demand in the U.S. (*The Straits Times* 2006). A description of the cognitive operations of both languages in the bilingual mind will have implications on fields such as education, speech-language therapy, second language acquisition, developmental psychology, cognitive theory, neuroscience and artificial intelligence.

Processing a logographic language like Chinese[1] and an alphabetic one like English may involve different mental operations due to the features of the different writing systems. Regarding the physical traits of Chinese, each character occupies the same square space evenly, and the space between compound characters is not differentiated from the space between simple characters. This structure allows Chinese to be written horizontally and vertically. In contrast, English words are different in length and each word forms a string. Additionally, English is only written and read horizontally. The elementary unit of reading Chinese is the character, which represents a syllable and a morpheme (McBride-Chang and Kail 2002; Lin and Akamatsu 1997), and happens to be better at representing meaning than sound (Chitiri, Sun, Willows and Taylor 1992; Chen 1996); but in English the elementary unit of reading is the letter, which represents a speech sound (McBride-Chang and Kail 2002). Furthermore, Chinese is orthographically deep compared to English because conversion rules between character and pronunciation are not unequivocally straightforward. Indeed, Chinese is a more homophonic and polysemic language than English inasmuch as the same pronunciation can be obtained from different characters, and the same character may have different meanings depending on the context. Finally, Chinese is not an inflected language, and the tone of some characters changes depending on the tone of the following character. Consequently, readers of Chinese must rely heavily on the context to figure out meaning and pronunciation.

Much research has been done on Chinese word recognition and lexical access. However, short-term memory (STM) employing Chinese words has hardly been studied from an information processing perspective. STM defines a limited capacity system that holds and manipulates information in a *special format* while performing cognitive tasks such as learning, retrieval, comprehension or thinking. It is important to figure out what format information is represented in STM and whether different languages make use of different formats.

Models of STM emphasise the role of phonological memory traces. In Baddeley's (2000) model, the *phonological loop* is the mechanism that transforms written information into phonological code automatically, and it is specialised for temporary maintenance of sound-based information and serial order. The performance of the phonological loop predicts vocabulary acquisition as long as it determines the quality of the phonological representations, capacity to retain phonological information, and the rate of information loss (Jarrold, Hewes, Leeke and Phillips 2004).

Moreover, the phonological similarity effect (recall impairment due to phonological resemblance of the words to be recalled), word-length effect (trade-off between the length of the material to be stored and memory capacity), unattended speech effect (retention impairment if the task is carried out against a background of speech; in this case, speech is gaining access to a limited phonological store at the same time as the words to be recalled), the modality effect (auditory over visual recall advantage) and, finally, the articulatory suppression effect (recall impairment due to preventing subvocalising at reading) demonstrate the use of a phonological device at memorizing information in alphabetic languages (for examples and further explanation of each effect, see Baddeley and Wilson 1988; Baddeley 1997).

Regarding Chinese word representation in STM, most of the studies have focused on memory span. Digit span is larger for Chinese speakers due to Chinese numbers being shorter in length and faster to rehearse than English numbers (Lau and Hoosain 1999; Ellis 1992; Hoosain 1984). Additionally, Hu (2003) carried out a longitudinal study with Chinese children and found that phonological memory and phonological awareness in Chinese predicted English learning. These results support phonological processing. However, Hue and Erickson (1988) showed that high frequency character-words were stored in STM in verbal form, but low frequency character-words were stored in visual form. This suggests that visual codes are also very important in memory for Chinese words. Moreover, Flaherty (1997) found that visual memory correlated with language proficiency in native children and adult learners of a logographic language such as Japanese. Moreover, Tavassoli (2002) asked English monolingual speakers and Chinese bilinguals (but dominant in Chinese) to read words/characters displayed sparsely on a sheet of paper. Tavassoli found that Chinese speakers recalled the position of the characters in the space better than the English sample did for words; however the overall word recall was similar for both groups. It is noteworthy remarking that visual memory has not been related with proficiency in alphabetic languages.

The results on memory suggest that English is recoded phonologically but Chinese can be stored phonologically and visually too. Differences between English and Chinese have also been demonstrated in the literature on visual encoding, word recognition, and phonological awareness. Regarding visual encoding, it appears that different written layouts require different visual encoding. English readers show saccadic eye-movement when reading. An interesting finding is that Chinese readers do not always evince this visual scanning pattern and, when they do, they make more regular saccades than English readers (Chen 1996). Green, Rickard-Liow, Tng, and Zielinski (1996) also reported different visual search procedures for English and Chinese words in both monolinguals and bilinguals. These findings suggest that if English and Chinese readers are using different strategies at encoding, it is probable that we may find differences in other more complex processes such as reading or memorising.

English word recognition is phonologically mediated. Standard phonological priming, masked priming, and backward masking paradigms demonstrate phonological recoding (Wu and Liu 1996; Brysbaert 2001). In the standard phonological priming procedure, a prime (word or pseudoword) is presented immediately before a target word; only those primes which are homophones (e.g., *brane*) of the target (e.g., *brain*), are expected to facilitate recognition of the target. The difference between the standard priming and the masked priming procedure is that, in the latter, the prime is displayed very briefly (40-50 ms) so that participants are not aware of it, but the presence of the prime usually facilitates target recognition. In the backward masking procedure, the prime is presented very briefly, immediately after the target. As in the masking task, participants are not conscious of the prime but when the prime is a homophone pseudoword of the target, target words are recognised faster.

In Chinese word recognition, phonological recoding has been demonstrated with standard phonological priming experiments (Wu and Liu 1996; Cheng 1992). However, priming effects are also revealed when the prime is graphically similar to the target. Chitiri, Sun, Willows and Taylor (1992) affirm that native readers of Chinese are very efficient at integrating phonological, visual and semantic information. Chen, Yung, and Ng (1988) found that orthographic similarity affected character recognition more than phonological similarity. Additionally, masked priming and backward masking tasks have not replicated the phonological priming effect found in English (Hong and Yelland 1992; Perfetti and Zhang 1991). Indeed, Perfetti and Zhang found that visually similar character-primes facilitated word recognition. However, phonological priming effects start being observed when target and masks are exposed for longer times in backward masking and naming tasks (Tan and Perfetti 1998). The tasks in priming experiments are lexical decisions and naming. The lexical decision task (LDT) requires participants to distinguish words and non-words, by pressing appropriate buttons on a response box. In naming tasks, participants read aloud words or non-words. Dependent variables are error rate and reaction time (RT). In English, monolingual participants take longer to respond in LDTs than in naming tasks. Hence, researchers (Chen 1996; Wu and Liu 1996) have suggested that, at naming, English speakers engage in recoding written words into sounds automatically without lexical access, that is, without accessing word meaning. However, in deciding between a word and non-word in LDT, participants need to access meaning, resulting in longer RTs. Contrary to English, RTs in Chinese LDT are faster than in naming (Chen 1996). These results suggest that Chinese participants need to know the character in order to be able to pronounce it, so lexical decision is made a priori, before recoding phonologically.

Standard phonological priming experiments are criticised because they seem to elicit phonological coding irremediably. One way of surpassing this limitation, and gauge phonological mediation without requiring it directly, is employing a semantic-decision task. In this type of task, participants are given a category name (e.g., flower) and have to decide whether words rapidly presented are members or not of the category. Many of the targets are members (rose), many are homophonic words (rows) and many are control words (cat). In English, the fact that homophonic words are more difficult to discard suggests phonological recoding. In contrast, Liu (1997) cited findings in semantic-decision tasks in Cantonese and in Mandarin showing not homophonic but graphemic interference. That is, participants took longer to respond to targets graphically similar to an example of the category than to a homophonic or control one.

The word recognition findings suggest that recoding is an automatic process in alphabetic languages that occurs independently, regardless of the nature of the task. However, Chinese is only recoded into phonological form in those tasks that require it, and graphemic characteristics of the words play an important role at recognition. Tan and Perfetti (1998) gathered results from different research on Chinese word recognition and suggested that phonology in Chinese is activated along with the complete identification of orthographic information. It might also be activated earlier than semantics—and probably influence meaning activation—but this does not imply that phonology mediates access to meaning necessarily. In contrast, in English, phonology is pre-lexical and mediates access to meaning. Another cognitive processing that can affect memory processing is phonological awareness, which refers to the knowledge about how a writing system might map phonological and acoustic properties of the language (Swan and Goswani 1997; Gernsbacher 1994). Examples of tasks used to measure phonological awareness are: manipulation of phonemes, phoneme identification, rhyme judgment, phoneme counting, phoneme deletion, etc.

Phonological awareness facilitates reading, spelling and phonological recoding strategies, and it is acquired faster in languages with shallow orthography (Rickard-Liow 1999; De Gelder and Vroomen 1992), where the letter-to-sound conversions are regular. English is a relatively shallow language compared to Chinese. Studies carried out with children suggest that reading instructions play an important role in the development of phonological awareness. McBride-Chang, Bialystok, Chong and Li (2004) compared phonological awareness of Chinese children who were being taught Chinese with the support of Pinyin (the phonetic romanisation system), Chinese children learning Chinese by the look-and-say method and English monolingual children. They found that Pinyin promotes phonological awareness but Chinese, in general, promotes more syllable awareness than phoneme awareness, contrary to English instruction methods which promote phoneme awareness. However, once children acquired a certain level of phonological awareness in Chinese, this knowledge positively affected the learning of alphabetic languages, so there is transfer across languages (Bialystok, McBride-Chang and Luk 2005; Hu 2003).

Rickard-Liow (1999) mentions one interesting study conducted in Singapore by Ho (1993), who found that nine-year-old Mandarin-English Singaporeans relied on visual strategies at reading and spelling English, although they had acquired basic levels of phonological awareness. However, good readers of English were using more phonological strategies. This suggests that greater experience with the Chinese script leads to reliance on graphemic features at reading, but greater experience with English leads to phonological processing.

In summary, many studies on visual encoding, word recognition and phonological awareness indicate that there may be cognitive processes differences due to the characteristics of Chinese and English. STM for Chinese has hardly been studied although it is important in processes such as language acquisition, thinking, problem-solving, and so on. Indeed, there is an absence of studies that describe how dominance in either English or Chinese in proficient bilinguals affects memory for English and Chinese words. Thus far, STM models account for phonological recoding of written material although some visual and spatial predominance over phonological traces have been shown by some studies on memory carried out in Chinese. The present study will examine the phonological and visual STM codification in English-Chinese bilinguals in more detail.

Experiment 1

Humphreys and Tehan (1999), and Tehan and Humphreys (1995, 1996, 1998) demonstrated that phonological and semantic codes are involved in STM cued recall. In cued recall, participants memorise a list of written words and are subsequently cued to recall only a word related to the cue. Phonological activation lasts approximately two seconds, whereas semantic activation lasts longer. When the recall cue subsumes two semantically related words, the phonological traces make the words distinctive from each other if their pronunciations are dissimilar.

Experiment 1 is an attempt to replicate Tehan and Humphreys' (1998) third experiment, but with Chinese words. Tehan and Humphreys created a series of trials made of four (one-block trials) and eight words (two-block trials). In one-block trials, a recall cue was presented immediately after the fourth word. In two-block trials, the cue was presented after the eighth word. The retrieval cue was the name of a category (e.g., cosmetic) and subjects had to respond with a word in the list that was semantically related to the cue (e.g., cream).

One-block and two-block trials were presented randomly. Participants had to consider all trials as a one-block trial until an exclamation mark (!) appeared after the fourth word indicating that the present trial was a two-block trial. Once the participants saw the exclamation mark, they were told to forget the first block and only concentrate on the second block because the cue only referred to the second block. Experimental conditions were composed of two-block trials. One-block trials were created with the purpose of ensuring attention to all stimuli. If they had presented only two-block trials, participants would have not paid attention to the first block.

There were three experimental conditions (see Figure 1). The *no interference* condition contained two-block trials in which the first block did not contain any word related to the cue, but the second block contained the target word. In the *standard* interference condition, the first and second blocks each included one word semantically related to the cue. The *phonological* interference condition was the same as the standard condition except that the phonemes of the foil (dog: /d/, /o/, /g/) were distributed among the filler words (/d/ in *dart*, /o/ in *mop*, /g/ in *fig*) of the second block, but not in the target word.

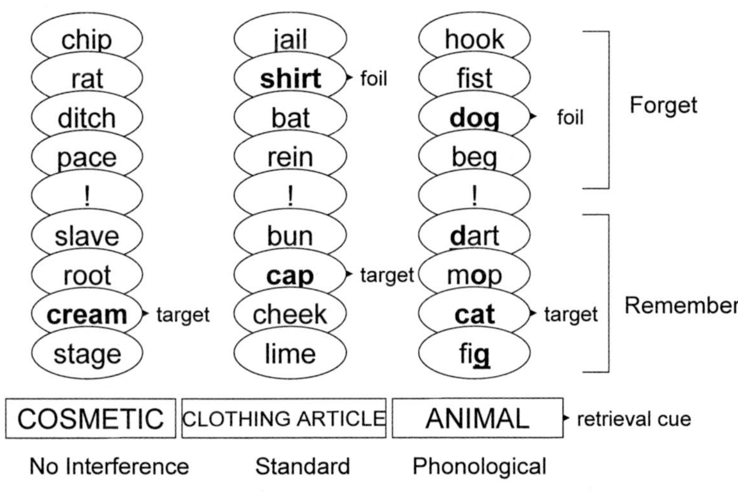

Figure 1. Experimental conditions in Tehan and Humphreys' (1998) third experiment.

Tehan and Humphreys (1998) demonstrated that information in STM is codified phonologically. Their participants made more interference errors (recall of the foil in the place of the target) in the phonological condition than in the standard condition, showing that the phonemes of the last block (in the phonological condition) mapped onto the foil and this facilitated its continued activation. In the phonological condition, activated phonological traces increased the interference between the foil and target. Furthermore, they demonstrated that memory is distributed because phonemes distributed among the fillers kept the foil word active.

We replicated Tehan and Humphreys' (1998) third experiment with Chinese characters (see the first three columns of Figure 2). Notice that in the phonological condition we have added Pinyin to show the phoneme repetition of the foil (/sh/, /ng/, and /u/) among the fillers of the second block. In the experiment, participants only saw character-words. We also conducted another experiment with English words.

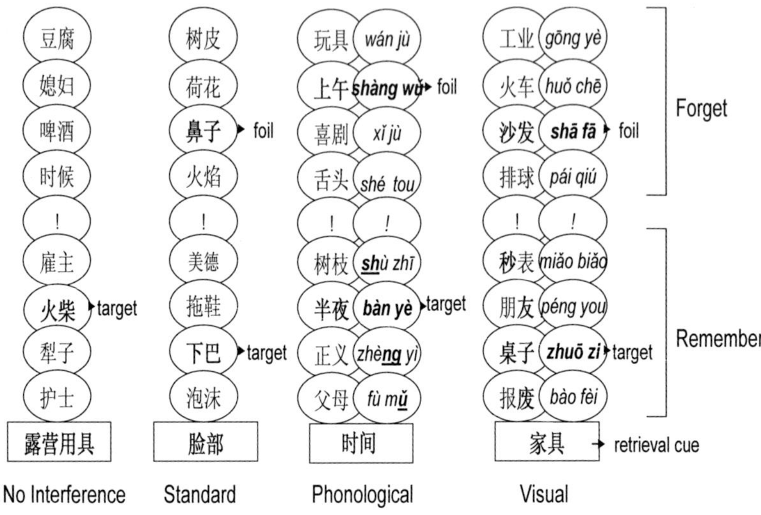

Figure 2. Experimental conditions.
No interference condition. English translation from top to bottom: bean, daughter-in-law, beer, time, employer, matches (target), pear, nurse, item of camping equipment (cue).
Standard condition. English translation from top to bottom: bark, lotus, nose (foil), flame, morality, slippers, chin (target), foam, part of a face (cue)
Phonological condition. English translation from top to bottom: toy, morning (foil), comedy, tongue, branch, midnight (target), justice, parents, time of day (cue).
Visual condition (experiment 2 only). English translation from top to bottom: industry, train, sofa (foil), volleyball, stopwatch, friend, table (target), scrap, house furniture (cue).

We believe that an immediate cued recall task may clarify some of the contradictory results obtained in Chinese language processing, specifically results supporting phonological recoding (Ellis 1992; Hoosain 1984) and those supporting direct lexical access prior to recoding (Liu 1997; Chen 1996).

The main hypothesis predicts that if Chinese words (and English words) are stored in distributed phonological traces, then there will be more foil interference errors in the phonological condition than in the standard condition because the phonemes in the second block will keep the phonological traces of the foil active. However, if Chinese words access meaning directly without necessarily requiring phonological recoding (also called the direct hypothesis), and then the proportion of errors in the phonological condition will be similar to the proportion of errors in the standard condition.

In addition, an exploratory hypothesis was that language dominance will affect the pattern of interference. Specifically, participants less proficient in Chinese will show more phonological interference than those more proficient in Chinese due to a greater phonological awareness and more phonemic-based language processing.

Method

1. Participants

The sample included 91 English-Mandarin undergraduate students from the National University of Singapore who participated for course credit. All of them had obtained a minimum score of B4 in Chinese at AO levels.

2. Material

Foils, targets and cues were selected from the normative data for taxonomic categories collected by McEvoy and Nelson (1982) and translated into Chinese. A total of 27 categories, 27 foils and 27 targets for two-block trials; and ten categories and ten targets for one-block trials were selected.

Our criteria for choosing foils and targets were that, within the same trial, both were single character or both were two-compound character words: one-character words composed by three phonemes and two-character words composed by four phonemes. The foil always was a more typical instance of the category in order to maximise the interference of the foil. Nineteen participants who did not participate in Experiment 1 ranked foil and target typicality. To do so, we presented a booklet with names of different categories (e.g., item of camping equipment) and several examples (e.g., backpack, lantern, matches, stove, and boots); they had to order the examples from the most typical to the less typical instance. Foils were selected from words mostly ranked as the first or second most typical instances, while targets occupied subsequent rankings. The nineteen participants also had to read aloud all the words that were initially selected for the experiment and indicate which ones they were not able to read or did not know the meaning of. This was to ensure that all stimuli were familiar to participants. Foils and targets were matched for number of strokes, and for word frequency (Wang et al. 1990; Loo 1992). In the phonological interference condition the first and last phoneme of the four-phoneme foils, plus either the second or the third phoneme were repeated among the fillers in the second block. In order to reduce the influence of primacy and recency effect, foils and targets were located in the second or third position. Foils and targets were always inserted in the same serial position within the same trial. In one-block trials, the targets were inserted in any position.

Fillers were obtained with the help of a Chinese-English online dictionary ("Xiao ma ci dian" 2005). Fillers matched the characteristics of the foils and targets of each trial; that is, one or two-compound characters with three or four phonemes, respectively.

The 27 categories for the critical two-block trials were divided into three lists (equated for average word frequency) of nine category retrieval cues and foil-target pairs. Each list was assigned to one of the three experimental conditions. For counterbalancing purposes, three versions of the experiment were created using a partial Latin-square procedure to rotate the lists through the different experimental conditions across different participants.

A simpler English version was also created. It contained two experimental conditions: the *standard* interference condition and the *phonological* interference condition, which nine trials in each one. Ten more categories were selected as one-block trials. The categories used were distinct to the ones used in the Chinese experiment. The rest of the details are common to the Chinese version. The word lists were equated on word frequency based on Kucera and Francis (1967).

3. Procedure

Presentation of four and eight-word lists were randomly interspersed and participants noticed that a trial was composed of eight words only when an exclamation mark (!) appeared after the fourth word. Once they realised that a trial was formed by eight words, they were instructed to forget the first four words and only pay attention to the next four words in order to respond to the cue. The cue was presented immediately after the fourth or eighth word. The cue was displayed in green in the Chinese version, and in upper-case in the English version. Words were presented in black and in lower case. The experiment was programmed with E-Prime 1.1. A trial sequence began with a READY sign displayed on the computer monitor for 2000 ms, then stimuli were displayed at a rate of one word per second. After the fourth or eighth word, a recall cue indicated that they should write the response immediately.

Participants wrote their answers in an answer sheet and were requested to answer all trials, or mark a cross if they were unable to recall the target. Participants pressed "enter" to start the next trial. In the Chinese version, participants were allowed to write in Pinyin whenever they felt incapable of writing the characters.

Participants were assigned randomly to one of the three versions of the Chinese experiment and one of the two versions of the English experiment. The presentation order of the Chinese and English versions was counterbalanced. Both the Chinese and the English versions were preceded by four practice trials. Once the experiment was over, we asked participants about their academic scores in Chinese at AO levels, their reading frequency, language used at home and subjective language dominance. The session lasted 30 minutes.

4. Results

The mean proportion of correct recall in the one-block trials for the Chinese experiment was .78 (*SD* = .17) and for the English experiment .93 (*SD* = .11). We eliminated participants who scored less than 2 standard deviations from the mean of one-block trials in the Chinese experiment; as such participants may not have paid attention to the first block of four words. Four participants failed to meet this criterion, and the rest of the analysis was performed with the remaining 87 participants[2].

The results of two trials were also discarded in the analysis because it was subsequently discovered that the cue subsumed not only the target but another filler of the second block. Parallel parametric and non-parametric tests were carried out because the features of the data (very few foil intrusions in the no interference condition) led to violation of some statistical assumptions. The results obtained with parametric and non-parametric methods were similar. Therefore, we choose to report only parametric results because analysis of variance (ANOVA) tends to be robust with respect to lack of normality and inequality of variances (Mickey, Dunn, and Clark 2004, p.65).

Figure 3 shows the proportion of interference errors. In the Chinese version, a one-way within-subjects ANOVA adjusted with Huynh-Feldt Epsilon for violation of the sphericity assumption was reliable, $F(1.84,157.98) = 21.69$, $MSE = .08$, $p < .001$. Planned comparisons revealed that participants significantly made more interference errors in the phonological ($M = .06$) condition than in the standard condition ($M = .04$), $t(86) = 2.29$, $p < .05$, and, not surprisingly, they made more interference errors in the standard interference condition than in the no interference condition ($M = 0$), $t(86) = 4.68$, $p < .001$. In the English version, a paired *t*-test revealed that there were significantly more foil intrusions in the *phonological* ($M = .09$) condition than in the *standard* condition ($M = .06$), $t(61) = 2.44$, $p < .05$.

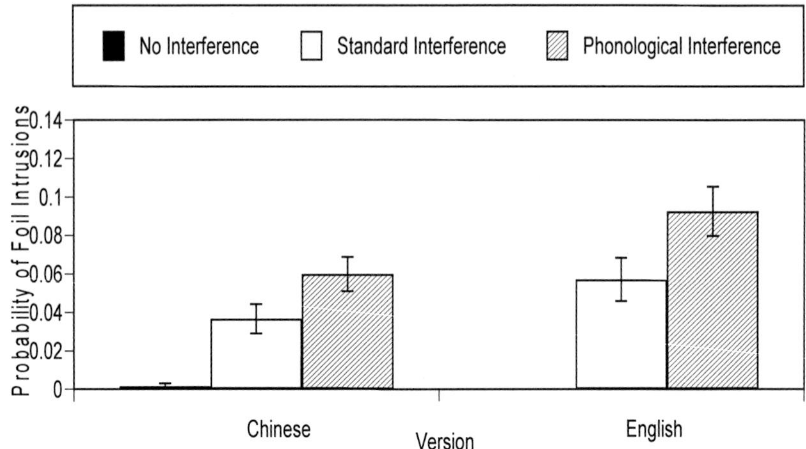

Figure 3. Average probability (+*SE*s) of foil intrusions for Experiment 1.

The exploratory hypothesis was studied by comparing the proportion of interference in the three experimental conditions of those *excellent* in Chinese (score of A in Chinese at AO levels, 53 participants) versus those just *good* in Chinese (score of B in Chinese at AO levels, 34 participants). Figure 4 shows the mean proportion of foil intrusions for the two groups in the Chinese and English experiments.

In the Chinese experiment we discarded the *no interference* condition because the proportion of errors in this condition was almost nonexistent, and a 2 x 2 mixed design ANOVA (Proficiency x Interference condition) was performed on the proportion of interference errors. *Proficiency* was the between-subjects factor, and *interference* was the within-subjects factor.

The main effect of interference was significant, $F(1,85) = 6.35$, $MSE = .03$, $p < .05$. As demonstrated previously, the proportion of interference errors was significantly larger in the phonological condition than in the standard condition. The proficiency and interference interaction was not significant, $F(1, 85) = 1.57$, ns, indicating that both groups showed the same pattern of interference. However, planned comparisons revealed that the *excellent* group did not show more interference in the phonological condition than in the standard one ($M = .05$ and $M = .04$, for the phonological and standard conditions, respectively), $t < 1$. In contrast, the *good* group showed a significant difference in the proportion of interference errors, they made more intrusions in the phonological condition ($M = .07$) than in the standard condition ($M = .03$), $t(33) = 2.48$, $p < .05$.

In the English version, 38 and 24 participants formed the *excellent* and *good* groups, respectively. A similar ANOVA yielded a significant main effect of interference, F (1, 60) = 6.84, MSE = .05, p < .05. The interaction was not significant, F (1, 60) = 1.13, *ns*. Planned comparison revealed that the *excellent* proficiency group did not show more interference in the phonological condition (M = .08) than in the standard one (M = .06), t (37) = 1.38, *ns*. However, the *good* proficiency group showed a significant difference in the proportion of interference errors, they made more intrusions in the phonological condition (M = .11) than in the standard condition (M = .06), t (23) = 2.06, p < .05.

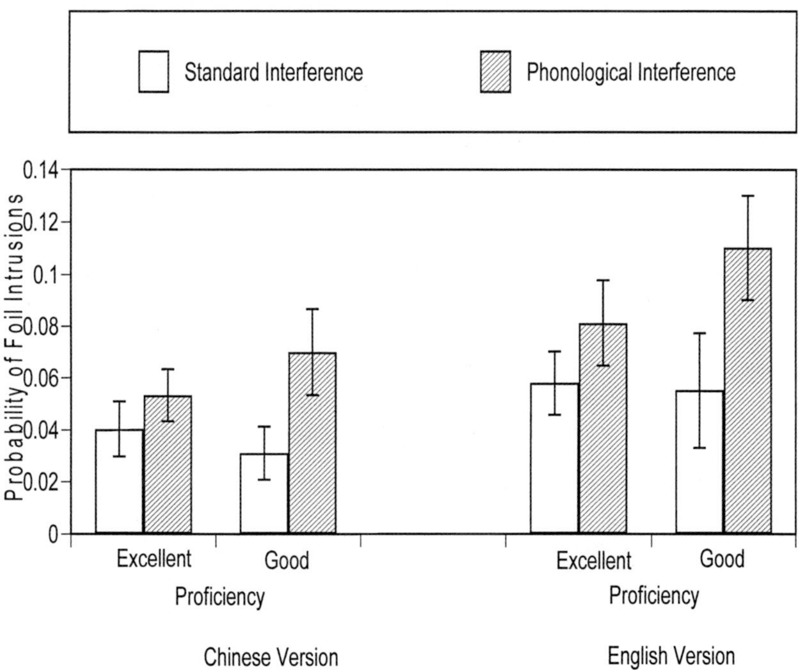

Figure 4. Average probability (+*SEs*) of foil intrusions by participants with different proficiency in Chinese for Experiment 1.

5. Discussion

The results showed that English-Chinese bilinguals seem to encode Chinese words in phonological form in STM. Phonological recoding in Chinese for this type of task was not necessary because the cue was a semantic category; hence, it was important to access meaning. In Chinese, lexical access is a step carried out prior to phonological recoding. So, phonological recoding was not necessary to succeed in the task. However, there is clear evidence for phonological recoding with Chinese words as the pattern replicated Tehan and Humphreys's (1998) findings with the English words; more foil intrusions were observed in the phonological interference condition than in the standard interference condition.

There was also some evidence to suggest that the exploratory hypothesis was supported. Participants with less proficiency in Chinese seem to apply a phonological strategy. In general, the level of English proficiency is very high in Singapore; it is almost certain that these participants were stronger in English and applied phonological recoding automatically as has been demonstrated with alphabetic languages. Participants whose proficiency in Chinese was excellent appeared to be immune to phonological interference. One possible explanation for this effect could be that those participants with great proficiency in Chinese access meaning directly and do not recode phonologically. Interestingly, the most proficient group did not show phonological interference in either the Chinese or English version of the experiment. Chinese proficient participants may access meaning in both Chinese and English experiments directly without phonological recoding.

If phonological recoding was not taking place in the most proficient group, we wondered if this group was mainly relying on the visual characteristics of the characters in order to access meaning. That is, we wanted to know if visual traces play a decisive role in Chinese language processing. The literature on Chinese language processing has showed the importance of visual traits in word recognition and even memory (Tavassoli 2002; Liu 1997; Perfetti and Zhang 1991; Hue and Erickson 1988). Moreover, we were not satisfied with employing merely the criteria of academic proficiency to discern between participants stronger in Chinese, and those stronger in English. These issues were addressed in Experiment 2.

Experiment 2

The main hypothesis was that English dominant participants would show more phonological interference than Chinese dominant participants due to a greater phonological awareness and a more phonemic-based language processing. In contrast, Chinese dominant participants would show more logographic interference because they rely on visual information at processing.

To test the hypothesis, the design of experiment 1 was replicated with one additional condition: the visual interference condition. This time, the experiment was run only in Chinese.

Language dominance was measured with a LDT (word vs. non-word) and a language questionnaire.

Method

1. Participants

A different sample of 86 English-Mandarin undergraduate students from the National University of Singapore participated for course credit.

2. Material

Thirty-six foils, targets and cues were selected from the normative data for taxonomic categories collected by McEvoy and Nelson (1982) and translated into Chinese. Eighteen more categories were picked for one-block trials. The characteristics of the trials pertaining to the *no interference*, *standard* and *phonological* interference experimental conditions were identical to those in experiment 1. We created the *visual* interference trials by inserting in the filler words characters very similar in shape to the characters of the foil (see last column of Figure 2). Fifteen subjects who did not take part in either experiment participated in the ranking of foils and targets, and read all the words selected for the present experiment. Four versions of the experiment were created to rotate all the categories through the different experimental conditions. The LDT used 50 words and 50 non-words with two-compound characters. The language questionnaire comprised six questions that asked about the language they generally use for speaking, reading and writing and used a 9-point Likert-scale (1 *exclusively English,* 2 *mostly English but Chinese on rare occasions,* 3 *frequently English but sometimes Chinese,* 4 *slightly more English than Chinese,* 5 *both languages equally,* 6 *slightly more Chinese than English,* 7 *frequently Chinese but sometimes English,* 8 *mostly Chinese but English on rare occasions,* 9 *exclusively Chinese*). Participants also rated their proficiency at speaking, reading and writing Chinese (1 *very low,* 2 *low,* 3 *average,* 4 *high,* 5 *very high*). They were also asked about their academic scores in English and Chinese at O and AO levels.

3. Procedure

The procedure of the immediate recall task was identical to experiment 1 (Chinese version). After completing the memory task, they performed a LDT. Participants were requested to respond as quickly and accurately as possible using appropriately labelled buttons, whether a compound-character was a word or a non-word. No feedback was provided to the subject. A READY sign (2000 ms) preceded each stimulus and participants had to response within 2000 ms of the onset of the stimulus. Participants practiced with six trials before starting the LDT. Stimuli were presented randomly and continuously. After the 50th trial, they were allowed to rest if necessary. They filled up a brief questionnaire on language use and proficiency at the end of the session. The whole experiment lasted approximately 50 minutes.

4. Results

Data of four subjects were discarded because they scored less than .32 (2 standard deviations) mean proportion of correct responses in one-block trials ($M = .70$, $SD = .19$). Two more subjects were also discarded due to their bad performance in the LDT (only 5 correct non-words out of 50, and 2 correct words out of 50). The data of 80 subjects were used in the subsequent analyses.

Figure 5 shows the proportion of foil intrusions in the different experimental conditions. A one-way within-subjects ANOVA was reliable, $F(2.77, 219.06) = 21.47$, $MSE = .16$, $p < .001$. Planned comparisons revealed that participants significantly made more interference errors in the phonological condition ($M = .10$) than in the standard one ($M = .06$), $t(79) = 3.20$, $p < .05$. They also made more interference errors in the visual condition ($M = .10$) than in the standard condition, $t(79) = 2.99$, $p < .05$.

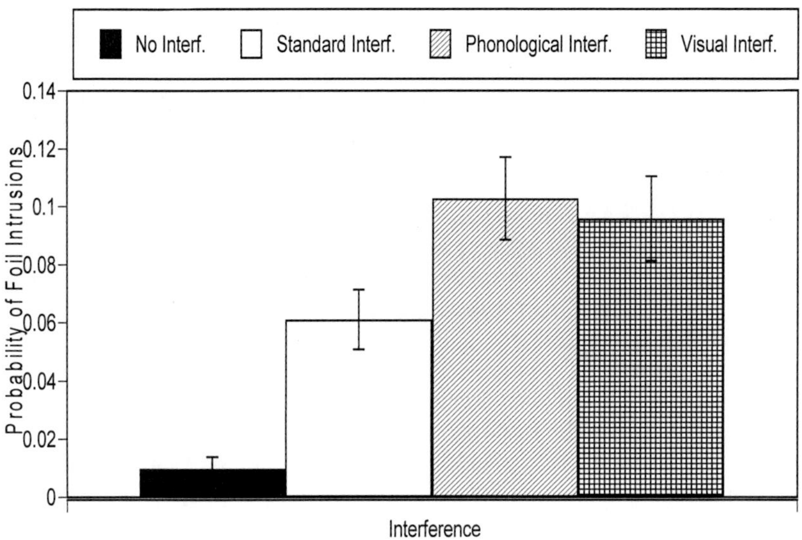

Figure 5. Average probability (+*SE*s) of foil intrusions for Experiment 2.

To differentiate between Chinese and English dominant participants, we considered their *academic proficiency* in Chinese and the *language they generally use at speaking*. *Preference* and *subjective proficiency* at reading and writing did not provide differential information because, generally, Singaporeans are more proficient in English than in Chinese at reading and writing. So, we categorised Chinese dominant participants as those who scored *A* in *Chinese at AO levels* and generally speak from *both languages equally* to *exclusively Chinese*. English dominant participants were those who scored less than *A* in *Chinese at AO levels* and speak from *frequently English but sometimes in Chinese* to *exclusively English*. We categorised as mixed dominant participants those who pertain to none of the previous groups.

Once we selected the three groups of language dominance, we examined their reading and writing practices as indicated in the language questionnaire. On balance, *Chinese dominant participants* tend to read in Chinese and write in Chinese; they also rank their proficiency at speaking and reading mainly as *high* or *very high* and their ability at writing as *average* or *high*. In contrast, those who were considered *English dominants* generally read and write *exclusively* or *almost exclusively* in English; they consider their proficiency at speaking Chinese *average* or *low,* and rate their proficiency at reading and writing Chinese *low* and *very low*. Mixed dominant participants tend to read and write more in English but they consider themselves to have an *average* proficiency in Chinese. This qualitative analysis showed no surprises. To objectively test the three groups, we analysed their dominance through the LDT. One-way between-subjects ANOVA (Chinese dominants, Mixed, and English dominants) was performed on proportion of errors. We found differences between groups: 0.10 of errors in the Chinese dominant group, 0.13 in the mixed, and 0.21 in the English dominant group, F (2, 77) = 15.63, MSE = 0.09, p <.001. All pairwise comparisons among means were tested using a Bonferroni correction at $\alpha = .01$. These comparisons revealed Chinese dominant and mixed made significantly fewer mistakes than the English dominant participants. No differences in RT on correct responses were found between the three groups.

We proceeded to split the foil interference data into the three groups of dominance. Since we were interested in knowing if Chinese dominants codify in STM visually—and English dominants phonologically—we employed t-test comparisons between the standard and the phonological condition, on one hand, and the standard and the visual condition, on the other hand, for each group. Figure 6 shows that Chinese dominant participants did display the same pattern of interference between the standard, the phonological and the visual experimental conditions. No differences were found between the standard (M = .05) and the phonological condition (M = .08), t (27) = 1, *ns*, and the standard and the visual condition (M = .08), t (27) = 1.69, *ns*. The mixed group showed phonological interference (M = .12) compared to the standard condition (M = .07), t (27) = 2.36, p < .05, but no visual interference (M = .08), $t < 1$. Finally, English dominant participants showed significant phonological interference (M = .12) when compared to the standard condition (M = .06), t (23) = 2.31, p < .05, and significant visual interference (M = .13), t (23) = 3.24, p < .05.

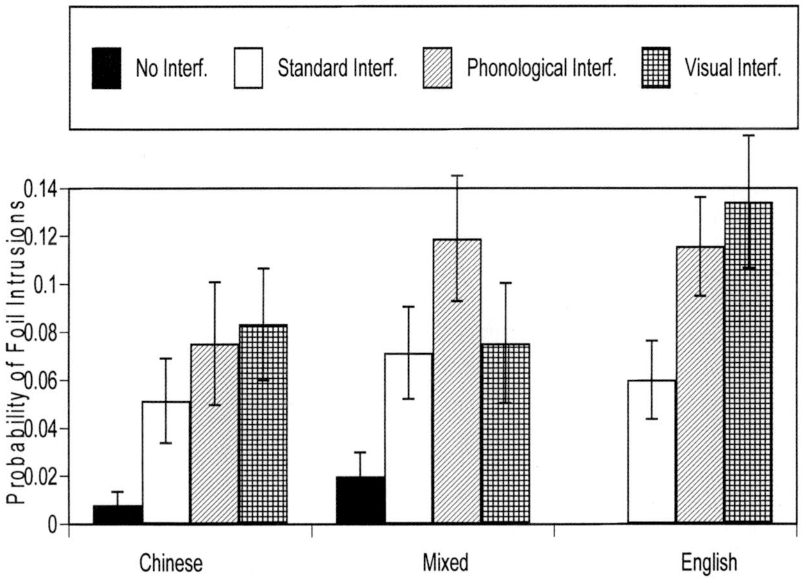

Figure 6. Average probability (+*SE*s) of foil intrusions for bilingual participants according to their language dominance.

5. Discussion

The hypothesis was partially supported. Chinese dominant participants did not show phonological or visual interference. We had expected them to show visual interference. Mixed dominant participants only showed phonological interference. Finally, the English dominant group showed both visual and phonological interference. We had not expected them to show visual interference.

One possible explanation would be that the Chinese dominant bilinguals were directly accessing meaning without phonological or visual encoding. Mixed dominant participants, however, because of being more English-oriented, tended to recode phonologically; however, they did not rely on visual codes because they recognised the characters as easily as the Chinese dominants. Finally, the English dominant group recoded phonologically and used visual codification. It is possible that low proficiency in Chinese did not allow English dominants to recode all the characters in the list, having to pay attention to the visual forms of the character and subsequently try to redintegrate the information from the visual traces.

General Discussion and Conclusion

The results suggest that bilinguals do not process each language as monolinguals do. Their dominance in one language leads them to process the weaker language the way they process the strongest language. English is processed phonologically so mixed and English dominant bilinguals seem to employ systematically a phonological-based strategy when dealing with English and Chinese. The results match Everson's (1998) findings of strong correlation between pronunciation and identification of Chinese words by English speakers learning Chinese as a second language. In a different type of experiment, Brandimonte and Gerbino (1993) found that once a drawing was given a name, mental transformations of the drawing were impeded. The same happened with the Chinese characters in the experiments, once the participants engaged in verbal recoding, they forgot the visual information. This mental operation is plausible because the visual cache—the component of WM that retains visual patterns—cannot retain sequential information; hence, the information seems to be rapidly recoded by the phonological loop, which can retain sequential information but in phonological code. However, when participants cannot easily recode all the words phonologically, as happened with our English dominant participants dealing with Chinese, visual features of the stimuli are available and not substituted by phonological codes. In scoring the responses, we accepted as visual interference errors those responses formed by one character of the foil and one character of the target, or a character of the foil plus an extra character. For example, the cue for one trial was FARM ANIMAL, the foil was *cow* and the target *turkey,* by combining the first character of the foil with the second character of the target, it can form the word *hen.* Some participants recalled *hen*, a word that was not presented in the list. These errors were prominent in the visual condition. English dominant participants were those who made this type of mistake, showing that they were redintegrating from visual codes. The intrusion of words composed by parts of the foils and targets show that visual memory has a very limited capacity; it also shows that English dominant participants are redintegrating from partial visual traces at retrieval. Harrington (1992) cites many other experiments that show reliance on graphic cues in second language (like the Chinese language for the English dominants).

Chinese dominant bilinguals, on the other hand, accessed meaning directly. The practice of accessing meaning directly without recoding while dealing with Chinese might have induced them to use the same strategy in English. Chinese dominant participants of our sample may have not recoded phonologically because recoding provided no extra advantage to perform the task successfully. The results also support the connectionist paradigm of language processing that conceives memory as associations represented by different patterns of connections in units and layers (phonological, semantic, context, etc.). Retrieval is accomplished by redintegration of the traces left in those units. The results of our experiments showed that the foil's phonemes distributed among other words kept the foil active, suggesting that a word is stored in memory as connections between phonemes, and the phoneme is the minimal phonological trace. Moreover, English dominant subjects also showed that they were redintegrating information from part of the compound-character words, suggesting that a word is kept in memory as single characters (or strokes). Chinese dominant subjects did not show phonological and visual distributed memory probably because their phonological, visual and semantic processes are so integrated that they do not rely exclusively on the phonemic or the visual system to access to meaning.

Chinese language represents meaning better than sound. Yet English dominant adults—and Mixed—bilinguals recode phonologically in order to access meaning. Moreover, Chinese dominant adults do not recode English automatically.

In conclusion, different languages are processed differently and dominance in one language affects the way the other language is processed. Chinese dominants seem not to use phonological nor visual strategies to memorise in a cued recall task. It is plausible that they access meaning directly. Mixed dominants, however, recode phonologically and store the information in phonological code. Their greater experience with English may have induced them to use phonological recoding as a strategy as demonstrated with alphabetic languages. Finally, the group less proficient in Chinese formed by English dominants show visual and phonological interference, suggesting that they use recoding to process known words and visual memory to retain words they do not how to pronounce or do not have time to recode into phonological form.

Notes

[1] The same Chinese script is used by all Chinese people (except in Taiwan and Hong Kong) although pronunciation varies due to the existence of different Chinese dialects. Mandarin is the spoken Chinese dialect taught at Singapore schools and is used for this experiment. In this paper, the term Chinese is used for spoken and written language interchangeably.

[2] Only 62 of the 87 participants took part in the English experiment because of technical problems with the English experiment at the start of data collection.

Acknowledgements

This work was supported in part by a Research Scholarship awarded to L. S. and in part by Research Grant R-581-000-048-112 awarded to W. D. G. by the National University of Singapore.

References

Baddeley, A. 1997. *Human memory* (Rev. ed.). Hove: Psychology Press.

—. 2000. The episodic buffer: a new component of working memory? *Trends in cognitive sciences* 4: 417-423.

Baddeley, A. and B. Wilson. 1988. Comprehension and working memory: A single case of neuropsychological study. *Journal of memory and language* 27: 479-498.

Bialystok, E., C. McBride-Chang and G. Luk. 2005. Bilingualism, language proficiency, and learning to read in two writing systems. *Journal of Educational Psychology* 97 (4): 580-590.

Brandimonte. M. A. and W. Gerbino. 1993. Mental image reversal and verbal recoding: When ducks become rabbits. *Memory & Cognition* 21: 23-33.

Brysbaert, M. 2001. Prelexical phonological coding of visual words in Dutch: Automatic after all. *Memory & Cognition* 29: 765-773.

Chen, H. C. 1996. Chinese reading and comprehension: A cognitive psychology perspective. In *The handbook of Chinese psychology*, edited by M. H. Bond, 43-62. Hong Kong: Oxford University Press.

Chen, M. J., Y. F Yung and T. W. Ng. 1988. The effect of context on perception of Chinese characters. In *Cognitive aspects of the Chinese language*, edited by I. M. Liu, H. C. Chen and M. J. Chen, 27- 40. Hong Kong: Asian Research Service.

Cheng, C. M. 1992. Lexical access in Chinese: Evidence from automatic activation of phonological information. In *Language processing in Chinese* edited by H. C. Chen and O. J. L.Tzeng, 67-91. Amsterdam: Elsevier Science Publishers B. V.

Chitiri H. F., Y. L Sun, D. M. Willows and I. Taylor. 1992. Word recognition in second-language reading. In *Cognitive processing in bilinguals* edited by R. J. Harris,283-298. Amsterdam: Elsevier Science Publishers B. V.

De Gelder, B. and J. Vroomen. 1992. Auditory and visual speech perception in alphabetic and nonalphabetic Chinese-Dutch bilinguals. In *Cognitive processing in bilinguals*, edited by R. J. Harris, 413-426. Amsterdam: Elsevier Science Publishers B. V.

Ellis, N. C. 1992. Linguistic relativity revisited: The bilingual word-length effect in working memory during counting, remembering numbers, and mental calculation. In *Cognitive processing in bilinguals*, edited by R. J. Harris, 137-156. Amsterdam: Elsevier Science Publishers B. V.

Everson, M. E. (1998). Word recognition among learners of Chinese as a foreign language: Investigating the relationship between naming and knowing. *The Modern Language Journal* 82: 194-2003.

Flaherty, M. 1997. The role of abstract visual memory in learning of kanji reading. In *Cognitive processing of Chinese and related Asian languages*, edited by H. C. Chen, 389-400. Hong Kong: The Chinese University Press.

Gernsbacher, M. A. 1994 (Ed.). *Handbook of psycholinguistics*. San Diego: Academic Press, Inc.

Green, D. W., S. J. Rickard-Liow, S. K Tng and S. Zielinski. 1996. Are visual search procedures adapted to the nature of the script? *British Journal of Psychology* 87: 311-326.

Harrington, M. 1992. Working memory capacity as a constraint on L2 development. In *Cognitive processing in bilinguals*, edited by R. J. Harris, 123-137. Amsterdam: Elsevier Science Publishers B. V.

Hong, E. L. and G. W. Yelland. 1997. The generality of lexical neighbourhood effects. In *Cognitive processing of Chinese and related Asian languages*, edited by H. C. Chen, 187-203. Hong Kong: The Chinese University Press.

Hoosain, R. 1984. Experiments on digits spans in the Chinese and English languages. In *Psychological studies of the Chinese language*, edited by H. S. R. Kao and R. Hoosain, 23-38. Hong Kong: Tao Dao Publishing Ltd.

Hu, C. F. 2003. Phonological memory, phonological awareness, and foreign language word learning. *Language Learning* 53 (3): 429-462.

Hue, C. W. and J. R. Erickson. 1988. Short-term memory for Chinese characters and radicals. *Memory & Cognition* 16: 196-205.

Humphreys, M. S. and G. Tehan. 1999. Cues and codes in working memory tasks. In *On human memory: evolution, progress, and reflections on the 30th anniversary of the Atkinson-Shiffrin model,* edited by C. Izawa, 127-150. Mahwah: Lawrence Erlbaum Associates.

Jarrold, C., A. D. Baddeley, A. K. Hewes, T. C. Leeke and C. E. Phillips. 2004. What links verbal short-term memory performance and vocabulary level? Evidence of changing relationships among individuals with learning disability. *Journal of Memory and Language* 50 (2): 134-148.

Lau, C. W. and R. Hoosain.1999. Working memory and language difference in sound duration: A comparison of mental arithmetic in Chinese, Japanese, and English. *Psychologia* 42: 139-144.

Lin, A.M.Y. and N. Akamatsu. 1997. The issue of prelexical phonology in the reading of Chinese characters. In *Cognitive processing of Chinese and related Asian languages*, edited by H. C. Chen, 369-387). Hong Kong: The Chinese University Press.

Liu, I. M. 1997. The issue of prelexical phonology in the reading of Chinese characters. In *Cognitive processing of Chinese and related Asian languages*, edited by H. C. Chen, 65-76. Hong Kong: The Chinese University Press.

Loo, S. C. 1992. *Xin jia po zhong xue hua wen jiao cia zi pin lü ci dian* [Frequency dictionary of Chinese characters, words and phrases used in Singapore secondary school textbooks]. Singapore: Chinese Language and Research Centre (National University of Singapore).

Kucera, H. and Francis, W. N 1967. *Computational analysis of present-day American English.* .MRC Psycholinguistic Database: Machine Usable Dictionary (Version 2.00). Available from http://www.psy.uwa.edu.au/mrcdatabase/uwa_mrc.htm.

McBride-Chang, C., E. Bialystock, K. K. Y Chong and Y. P. Li. 2004. Levels of phonological awareness in three cultures. *Journal of Experimental Child Psychology* 89: 93-111.

McBride-Chang, C. and R. V. Kail. 2002. Cross-cultural similarities in the predictors of reading acquisition. *Child development* 73: 1392-1407.

McEvoy, C. L. and D. L. Nelson. 1982. Category name and instance norms for 106 categories of various sizes. *American Journal of Psychology* 95: 581-634.

Mickey, R. M., O. J. Dunn and V. A. Clark. 2004. *Applied statistics: analysis of variance and regression* (3rd ed.). Hoboken, NJ: John Wiley & Sons, Inc.

Perfetti, C. A. and S. Zhang. 1991. Phonological processes in reading Chinese characters. Journal *of Experimental Psychology: Learning, Memory and Cognition* 17: 633-643

Rickard-Liow, S. 1999. Reading skill development in bilingual Singaporean children. In *Learning to read and write: a cross-linguistic perspective,* edited by M. Harris and G. Hatano, 196-213. Cambridge: Cambridge University Press.

Swan, D. and U. Goswami. 1997. Phonological awareness deficits in developmental dyslexia and the phonological representations hypothesis. *Journal of Experimental Child Psychology* 66: 18-41.

Tan, L. H. and C. A. Perfetti. 1998. Phonological codes as early sources of constraint in Chinese word identification: A review of current discoveries and theoretical accounts. *Reading and Writing* 10 (3-5): 165-200.

Tavassoli, N. T. 2002. Spatial memory for Chinese and English. *Journal of Cross-cultural Psychology* 33 (4): 415-431.

Tehan, G. and M. S. Humphreys. 1995. Transient phonemic codes and immunity to proactive interference. *Memory & Cognition* 23: 181-191.

Tehan, G. and M. S. Humphreys. 1996. Cuing effects in short-term recall. *Memory & Cognition* 24: 719-731.

Tehan, G. and M. S. Humphreys. 1998. Creating proactive interference in immediate recall: building a DOG from a DART, a MOP, and a FIG. *Memory & Cognition* 26: 477-489.

The Straits Times. 2006. Mandarin lessons for all–in UK school, January 21.

Wu, J. T. and I. M. Liu. 1996. Chinese lexical access. In The handbook of Chinese psychology, edited by M. H. Bond, 30-42. Hong Kong: Oxford University Press.

Wang, H., B. R. Chang, Y. S. Li, L. H. Lin, J. Liu, Y. L. Sun, Z. W. Wang, Y. X. Yu, and J. W. Zhang (Eds.) 1990. Xian dai hun yu pin lu ci dian [Frequency dictionary of modern Chinese words] (2nd ed.) Beijing: Beijing yu yan xue yuan chu ban she [Beijing Language Institute].

Xiao ma ci dian (Version 2.2.7). 2005. Available from: http://hmarty.free.fr/hanzi/

CHAPTER 10

MULTILINGUAL PROCESSING OF RELATIVE CLAUSES

Maurits van den Noort, Peggy Bosch and Kenneth Hugdahl

The processing of relative clauses has been well investigated in L1 research, showing that subject relatives are often easier to comprehend than object relatives (Clancy et al. 1986; Demuth 1995). Miller and Chomsky (1963) were among the first to notice that there are sentences whose syntactic structures are quite similar, but whose processing demands are not. For example:

(1) *The reporter who harshly attacked the senator admitted the error.*
(2) *The reporter who the senator harshly attacked admitted the error.*

Both sentences contain a relative clause modifying the subject of the sentence, but differ in the role that the main subject NP ('the reporter') plays in the relative clause; in subject relatives, as in example (1), the main-clause subject is also the subject (and agent) of the verb in the relative clause, while in object relatives, as in example (2), it is the object (and patient) (King and Kutas 1995).

There is a large body of literature on the processing of relative clauses in Germanic languages showing that subject relatives are easier to comprehend than object relatives. This has, for instance, been found for English, in which the clause is disambiguated at the word (noun vs. verb) following the relative pronoun (Caplan et al. 1999; Grodzinsky et al. 1999; Just et al. 1996b; King and Just 1991; King and Kutas 1995). Moreover, it was found for German, in which the clause is disambiguated either at a case-marked element or at the clause-final verb (Mecklinger et al. 1995; Schriefers et al. 1995; Vos et al. 2001). In addition, it was also found for Dutch, in which relative clauses are either disambiguated by case-marking on a pronoun or at the clause-final verb (Mak 2001; Van Gompel 1995). However, recent Cross-linguistic research has shown that object relatives are not always more difficult to process than subject relatives. For Chinese, for example, it was found that object relatives are less complex than subject relatives (Hsiao and Gibson 2003; Hsu 2004).

The reason for subject relatives, at least in Germanic languages, being easier to comprehend than object relatives has been the subject of much research, and many factors appear to contribute (Just and Carpenter 1992; King and Just 1991). Historically, one of the more prominently mentioned hypothesis is that sentences with object relatives induce a greater working memory load. One argument for this working memory load hypothesis is that the syntactic processing of the initial NP in the sentence with an object relative is interrupted by the need to process an (self-) embedded NP which requires the temporary storage of the sentence initial NP in working memory until its processing can resume (Miller and Chomsky 1963). This proposal correctly predicts the increasing difficulty of processing sentences containing object relatives compared to subject relatives, as clauses become more deeply embedded (Müller et al. 1997).

There have been two approaches to study the specificity of the working memory system underlying language comprehension. The first proposal is the capacity theory of language comprehension of Just and Carpenter (1992), which assumes a single verbal resource underlying all processes involved in language comprehension. In case of a shortage of capacity, language processing will slow down and comprehension will deteriorate. Just and Carpenter favour an approach to language comprehension in which information from different levels of representation is allowed to interact during processing (Just and Carpenter 1987). Their model permits several productions to fire at the same time within a given processing cycle and allows for gradual instantiations of information in working memory. Information in working memory is assigned to a numerical activation (or confidence) level, and information without sufficient activation decays from working memory. During the processing of a sentence, the model uses the items in working memory to build explicit syntactic and semantic representations for the purpose of interpretation. This information may be used by several different kinds of productions (lexical, syntactic, etc.), permitting interaction across levels of processing when productions from different levels are executed in parallel (MacDonald and Christiansen 2002).

The second proposal is the separate sentence interpretation resource (SSIR) theory of Waters and Caplan (1996). According to this theory, there are at least two specialised resources: A first resource is used in processes such as constructing syntactic representations and assigning thematic roles. The second resource is used in controlled verbally mediated tasks, for instance in reading span tasks (Desmette et al. 1995). The SSIR theory is more closely tied to generative linguistic theory (e.g. Chomsky 1965), particularly to claims about the modular nature of language processes and the linguistic knowledge people use (Fodor 1983; Frazier 1987). Apart from a module for syntactic processing, Waters and Caplan (1996) envisaged components for other functions, including 'acoustic-phonetic conversion, lexical access, assignment of intonational contours, determination of sentential semantic values such as thematic roles, and determination of discourse-level semantic values such as topic and coherent coreference'. Information from these different components is brought together and processed in a common working memory to build explicit syntactic and semantic representations for the purpose of interpretation. Thus, the representation of linguistic knowledge is highly modularised and separated from processing in working memory (MacDonald and Christiansen 2002).

The capacity theory and the SSIR theory have led to different, and inconsistent, findings (Caplan and Waters 1995, 1999; Just et al. 1996a; Miyake et al. 1995; Waters and Caplan 1996). In this study, the capacity theory and the SSIR theory will be tested on multilinguals, who conduct a relative clause task in three languages. Before discussing the specific aims of this study, we would like to briefly discuss what we know about the L1 and L2 acquisition of relative clauses in Germanic languages.

The acquisition of relative clauses has been subject to numerous L1 investigations. The majority of these investigations are concerned with children's comprehension of relative clauses in English (Kidd and Bavin 2002; McKee and McDaniel 2001; Schuele and Nicholls 2000). The L1 acquisition of relative clauses has been studied by using both natural speech samples and controlled experimental material (Goodluck and Tavakolian 1982; Hamburger 1980; Hamburger and Crain 1982; Lust et al. 1987; Lust et al. 1996). Flynn and Lust (1981), for example, compared children's production of three relative clause types. In this study, a primacy of the free relative clause construction in the early development of subordination in child L1 acquisition was found. Moreover, it was found that subject relatives are easier to acquire than object relatives.

The acquisition of relative clauses has also been subject to second language research (Omaki 2005; Papadopoulou and Clahsen 2003). A number of second language studies were conducted, in which the processing of relative clauses was tested on second language learners of a Germanic language. For example, Flynn tested adult L2 acquisition of English by L1 speakers of Japanese and Spanish (Flynn 1983; 1987). The results showed that the L1 Japanese and Spanish speakers were at one of three levels of English proficiency as measured by the Michigan Test. More recently Felser, Roberts, Marinis and Gross (2003) tested two groups of advanced second language learners of English whose first language (Greek or German) showed a non-local attachment preference. Their second language learners as a group showed no clear attachment preference in the off-line and on-line experiments, while the native speaker controls showed a local attachment preference in on-line processing.

In the present study, adults, who are at an early stage of L3- and adults, who are at a more advanced stage of L3 acquisition will be compared in the processing of subject- and object relatives. The L3 acquisition of relative clauses in Germanic languages is a new research topic. So far, only one study was conducted by Flynn, Foley, and Vinnitskaya (2004), in which subtle differences between adults and children in the processing of relative clauses were found. Contrary to their study, we will focus both on differences in relative clauses comprehension and speed of processing in L1, L2, and L3. In addition, we would like to investigate the role of working memory in third language acquisition of relative clauses. To investigate this, not only a relative clause task in all languages, but also two working memory tests will be conducted. Which working memory theory (the SSIR- or the capacity theory) can better explain our experimental results? Our hypotheses will be discussed in detail below.

With respect to relative clauses comprehension, it is expected that both for the early stage L3 learners and the more advanced L3 learners no significant differences in relative clauses comprehension between L1 and L2 will be found. For the more advanced L3 learners, this will also be the case in L3. For the early stage L3 learners, however, significant differences in relative clauses comprehension between L1/L2 on the one hand and L3 on the other hand are expected.

With respect to processing speed of relative clauses, it is expected that both the early stage L3 learners and the more advanced L3 learners read sentences with relative clauses fastest in L1 followed by L2 and L3. Moreover, it is expected that the more advanced L3 learners process relative clauses in L3 significantly faster than the early stage L3 learners. In line with previous research on processing speed of relative clauses in Germanic languages (Mak 2001; Vos et al. 2001), it is expected that for both groups in L1; subject relatives are processed faster than object relatives. Since all participants of this experiment are highly skilled in their L2, it is expected that sentences containing subject relatives will also be read faster than sentences with object relatives in L2. For the more advanced L3 learners this will also be the case in L3. However, for the early stage L3 learners, on the one hand, a significant difference between subject and object relatives could be expected since early stage L3 learners still process subject relatives faster than object relatives. On the other hand, it could also be the case that for the early stage L3 learners, the difference between subject and object relatives is not significant since both sentence types are very difficult to process, because of the early stage of foreign language acquisition. Finally, in line with previous findings (Mak et al. 2002), any differences in reading time between sentences with subject relatives and object relatives are only expected for relative clauses with animate objects and not for inanimate objects in all languages.

To investigate the role of working memory in third language acquisition of relative clauses, a correlation test will be conducted between the scores on the working memory tasks and the comprehension scores on the relative clause task in L1, L2, and L3. The SSIR theory (Waters and Caplan 1996) would predict no significant correlation between the scores on the working memory tasks and the comprehension scores on the relative clause task in all languages. According to this theory, any individual difference in working memory capacity for language should not interfere with the processing of complex sentences. In contrast to the SSIR theory, the capacity theory (Just and Carpenter 1992) would at least predict a correlation between the working memory tests and the comprehension scores on the relative clause task in L1.

Method

Participants

Twenty healthy adults participated in this study, who were all native Dutch speakers (L1) and fluent in German (L2). Ten subjects started their free acquisition of Norwegian (L3) in the last 6 months, whereas ten other subjects lived in Norway and started their acquisition of Norwegian more than 3 years ago. It is important to note that the languages that were used in this study were all Germanic languages, which made comparisons between languages easier. Dutch and German both belong to the West Germanic linguistic group, whereas Norwegian belongs to the North Germanic linguistic group (König and Van der Auwera 1994). In addition, all participants had learned English at school. To further determine language background and proficiency, the participants completed a language background questionnaire (Vingerhoets et al. 2003).

The first part of this questionnaire assessed first experience with, age of acquisition, and general exposure to German and Norwegian. It also included a self-rating of the participants' subjective proficiency of the two foreign languages. None of the participants was regularly exposed to; or had acquired German or Norwegian during early childhood. No one had spent more than one continuous month in a German speaking (part of the) country. All participants had started to learn German as a foreign language at a mean age of respectively 12.90 (SD = .45) at school. All participants had learned Norwegian during a language course and by free acquisition in the country. The 10 participants, who were at an early stage of third language acquisition had a mean age of 26.8 (SD = 3.10) years compared to 24.3 (SD = 3.10) years for the other group (see Table 1). In total, 10 males and 10 females participated in the study. Exposure to the foreign languages was estimated by interrogating the frequency of active and passive use (see Table 1).

Subject	Age	Age of acquisition		Estimated exposure active/passive[b]		Subjective proficiency[c]		Translation into Dutch[d]		Translation into FL[e]	
		G[a]	N[a]	G	N	G	N	G	N	G	N
Group 1											
1	25	13	24	-/+	++/++	+	-	93	93	87	40
2	26	13	26	-/+	++/++	++	+	87	93	93	47
3	25	13	25	+/+	++/+++	++	+	100	93	93	60
4	31	13	31	+/+	+++/+++	++	+	100	87	93	67
5	32	12	31	-/-	+++/++	++	++	93	93	93	73
6	25	13	25	+/+	++/+++	++	++	100	93	93	67
7	26	13	26	++/++	++/++	+++	+	100	93	100	53
8	28	13	28	+/++	+++/+++	++	+	100	100	93	60
9	26	12	25	-/-	++/+++	++	+	93	87	87	60
10	32	13	27	-/+	+++/+++	++					
	+	87	93	100	60						
Mean	27.6	12.8	26.8					95.3	92.5	93.2	58.7
SD	3.0	.4	2.5					5.4	3.6	4.3	9.8
Group2											
11	27	13	24	+/+	++/++	++	++	87	93	80	67
12	25	13	23	-/+	++/+++	++	++	93	93	87	60
13	27	13	24	+/+	++/++	+	+	100	80	93	73
14	27	12	26	+/+	+++/+++	+++	++	100	93	93	67
15	31	13	26	-/-	+++/++	++	++	87	93	100	73
16	30	13	22	-/+	++/+++	++	++	100	93	93	67
17	25	13	23	+/++	++/+++	++	++	100	93	100	73
18	26	13	25	+/++	+++/+++	++	++	100	100	100	73
19	25	13	23	-/-	++/++	++	+	93	93	87	67
20	30	13	27	+/+	+++/+++	++	++	93	93	100	73
Mean	27.3	12.9	24.3					95.3	92.4	93.3	69.3
SD	2.3	.3	1.6					5.4	4.9	7.0	4.4

Table 1 Age of acquisition, estimated exposure, proficiency, and performance for each individual participant

Note.
[a] G = German; N = Norwegian.
[b] Less than once a year (--); yearly (-); monthly (+); weekly (++); daily (+++).
[c] Poor (-); fair (+); good (++); excellent (+++).
[d] Percentage correctly translated words from the foreign language into Dutch.
[e] Percentage correctly translated words from Dutch into the foreign language.

The participants had to indicate whether speaking and writing in each language occurred daily, weekly, monthly, yearly, or less than once a year. Estimation of the average active use was based on these answers. Participants also had to indicate their passive use of the languages by judging the frequency of reading, or listening to (radio) or watching (TV) programs in German and Norwegian. Estimation of average passive use was based on these answers. The participants' subjective proficiency of the foreign languages was evaluated with four questions regarding speaking, writing, reading, and understanding. Subjective proficiency for each of these skills was indicated on a fourpoint scale (poor/fair/good/excellent). The results of the self-ratings as can be seen in Table 1, indicated that all participants perceived themselves on average as having good command of German. The early stage L3 learners perceived themselves on average as having fair command of Norwegian, whereas the more advanced L3 learners percieved themselves as having good command of Norwegian.

The second part of the questionnaire estimated the participants' objective proficiency of each foreign language as assessed by translations of 30 high to low frequent words and free written production. For each foreign language, this test consisted of five parts. In the first part, participants received a list of 5 German or Norwegian words, and a list of 10 Dutch words. They then had to select those Dutch words that matched in meaning with the German or Norwegian ones. In the second part, participants received a list of 5 Dutch words, and a list of 10 German or Norwegian words. They then had to select those German and Norwegian words that matched in meaning with the Dutch ones. In a third part, free translation of 10 German or Norwegian words into Dutch was required. In a fourth part, free translation of 10 Dutch words into German or Norwegian was required. Finally, all participants had to write a text about their study and/or profession in German and Norwegian. The translation performance, as can be seen in Table 1, revealed that all participants had a good command of German. No significant differences in German to Dutch or Dutch to German translation were found between the groups. As could be expected, a significant difference in translation performance for the early stage L3 learners compared to the more advanced L3 learners was found for the Dutch to Norwegian translation [$t\ (9) = 10.11$, $p < 0.001$], but not for the Norwegian to Dutch translation. Finally, in line with our selection criteria, the analysis of the written production showed that the early stage L3 learners produced shorter texts and made more grammatical mistakes in their L3 than the more advanced L3 learners.

Materials and procedure

1.General procedure

The participants were tested individually in an experimental room. After receiving a general instruction, a detailed instruction was given for each separate task. First, the participants filled out a language background questionnaire (Vingerhoets et al. 2003). Then, the experiment, which consisted of three different parts, started: three self paced reading task of relative clauses (in Dutch, German, and Norwegian), a reading span task (only in L3) and a number ordering task. The order of the experimental tasks was semi-randomised over the participants. After finishing all experimental tasks, participants received feedback about the aim of the experiment. The duration of the experiment was +/- 60 minutes. The experimental material will be discussed in detail below.

2. Relative clause tasks

Participants had to read relative clauses and filler sentences in Dutch, German, and Norwegian. For every language, a different relative clause task was developed. The order in which the participants had to complete the three relative clause tasks was semi-randomised. The sentences were presented on a computer screen and were programmed in E-Prime (Schneider et al. 2002). All relative clauses were developed in such a way that the semantic content of the past participle in the relative clause was consistent with the correct syntactic analysis of the relative clause. As can be seen in Figure 1, the first line contained the main clause up to the antecedent NP, the second line contained the relative clause and at least two words of the continuation of the main clause. When a participant had finished reading a sentence, he/she pressed the space bar, after which another sentence appeared on the screen. The 48 experimental items were mixed with 48 unrelated filler sentences. The experimental items consisted of 24 sentences with subject relatives and 24 sentences with object relatives (See Appendix A for examples). The 48 experimental items and 48 fillers were pseudo randomly divided into two blocks of trials. To make sure that the participants read the sentences carefully and to test their sentence comprehension, verification statements were included after the experimental and filler trials (Mak 2001). At the beginning of the experiment, there was a practice block of 2 x 5 trials. The practice items had constructions similar to the ones used in the experiment. There were no significant differences in mean number of syllables of both the filler sentences and the experimental sentences between the three languages.

3.Reading span task

The Reading span task (RST) started with an instruction on the computer screen and two exercise trials, after which the experimental material was presented. The new standard computerized RST was used (Van den Noort et al. submitted). The instruction emphasized the importance of reading the sentences as fast as possible while reading for content. The 100 experimental sentences were controled for length, ranging from 12 to 17 words and 20 to 22 syllables. Moreover, the number of syllables, the number of letters, and the frequency of the sentence-final words were controlled for. Within the sets, the sentences and sentence-final words were controlled for semantic relations. The experimental sentences were presented in different set sizes (2, 3, 4, 5 or 6 sentences) and in random order. As a result, participants did not know how many sentences were presented in a set and could therefore not anticipate. Participants read sentences aloud. When a participant had finished reading a sentence, the participant pressed the space bar, after which another sentence appeared on the screen. If the participant could not finish the sentence within 6.5 seconds, the computer automatically presented the following sentence. When a participant had completed all the sentences of a set, the word 'recall' was presented. At that point, participants had to recall the last word of each sentence in the set. The order of recall was free. This is important since free recall gives important information of possible primacy- and recency effects (Baddeley 1999). The participants completed all 5 different series of 2, 3, 4, 5, or 6 sentences. The reading span task was conducted in Norwegian, which was the third language of the participants.

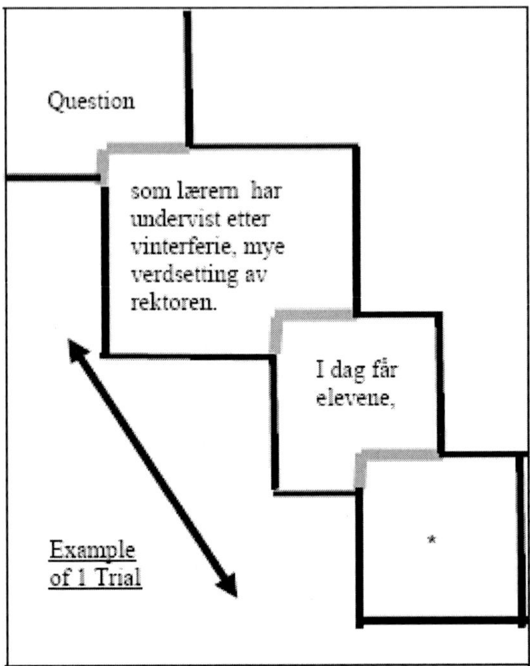

Figure 1 An example of how experimental sentences in the relative clause task were presented on the screen. The first line contained the main clause up to the antecedent NP, the second line contained the relative clause and at least two words of the continuation of the main clause

4. Number ordering task

Since the reading span task is a typical language based working memory task, we decided to use a number ordering task as a second working memory task; to better understand the role of working memory in third language acquisition of relative clauses. Note that the number ordering task is a non-verbal working memory task, whereas the reading span task is a typical verbal working memory task. During the number ordering task, one number after the other was presented on a computer screen after which the participant had to write down these numbers in a special order, namely: first the even numbers in order of increasing magnitude and then the odd numbers in order of increasing magnitude. For example, when the computer presented: 6-9-2-3, the participant wrote down 2-6-3-9. There were three sets of 2, 3, 4, 5, 6, 7, and 8 even and odd numbers. If a participant failed three following trials, the computer did not move on to the next trial. The maximum score on the number ordering task was 21.

Results

Reading times shorter than 2000 ms and longer than 9000 ms were excluded from further analysis. The rationale behind this decision was that, if a participant read a sentence extremely fast or slow in comparison with other sentences, one cannot be sure that the participant read the sentence in a normal, comprehensive way. From the remaining reading times, those that were more than two standard deviations away from a participant and item means at a given position in each condition were excluded. In total: 6 cases (0.3%) were excluded in the Dutch relative clause task, 45 cases (2.3%) in German and 56 cases (2.9%) in Norwegian.

Relative clause tasks

1. Comprehension

As can be seen in Table 2, the analysis of the verification statements after all sentences (both experimental- and filler sentences) showed that all participants performed well on the Dutch- and German relative clause task. The more advanced L3 learners also performed well on the Norwegian relative clause task, but the early stage L3 learners did not. A significant difference in percentage correct between the early stage L3 learners and the more advanced L3 learners was only found on the Norwegian- [t (9) = -6.96, $p < 0.001$], but not on the Dutch or German relative clause task.

In addition, it was found that the answers to the verification statements were significantly better after the filler sentences compared to the sentences with relative clauses in the Dutch- [t (19) = 2.77, $p < 0.2$] and German- [t (19) = 2.30, $p < 0.04$], but not in the Norwegian relative clause task.

For the more advanced L3 learners no significant differences in relative clauses comprehension were found on the Dutch, German, and Norwegian relative clause task. For the early stage L3 learners, this was also the case on the Dutch- and German task. However, significant differences in relative clauses comprehension between L1/L2 on the one hand and L3 on the other hand were found. The early stage L3 learners performed significantly better both on the Dutch- [t (9) = -17.96, $p < 0.001$] and German relative clause task [t (9) = -16.54, $p < 0.001$] than on the Norwegian one.

	Group 1	Group 1	Group 2	Group 2
	RC[a]	**Filler**	**RC**	**Filler**
Dutch	91.9 (4.4%)	93.6% (3.1%)	91.6% (3.0%)	93.3% (2.9%)
German	90.2 (6.1%)	92.5% (3.9%)	89.9% (3.6%)	91.8% (4.1%)
Norwegian	65.4 (9.3%)	65.8% (14.2%)	89.6% (5.9%)	90.1% (6.8%)

Table 2 Overview of the percentage verification statements correct for the sentences with relative clauses and the filler sentences in Dutch, German, and Norwegian. The group with the early stage L3 learners (group 1) is compared to the group with the more advanced L3 learners (group 2). *Note.* [a] RC = Relative Clause.

2. Processing speed

The mean reading time of sentences with relative clauses was analysed in a 3 (language) x 2 (relative clause type) x 2 (animacy) within-subjects MANOVA. A significant main effect for language was found, $F(2, 18) = 36.42$, $p < 0.001$. Participants in both groups read sentences with relative clauses significantly faster in Dutch compared to German [t (9) = -6.12, $p < 0.001$] and [t (9) = -13.04, $p < 0.001$]. Moreover, in both groups these sentences were read significantly faster in Dutch compared to Norwegian [t (9) = -10.31, $p < 0.001$] and [t (9) = -10.21, $p < 0.001$]. In addition, no significant differences in mean sentence reading time were found between the L2 in comparison with the L3 in both groups. Participants read sentences with relative clauses in German not significantly faster than in Norwegian. Finally, the analysis of the mean reading time of sentences with relative clauses showed a significant difference between the early stage L3 learners and the more advanced L3 learners in Norwegian [t (9) = 2.36, $p < 0.05$], but not in Dutch and German.

In addition, a significant main effect for relative clause type was found, F (1, 19) = 6.72, $p < 0.04$. As Table 3 shows, participants in both groups read subject relatives significantly faster than object relatives in Dutch [t (9) = -3.98, $p < 0.01$] and [t (9) = -3.09, $p < 0.02$]. Moreover, participants in both groups read subject relatives significantly faster than object relatives in German [t (9) = -2.87, $p < 0.02$] and [t (9) = -2.92, $p < 0.02$], but not in Norwegian. In addition, no significant differences were found between the group with the early stage L3 learners and the group with the more advanced L3 learners in mean sentence reading of subject- and object relatives in Dutch, German, and Norwegian.

Language	Group 1	Group 1	Group 2	Group 2
	SR[a]	OR[b]	SR	OR
Dutch	5257 (331)	5534 (412)	5201 (328)	5445 (449)
German	6148 (372)	6476 (464)	6182 (396)	6454 (476)
Norwegian	6604 (557)	6837 (618)	6461 (553)	6704 (327)

Table 3 Overview of the mean sentence reading time in milliseconds per type of relative clause in Dutch, German and Norwegian. The group with the early stage L3 learners (group 1) is compared to the group with the more advanced L3 learners (group 2)

Note.
[a] SR = Subject Relative.
[b] OR = Object Relative.

Finally, no significant main effect for animacy was found, $F\,(1, 19) = 2.09$, $p > .15$. However, the analysis of the relative clauses with animate objects compared to inanimate objects per language showed that participants read relative clauses with inanimate objects significantly faster than relative clauses with animate objects in both Dutch [$t\,(19) = -4.97$, $p < 0.002$] and German [$t\,(19) = -6.59$, $p < 0.001$], but not in Norwegian.

3. Filler sentences

An ANOVA on the mean reading time of the filler sentences in Dutch, German, and Norwegian was conducted. A significant main effect for language was found, $F\,(2, 18) = 82.17$, $p < 0.001$. The analysis of the filler sentences showed a significant difference in mean sentence reading time between the languages in both groups. The early stage L3 learners read the filler sentences significantly faster in Dutch compared to German [$t\,(9) = -10.68$, $p < 0.001$] and Norwegian [$t\,(9) = -9.47$, $p < 0.001$]. Moreover, participants read the filler sentences significantly faster in German compared to Norwegian [$t\,(9) = -2.89$, $p < 0.02$]. The more advanced L3 learners also read the filler sentences significantly faster in Dutch than in German [$t\,(9) = -10.18$, $p < 0.001$] and Norwegian [$t\,(9) = -9.37$, $p < 0.001$]. However, no significant differences in mean sentence reading time were found for German compared to Norwegian. Finally, the analysis of the filler sentences showed that no significant difference in mean sentence reading time was found between the two groups in all languages.

Reading span task

The mean total score on the Norwegian reading span task was 59.3 ($SD = 6.3$) for the early stage L3 learners and 62.8 ($SD = 5.6$) for the more advanced

L3 learners. The analysis of the Norwegian reading span task showed that the more advanced L3 learners performed significantly better than the less skilled L3 learners [t (9) = 2.61, $p < 0.03$]. A Pearson correlation was conducted between the scores on the Norwegian reading span task and the comprehension scores on the relative clause tasks in Dutch, German, and Norwegian. No significant correlations were found between the total score on the Norwegian reading span task and the total comprehension score on the relative clause tasks in Dutch, German, and Norwegian.

Number ordering

The mean total score on number ordering was 13.9 (SD = .4) for the less skilled L3 learners and 14.2 (SD = .6) for the more advanced L3 learners. Paired-samples t-tests showed that this difference was not significant. In addition, a Pearson correlation was conducted between the total score on the number ordering task and the total comprehension scores on the relative clause tasks in all three languages. Again, no significant correlations were found.

Discussion

In this study, adults, who are at an early stage of L3- and adults, who are at a more advanced stage of L3 acquisition were compared in the processing of subject- and object relatives. The L3 acquisition of relative clauses in Germanic languages is a new research topic. So far, only one study was conducted by Flynn, Foley, and Vinnitskaya (2004). Contrary to their study, we focused both on differences in relative clauses comprehension and speed of processing in L1, L2, and L3. In addition, we wanted to investigate the role of working memory in third language acquisition of relative clauses. To investigate this, not only a relative clause task in all languages, but also two working memory tests were conducted. We used the reading span task (Van den Noort et al. submitted), which is a typical verbal working memory test, and a number ordering test, which is a less language based working memory task. Which working memory theory (the SSIR- or the capacity theory) is better able to explain our experimental results?

With respect to relative clauses comprehension, it was expected that both for the early stage L3 learners and the more advanced L3 learners no significant differences in relative clauses comprehension between L1 and L2 would be found. For the more advanced L3 learners this would also be the case in L3. For the early stage L3 learners, however, significant differences in relative clauses comprehension between L1/L2 on the one hand and L3 on the other hand were expected. The results of the verification statements after all sentences (both experimental- and filler sentences) showed that all participants performed well on the Dutch- and German relative clause task, showing that they understood both the filler sentences and the sentences with relative clauses constructions. As we expected according to our hypothesis, the more advanced L3 learners performed well on the Norwegian relative clause task, but the early stage L3 learners did not. Conform our hypotheses, for the more advanced L3 learners and the early stage L3 learners no significant differences in relative clauses comprehension were found on the Dutch and German relative clause task. On the Norwegian relative clause task the more advanced L3 learners performed well, whereas the early stage L3 learners did not. This is what we could expect according to our selection criteria. Finally, as we expected, for the early stage L3 learners, significant differences in relative clauses comprehension between L1/L2 on the one hand and L3 on the other hand were found. However, it seems that the early stage L3 learners had difficulties with understanding the Norwegian sentences in general since they also had problems with the filler sentences.

With respect to processing speed of relative clauses, it was expected that both the early stage L3 learners and the more advanced L3 learners read sentences with relative clauses fastest in L1 followed by L2 and L3. The reading time results showed that this was indeed the case. Moreover, it was expected that the more advanced L3 learners process relative clauses in L3 significantly faster than the early stage L3 learners and that was also what we found. In line with previous research on processing speed of relative clauses in Germanic languages (Mak 2001; Vos et al. 2001), it was expected that for both groups in L1 and L2; subject relatives are processed faster than object relatives. The results showed that in L1 and L2, the participants in both groups indeed read sentences containing subject relatives significantly faster than sentences containing object relatives. We expected that this would also be the case for the more advanced L3 learners, whereas for the early stage L3 learners, on the one hand, a significant difference between subject and object relatives could be expected since early stage L3 learners still process subject relatives faster than object relatives. On the other hand, it could also have been the case that for the early stage L3 learners, the difference between subject and object relatives is not significant since both sentence types are very difficult to process, because of the early stage of foreign language acquisition. Contrary to our hypothesis in L3, none of our participants read subject relatives significantly faster than object relatives in Norwegian, independent of language proficiency. Finally, in line with previous findings (Mak et al. 2002), any differences in reading time between sentences with subject relatives and object relatives were only expected for relative clauses with animate objects and not for inanimate objects in all languages. Strangely, in this study, these results could not be replicated.

Differences between subject- and object relatives were found both for animate- and inanimate objects in L1 and L2. Whereas in L3, no differences were found both for relative clauses with animate- and inanimate objects. With respect to this, it is important to note that we used the same L1 (Dutch) as in the original study.

To investigate the role of working memory in third language acquisition of relative clauses, a correlation test was conducted between the scores on the working memory tasks and the comprehension scores on the relative clause task in L1, L2, and L3. The SSIR theory (Waters and Caplan 1996) would predict no significant correlation between the scores on the working memory tasks and the comprehension scores on the relative clause task in all languages. According to this theory, any individual difference in working memory capacity should not interfere with the processing of complex sentences. In contrast to the SSIR theory, the capacity theory (Just and Carpenter 1992) would at least predict a correlation between the working memory tests and the comprehension scores on the relative clause task in L1. A Pearson correlation was conducted between the total score on the Norwegian reading span task and the total comprehension score on the relative clause task in Dutch, German, and Norwegian. In this study, no significant correlations were found for all languages. In addition, a Pearson correlation was conducted between the total score on the number ordering task and the total comprehension score on the relative clause task in Dutch, German, and Norwegian. Again, no significant correlations were found. These results are in line with the SSIR theory.

There are, however, some restrictions within this multilingual study. First, it would have been better if the L3 acquisition of the participants in this study had even been better controlled for. In this study, care was taken that only participants with the same native- and second language background were selected. Moreover, all the participants had followed a Norwegian language course and stayed in Norway for 6 months for the early stage L3 learners and for more than 3 years for the more advanced L3 learners. However, factors like the exact amount of acquisition and motivation were not completely controlled for. Although these are indeed important factors; it was not possible to further control these factors due to practical reasons.

Moreover, care was taken that the languages of investigation were all Germanic languages, but there was still a small difference, since Norwegian is a North Germanic language, whereas Dutch and German are West Germanic languages (König and Van der Auwera 1994). In future research it would be interesting to replicate this study with either an even closer related language than Norwegian and/or with a language that is not related to the West Germanic languages. This could give us more information on how important the L1 and L2 transfer factor is in the processing of subject- and object relatives in the different stages of L3 acquisition. With respect to the present study there was a difference between the three languages with respect to case. German has a more active case system than Dutch and Norwegian and perhaps this has influenced our relative clauses reading time results?

In addition, we wanted to investigate the role of working memory in third language acquisition of relative clauses. We decided to use the reading span task, which is a typical language based working memory test (Van den Noort et al. submitted), and a number ordering test, which is a less language based working memory task. Although the number ordering test is less language based than the reading span task, there is, of course, still a language component. Participants have to write down their answers and they can internally verbalize their answers. On the other hand, it will be difficult to find a working memory test that is completely language independent.

For future research it would also be interesting to conduct a follow-up study with the same participants; to investigate whether the mean reading time of sentences with relative clauses in the L3 improves towards the L1 and/or L2 level. This is what could be expected, since second language acquisition is not a static, but a dynamic process (Wang et al., in press). With respect to this it could also be interesting to conduct a follow-up study by using another methodology, for example, a production paradigm instead of a reading paradigm.

Finally, it would be highly interesting to conduct both an functional- and a structural MRI-study on the multilingual processing of relative clauses during the process of L3 acquisition. Perhaps both functional- and structural differences in the brain between the early stage- and the more advanced L3 learners can be found? This might be expected because recently, a structural bilingualism study showed that the acquisition of a second language increases the density of grey matter in the left inferior partietal cortex (Mechelli et al. 2004; Van den Noort et al. 2005).

Appendix A

For every language (Dutch, German, and Norwegian) there were four different conditions: The first sentence contained a subject relative clause with an animate object, the second sentence contained an object relative clause with an animate object, the third sentence contained a subject relative clause with an inanimate object, and the fourth sentence contained an object relative clause with an inanimate object. The fifth- and sixth sentences are examples of two filler sentences.

Norwegian examples of the four experimental conditions:

1) I sykehuset blir den nye legen, som har fått store feil med pasientene, besøkt av mange journalister.

(In the hospital, the new doctor, who has made large mistakes with patients, was visited by many journalists.)

2) I dag får elevene, som læreren har undervist etter vinterferie, mye verdsetting av rektoren.
(Today, the pupils, whom the teacher has taught after the winter holiday, received a lot of praise from the director.)

3) I går reiste generalen, som har gjort topografiske kart i stand etter øvingen, til kasernen i Stavanger.
(Yesterday, the general, who fixed the topographical cards after the exercise, traveled to the base in Stavanger.)

4) Noen mener at prekene, som kardinalen har gitt i domkirken, blir for mye for de troende.
(Some people think that the preaches, which the cardinal has given in the cathedral, were too much for the believers.)

Norwegian examples of two filler sentences:

5) En 76 år gammel kvinne ble i går kveld alvorlig skadet i en kollisjon på E6 i Soknedal.
(A 76 years old woman was severely injured in a collision at the E6 in Soknedal, yesterday evening.)

6) Det er nesten dobbelt så mange med psykiske lidelser blant fremmedkulturelle som etniske nordmenn.
(There are almost twice as many people with psychological disorders among foreigners than among ethnic Norwegians.)

Acknowledgments

The authors would like to thank the Max Planck Institute for Psycholinguistics in Nijmegen, the Netherlands for allowing the use of the CELEX lexical database.

References

Baddeley, A. D. 1999. *Human Memory: Theory and Practice.* Hove: Psychology Press.

Caplan, D., Alpert, N. and Waters, G. 1999. PET studies of syntactic processing with auditory sentence presentation. *NeuroImage* 9: 343-351.

Caplan, D. and Waters, G. S. 1995. Aphasic disorders of syntactic comprehension and working memory capacity. *Cognitive Neuropsychology* 12: 637-649.

Caplan, D. 1999. Verbal working memory and sentence comprehension. *Behavioral and Brain Sciences* 22: 77-126.

Chomsky, N. 1965. *Aspects of the theory of syntax*. Cambridge, M.A.: MIT Press.

Clancy, P. M., Lee, H. and Zoh, M. H. 1986. Processing strategies in the acquisition of relative clauses: Universal principles and language-specific realizations. *Cognition* 24: 225-262.

Demuth, K. 1995. Questions, relatives, and minimal projection. *Language Acquisition* 4: 49-71.

Desmette, D., Hupet, M., Schelstraete, M. A. and Van der Linden, M. 1995. Adaptation en langue française du 'Reading Span Test' de Daneman et Carpenter. *L'Annee Psychologique* 95: 459-482.

Felser, C., Roberts, L., Marinis, T. and Gross, R. 2003. The processing of ambiguous sentences by first and second language learners of English. *Applied Psycholinguistics* 24: 453-489.

Flynn, S. 1983. A Study of the Effects of Principal Branching Direction in Second Language Acquisition: The Generalization of a Parameter of Universal Grammar from First to Second Language Acquisition. PhD thesis, Cornell University.

—. 1987. *A Parameter-Setting Model of L2 Acquisition: Experimental Studies in Anaphora.* Dordrecht: Reidel.

Flynn, S., Foley, C. and Vinnitskaya, I. 2004. The Cumulative-Enhancement Model for Language Acquisition: Comparing Adults' and Children's Patterns of Development in First, Second and Third Language Acquisition of Relative Clauses. *International Journal of Multilingualism* 1: 3-16.

Flynn, S. and Lust, B. 1981. Acquisition of relative clauses in English. *Cornell Working Papers in Linguistics, 1*, 1. Ithaca, NY: Department of Modern Languages and Linguistics, Cornell University.

Fodor, J. A. 1983. *Modularity of mind*. Cambridge, M.A.: MIT Press.

Frazier, L. 1987. Sentence processing: A tutorial review. In *Attention and performance XII: The psychology of reading*, edited by M. Coltheart, 559-586. Hillsdale, N.J.: Erlbaum.

Goodluck, H. and Tavakolian, S. 1982. Competence and processing in children's grammar of relative clauses. *Cognition* 11: 1-27.

Grodzinsky, Y., Pinango, M., Zurif, E. and Drai, D. 1999. The critical role of group studies in neuropsychology: comprehension regularities in Broca's aphasia. *Brain and Language* 67 (2): 134-147.

Hamburger, H. 1980. A deletion ahead of its time. *Cognition* 8: 389-416.

Hamburger, H. and Crain, S. 1982. Relative acquisition. In *Language Development.* Vol. 1, *Syntax and Semantics*, edited by S. Kuczaj, 245-274. Hillsdale, NJ: Erlbaum.

Hsiao, F. and Gibson, E. 2003. Processing relative clauses in Chinese. *Cognition* 90: 3-27.

Hsu, C. 2004. Revisiting the processing of pre-nominal relative clauses in Chinese. MA thesis, University of Delaware.

Just, M. A. and Carpenter, P. A. 1987. *The psychology of reading and language comprehension.* Newton, M.A.: Allyn & Bacon.

Just, M. A. and Carpenter, P. A. 1992. A capacity theory of comprehension: Individual differences in working memory. *Psychological Review* 99: 122-149.

Just, M. A., Carpenter, P. A. and Keller, T. A. 1996a. The capacity theory of comprehension: New frontiers of evidence and arguments. *Psychological Review* 4: 773-780.

Just, M. A., Carpenter, P. A., Keller, T. A., Eddy, W. and Thulborn, K. 1996b. Brain activation modulated by sentence comprehension. *Science* 274 (5284): 114-116.

Kidd, E. and Bavin, E. L. 2002. English-speaking children's comprehension of relative clauses: Evidence for general-cognitive and language specific constraints on development. *Journal of Psycholinguistic Research* 31 (6): 599-617.

King, J. W. and Just, M. A. 1991. Individual differences in syntactic processing: The role of working memory. *Journal of Memory and Language* 30: 580-602.

King, J. W. and Kutas, M. 1995. Who did what and when? Using word- and clause-level ERPs to monitor working memory usage in reading. *Journal of Cognitive Neuroscience* 7: 376-395.

König, E. and Van der Auwera, J. 1994. *The Germanic Languages.* London: Routledge.

Lust, B., Chien, Y-C. and Flynn, S. 1987. What children know: Methods for the study of first language acquisition. In *Studies in the Acquisition of Anaphora, Volume 2: Applying the Constraints*, edited by B. Lust, 271-356. Dordrecht: Reidel.

Lust, B., Flynn, S. and Foley, C. 1996. What children know about what they say: Elicited imitation as a research method for assessing children's syntax. In *Methods for Assessing Children's Syntax*, edited by D. McDaniel, C. McKee and H. S. Cairns, 55-76. Cambridge, MA: MIT Press.

MacDonald, M. C. and Christiansen, M. H. 2002. Reassessing Working Memory: Comment on Just and Carpenter (1992) and Waters and Caplan (1996). *Psychological Review* 109: 35-54.

Mak, W. M. 2001. Processing Relative Clauses: Effects of Pragmatic, Semantic, and Syntactic Variables. PhD thesis, Radboud University Nijmegen.

Mak, W. M., Vonk, W. and Schriefers, H. J. 2002. The influence of animacy on relative clause processing. *Journal of Memory and Language* 47: 50-68.

McKee, C. and McDaniel, D. 2001. Resumptive pronouns in English relative clauses. *Language Acquisition* 9: 113-156.

Mechelli, A., Crinion, J. T., Noppeney, U., O'Doherty, J., Ashburner, J., Frackowiak, R. S. and Price, C. J. 2004. Structural plasticity in the bilingual brain. *Nature*: 757.

Mecklinger, A., Schriefers, H., Steinhauer, K. and Friederici, A. D. 1995. Processing relative clauses varying on syntactic and semantic dimensions: An analysis with event-related potentials. *Memory & Cognition* 23: 477-494.

Miller, G. A. and Chomsky, N. 1963. Finitary models of language users. In *Handbook of Mathematical Psychology*, edited by D. Luce, R. Bush and E. Galanter, 419-492. New York: Wiley.

Miyake, A., Carpenter, P. A. and Just, M. A. 1995. Reduced resources and specific impairments in normal and aphasic sentence comprehension. *Cognitive Neuropsychology* 12: 651-679.

Müller, H. M., King, J. W. and Kutas, M. 1997. Event-related potentials elicited by spoken relative clauses. *Cognitive Brain Research* 5: 193-203.

Omaki, A. 2005. Working memory and relative clause attachment in first and second language processing. MA thesis, University of Hawaii.

Papadopoulou, D. and Clahsen, H. 2003. Parsing strategies in L1 and L2 sentence processing: A study of relative clause attachment in Greek. *Studies in Second Language Acquisition* 25: 501-528.

Schneider, W., Eschman, A. and Zuccolotto, A. 2002. *E-Prime reference guide.* Pittsburgh: Psychology Software Tools Inc.

Schriefers, H., Friederici, A. D. and Kühn, K. 1995. The processing of locally ambiguous relative clauses in German. *Journal of Memory and Language* 34: 499-520.

Schuele, C. M. and Nicholls, L. M. 2000. Relative clauses: Evidence of continued linguistic vulnerability in children with specific language impairment. *Clinical Linguistics and Phonetics* 14: 563-585.

Van den Noort, M. W. M. L., Bosch, M. P. C., Haverkort, M. and Hugdahl, K. submitted. The reading span test: A standard computerized version. *International Journal of Testing*.

Van den Noort, M. W. M. L., Nordby, H., Bosch, M. P. C. and Hugdahl, K. 2005. Understanding Second Language Acquisition: Can Structural MRI bring the Breakthrough? *Proceedings of the International Conference on Cognitive Systems*. New Delhi: NIIT.

Van Gompel, R. P. G. 1995. The processing of subject and object relative clauses in Dutch. MA thesis, Radboud University Nijmegen.

Vingerhoets, G., Van Borsel, J., Tesink, C., Van den Noort, M. W. M. L., Deblaere, K., Seurinck, R., Vandemaele, P. and Achten, E. 2003. Multilingualism: An fMRI study. *NeuroImage* 20: 2181-2196.

Vos, S. H., Gunter, T. C., Schriefers, H. and Friederici, A. D. 2001. Syntactic parsing and working memory: The effects of syntactic complexity, reading span, and concurrent load. *Language and Cognitive Processes* 16: 65-103.

Wang, Y., Jongman, A. and Sereno, J. A. in press. L2 acquisition and processing of Mandarin Chinese tones. In *Handbook of Chinese Psycholinguistics*, edited by E. Bates, L. H. Tan and O. Tseng. Cambridge, U.K.: Cambridge University Press.

Waters, G. S. and Caplan, D. 1996. The capacity theory of sentence comprehension: Critique of Just and Carpenter (1992). *Psychological Review* 4: 761-772.

CHAPTER 11

A PARALLEL DEVELOPMENTAL SEQUENCE (PDS) MODEL IN SECOND LANGUAGE ACQUISITION (SLA)

Yong Myeong Kim and Oryang Kwon

For the last quarter of the century, research on Second Language Acquisition (SLA) has explored what has come to be known as both the logical problems (Hornstein & Lightfoot, 1981) and the developmental problems (Flex, 1984) to SLA[1]. In fact, UG-based SLA theories on Universal Grammar (Chomsky, 1986) have surely given a valid explanatory power to the logical problems, and sequence-based SLA theories on language processing have provided reasonable explanations for the developmental problems. However, Gregg (1996, p.74) pointed out that there is a serious imbalance between SLA research on the logical problems and on the developmental problems, and that there should be an interface between these two theories. Thus, considering the pictures drawn by the research to date, it can be argued that each theory has its own complementary limitations to each other in that UG-based SLA research has some limitations to explain the developmental problems, whereas sequence-based SLA research has difficulties in explaining the logical problems.

On the other hand, from the perspectives of language knowledge, there is a debate as to whether or not declarative knowledge and procedural knowledge are interfaced with each other in interlanguage (IL) development. Anderson proposed the Adaptive Control of Thought Models (1976, 1980, 1983) based on the distinction between declarative and procedural knowledge. He argued in his Models that declarative knowledge is converted into procedural knowledge through three stages (i.e., the declarative, the associative, and the autonomous stage). For Anderson, procedural knowledge accounts for how learners accumulate and automatise rules and how they restructure their internal representations. As opposed to Anderson's interface position, Paradis (1994) argued for the dissociation of procedural and declarative knowledge on neuropsychological evidence. Similarly, Squire (1992) maintained that the two knowledge bases are qualitatively different and non-interfaced. Until recently, such arguments and counter-arguments on the question of whether or not declarative and procedural knowledge are interfaced have remained unsettled and will go on for the time being. Thus, an alternative we are taking in all this is to consider the possibility that declarative and procedural knowledge take on complementary roles for IL development.

A question can be raised as to how each theory which provides explanatory power for its own domain but has complementary limitations to the other domain related to IL development can come to be in complementary relations with each other for explaining IL developmental processes.

In order to explore this question, the present study will propose three separate L2 developmental modules, i.e., (a) Procedural Developmental Sequence, (b) Syntactic Developmental Sequence, and (c) Morphological Developmental Sequence. Each of these modules will be derived from the Developmental Sequence by Pienemann and Johnston (1987), the Minimal Tree Hypothesis by Vainikka and Young-Scholten (1998), and the Processability Theory of Pienemann (1998) respectively. By integrating these three separate modules into one according to the Modular Approach (Ellis, 1994; Gregg, 1996; Pienemann, 1998; White, 1989), the present study will also propose a modular model called the Parallel Developmental Sequence (PDS) Model as illustrated in Figure 1.

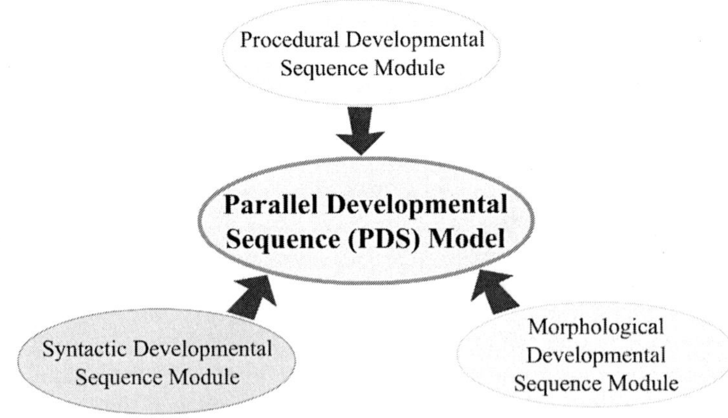

Figure 1. Parallel Developmental Sequence (PDS) Model

In essence, the PDS Model will constitute implicational Parallel Developmental Stages (1X, 2X, $1X^2$, ..., $1X^3$, ..., kX^n.), each of which incorporates three different dimensions of sequential development: the

Procedural, the Syntactic, and the Morphological Developmental Sequence. On the logic of the parallel connections of the Parallel Distributed Processing Model (Rumelhart, McClelland & PDP Research Group, 1986), one of three sub-stages of a Parallel Stage is assumed to be activated first, and then interconnected, and finally synchronized with each other through the synchronization process. Thus, the PDS will allow the complementary limitations to have complementary explanations for each other module, and hence it will have an interface between the three sub-developmental sequences. Therefore, the PDS is on the assumption that L2 learners at any Parallel Stage will first activate one of the three parallel mechanisms (i.e., the procedural, the syntactic, and the unificational mechanism), and then interconnect, and finally synchronize each other only to move to the next stage of the PDS, and, by repeating these processes recursively, to pass through all the stages of the PDS up to the last Parallel Stage kX^n.

The question then is whether or not the theoretically built Parallel Developmental Stages of the PDS does reflect the actual developmental stages of L2 learners. The PDS Model thus will be put to the test by empirical research on Sentence Construction Tests through a real-time experimental method called the Flash Window Method, which is specially devised to elicit more spontaneous responses from L2 learners in real time. Finally, the results and implications will be discussed.

Three Sub-Developmental Sequences (Modules)

In this section, Pienemann and Johnston's Sequence (1987), Vainikka and Young-Scholten's Sequence (1998), and Pienemann's Morpheme Processability (1998) will be examined and three separate developmental sequences will be proposed.

1. Procedural Developmental Sequence (ProDS)

Based on the Multidimensional Model from the Zweitsprachenerwerb Italienischer und Spanischer Arbeiter Projekt (Meisel, Clahsen & Pienemann, 1981; Clahsen, Meisel & Pienemann, 1983), Pienemann and Johnston (1987) suggested the Developmental Sequence for English as a Second Language (ESL). The Sequence can be summarized as illustrated in Table 1.

Stages	SPS			Critical Structures	Examples
	[COS]	[IFS]	[SCS]		
X	+	•	•	Canonical SVO	[I kissed Mary] yesterday.
X+1	+	+	+	Adv/Do/Wh/-Fronting	*In the park,* [I kissed Mary] __.
X+2	-	+	+	Aux-en/-ing, Y/N-Inversion	Did [you kiss(-*ed*) Mary]?
X+3	-	-	+	Aux/Do-2nd, 3sg-S	Who *did* [you kiss(=*ed*) _] yesterday?
X+4	-	-	-	2-Sub-Comp, Subordinate Clauses	[I don't know [whether I'll retire here]].

Table 1. The Developmental Sequence of English as a Second Language

As seen in Table 1, the Sequence consists of five implicational stages of X, X+1, X+2, X+3, and X+4 on the hierarchical combinations of three components of the Speech Processing Strategies (SPSs) proposed by Clahsen (1984), which act as constraints on IL development. Therefore, IL learners pass through from one stage to the subsequent on the Sequence only if they can operate the SPS imposed hierarchically on each stage. In this respect, the SPS can function as a procedural mechanism for determining an IL developmental sequence of what Anderson (1976) calls procedural knowledge. Thus, the Sequence can be considered as the first procedural developmental sequence on procedural mechanisms, and therefore can provide a reasonable explanation for what has come to be known as developmental problems to SLA (Flex, 1984).

However, with all its contributions to SLA, the Sequence is too sparse to explain the IL developmental processes of embedded clauses in stages higher than Stage X+4. Consider the following embedded clauses.

(1) a. I know that John loved Mary at that time.
b. I wonder who loved Mary at that time.
c. I know the girl whom John loved at that time.
d. Do you know who John loved at that time?
e. Who do you think John loved at that time?

Since all the examples in (1) contain embedded clauses, they are represented by [-COS], [-IFS], and [-SCS] according to the SPS as seen in Table 1, and hence they are the structures belonging to Stage X+4. What this implies is that the examples (1a-1e) all belong to the same developmental stage, thereby assuming that their processing complexity will also be the same. Even though all the examples of (4) have embedded clauses, there will be some differences in the degrees of procedural complexity, depending on whether the embedded clause in question is an object of a matrix verb, a relative, an indirect-question, and this is compatible with our linguistic intuition. Thus, these differences should also be represented on the developmental sequence of procedural knowledge.

As a possible prescription for this limitation, this study proposes the Speech Processing Mechanisms (SPM) which consists of three components (i.e., [αIFM], [βCOM], [γSCM]) derived from the SPS of Clahsen (1984), and makes an operational definition for each of the three components so as to formalize the values of the variables α, β, and γ as seen in (2).

(2) SPM (Speech Processing Mechanisms)

(a) [αIFM]: Initialization Finalization Mechanism

[αIFM] is a mechanism operating on constituent movements to realize grammatical changes and sentential forces. Hence, the variable α of [αIFM] will have a positive value (+) if a certain constituent moves from an internal position to an external position, and vice versa, and the variable α will have a negative value (-) if one moves from an internal position to another internal position within a sentence.

(b) [βCOM]: Canonical Order Mechanism

[βCOM] is a mechanism operating on word order changes within a sentence. Hence, the variable β of [βCOM] will have a positive value (+) if no change takes place in the canonical order, and the variable β will have a negative value (-) if any change takes place in the order as a result of the movements of any constituent.

(c) [γSCM]: Sentence Combination Mechanism

[γSCM] is a mechanism operating on an embedded clause when more than two sentences are combined to form a complex sentence. Hence, as a result of combining two sentences, the variable γ of [γSCM] will have a positive value (+) if a certain constituent moves only within the embedded clause, and the variable γ will have a negative value (-) if one moves to the outside of the embedded clause, i.e., moves to the matrix.

In a nutshell, the SPM in (2) is a mechanism that can quantify the degrees of constituent movements and word order changes to realize grammatical changes (e.g. modality, tense) and sentential forces (e.g. declaratives, interrogatives). First, [αIFM] in (2a) is a mechanism whose operation depends on whether or not there is a movement of constituents, and if there is, whether it is a single movement (when the grammatical change can be completed with one movement) or a double movement (when the grammatical change can not be completed with one movement, another movement is induced) as seen in (3a-3b) below. Second, [βCOM] in (2b) is a mechanism governing whether or not there is a word order change in a sentence as a result of an operation on [αIFM] as seen in (3c-3d) below. Finally, [γSCM] in (2c) is a mechanism whose operation depends on whether or not there is a movement within an embedded clause, and if it is, whether the final destination (the landing site) of the movement is within or without the embedded clause (i.e., moves to the matrix) as seen in (3e-3f) below.

(3)a. Can [you _ do it]? ([+IFM])
 b. What are [you _ doing _] now? ([-IFM])
 c. Yesterday, [John kissed Mary] ___. ([+COM])
 d. What are [you _ doing _] now? ([-COM])
 e. [Do you know [who(m) Mary loved __ at that time]]? [+SCM])
 f. [Who(m) do you think [__ Mary loved __ at that time]]? ([-SCM])

Thus, the processing complexity of utterances can be quantified by each variable value of the three components of the SPM. Therefore, the SPM can play a role as a procedural mechanism governing the IL developmental sequence of procedural knowledge. However, the SPM itself can not determine the IL developmental stages of procedural knowledge.

Thus, in order for a procedural developmental stage to be sequentialized, this study deviss a set of developmental-stage-functions called the SPM functions, which are formularized in a form of implicational recursive connection combinations of three components of the SPM as seen in (4).

(4) Developmental-Stage Functions (SPM functions)
 a. SPM $f(\alpha, \beta)$ = [αIFM]/ [βCOM]
 b. SPM $f(\alpha, \beta, \gamma)$ = [γSCM ([αIFM]/ [βCOM]) *]
 ('*' indicates that [([αIFM]/ [βCOM]) is recursive. The value of variable α, β, and γ is '+' or '-')

(4a), as serial connection combinations of [αIFM] and [βCOM] among the SPM's three components, is the SPM function of non-embedded clauses, which can quantify the procedural complexity of simple or matrix clauses, and according to which the developmental sequence of simple or matrix clauses can be ordered into stages. On the other hand, (4b), as implicational recursive connection combinations of the components derived from inserting the serial combinations of (4a), i.e., the '[αIFM]/[βCOM],' into the implicational components of the '[γSCM [/]*]', is the SPM function of embedded clauses, which can quantify the procedural complexity of embedded clauses, and depending on which the developmental sequence of embedded clauses can be ordered into stages.

First, consider how the developmental sequence of non-embedded clauses can be ordered into stages. The substitution of the values ('+' or '-') of the variables α and β hierarchically for the function of non-embedded clauses (i.e., 4a) can result in four types of [αIFM]/[βCOM] combinations as seen in Table 2. Depending on these implicational values of the SPM combinations, the procedural complexity of non-embedded clauses can be quantified, and consequently the developmental stages of simple or matrix sentences can be sequentialised in the order of '1x', '2x', '3x', and '4x'.

SPM *f* (α, β) =	[α IFM]/[β COM]	Stages
If α = ・, β = +,	・/+	1x
If α = +, β = +,	+/+	2x
If α = +, β = −,	+/−	3x
If α = −, β = −,	−/−	4x

Table 2. Developmental Sequence for Non-embedded Sentences

(' ・ ' indicates non-application of the component in question.)

Now, let us examine how the developmental sequence of embedded clauses can be ordered into stages. Five types of [SCM([IFM]/[COM])] combinations can be derived from the substitution of the values of variable α, β, and γ hierarchically for the SPM function of embedded clauses (i.e., 4b) as shown in Table 3. According to these implicational values of the SPM combinations, the procedural complexity of embedded clauses can be quantified, and therefore the developmental stages of embedded clauses can be sequentialised in the order of '$1x^2$', '$2x^2$', '$3x^2$', '$4x^2$', '$5x^2$'.

SPM *f* (α, β, γ) =	[γ SCM([α IFM]/[β COM])]	Stages
If α= ・, β= +, γ= ・,	[・ ([・ /+])]	$1x^2$
If α= +, β= +, γ= +,	[+ ([+/+])]	$2x^2$
If α= +, β= −, γ= +,	[+ ([+/−])]	$3x^2$
If α= −, β= −, γ= +,	[+ ([−/−])]	$4x^2$
If α= −, β= −, γ= −,	[− ([−/−])]	$5x^2$

Table 3. Developmental Sequence for Embedded Sentences

(' ・ ' indicates non-application of the component in question.)

On the other hand, since a complex sentence consists of a matrix and embedded clauses, the developmental stage of a complex sentence can be formalized by combining that of the matrix clause by the simple SPM function (4a) and those of the embedded clauses by the embedded SPM function (4b).

Thus the developmental stages of complex sentences can be represented in the form 'kx^n+kx^{n-1}... kx' (here, 'n' is the number of embedded clauses). According to the SPM functions discussed so for, a developmental stage can be assigned to each sentence of the above examples (1) as follows: (1a) is represented as '$1x^2+1x$', (1b) as '$2x^2+1x$', (1c) as '$3x^2+1x$', (1d) as '$4x^2+3x$', and (1e) as '$5x^2+3x$', respectively.

To sum up, the SPM can quantify the relative procedural complexity of the construction and the processing of utterances. In addition, the SPM functions not only determine an IL developmental sequence of procedural knowledge called Procedural Developmental Sequence (ProDS), but also predict the critical structures and the error patterns at each stage of the ProDS as illustrated in Table 4. Thus, the SPM, its functions and the ProDS can extend beyond Pienemann and Johnston's Sequence to constructing the developmental stages of embedded clauses, and provide a clear definition, or at least an operational one for what Anderson calls the procedural knowledge as well as a theoretical framework for the sequence-based SLA research.

Stages		**Procedural Developmental Sequence**			
		SPM $f(\alpha, \beta)$ = [αIFM]/[βCOM]	**SPM $f(\alpha, \beta, \gamma)$ = [γSCM([αIFM]/[βCOM])*]**	**Critical Structures**	**Error Patterns**
Simple Sentence	**1x**	[· /+]	•	SVO	...
	2x	[+/+]	•	*Adv/wh/Do*-fronting	...
	3x	[+/−]	•	*Aux-en/-ing*, Y/N-Inv, Comp-to	...
	4x	[−/−]	•	*wh*-questions	...
Complex Sentence	**$1x^2$**	[±/±]	[· (· /+])]	*that*-clause, 2-Sub-Comp,	...
	$2x^2$	[±/±]	[+ ([+/+])]	Indirect-question/Relatives (subject)	...
	$3x^2$	[±/±]	[+ ([+/−])]	Relatives (object)	...
	$4x^2$	[±/±]	[+ ([−/−])]	Indirect-question (object)	...
	$5x^2$	[±/±]	[− ([−/−])]	Long distance-questions	...
Double Complex Sentence	⋮	⋮	⋮	⋮	⋮
	kx^n	±/±	(±/±)+(±/±)+...	•••	...

Table 4. Procedural Developmental Sequence on the SPM

However, as Pienemann (1998, p. 51) pointed out, the SPM and its functions cannot play a "grammar" role in the explanation of the IL development of linguistic knowledge (i.e., grammaticality) on the ProDS. For example, at Procedural Stage $2x^2$, the operation of SPM [+SCM([+IFS]/[+COM])] can predict critical structures such as subject indirect-questions and relatives clauses (see Table 4.). However, this SPM in itself can not explain the grammaticality inherent in such structures. From this point of view, it might be more accurate to say that the ProDS represents the sequence of the SPM itself rather than that of grammatical knowledge. Therefore, the ProDS needs to be in a complementary relation to a syntactic developmental sequence on syntactic mechanisms as in the studies of Vainikka and Young-Scholten (1994, 1996, 1998).

2.Syntactic Developmental Sequence (SynDS)

Vainikka and Young-Scholten (1994, 1996, 1998) studied the acquisition processes of L2 German on the Minimal Tree Approach. According to the results of the studies, Vainikka and Young-Scholten‘s Syntactic Sequence can be represented as in (5).

(5) Vainikka & Young-Scholten‘s Syntactic Sequence: VP → IP → CP

According to Vainikka and Young-Scholten, the Sequence (5) forms an implicational scale in which the emergence of IP requires the acquisition of VP and the development of CP is dependent on the previous acquisition of IP. In addition, this development is driven by interaction between UG (i.e., X-bar theory) and the L2 input. In this respect, Vainikka and Young-Scholten's Sequence can be regarded as the first syntactic IL developmental sequence on syntactic mechanisms. Thus, the Sequence can provide a significant explanation for the developmental problems as well as the logical problems to SLA, and hence it may give a possible interface for the UG-based and the sequence-based SLA research. However, despite such implications for SLA, the Sequence is too sparse to explain the developmental processes of double or multiple CP structures, and hence to sequentialise the developmental stages of these structures. Consider the following double CP structures in (6).

(6) a. Who(m) did Mary love at that time?
b. I wonder who loved Mary at that time.
c. I know the girl whom John loved at that time.
d. Do you know who(m) John loved at that time?
e. Who(m) do you think John loved at that time?

Since all the examples in (6) contain CP structures, they belong to the CP Stage on the Sequence in (5). This implies that the examples (6a-6e) are all at the same developmental stage, thereby assuming that their syntactic complexity will also be same. But, in spite of all the examples of (6) having CP structures, depending on whether the CP in question is a simple sentence or an embedded clause, and if it is an embedded, is it an object of a matrix verb, a relative clause, or an indirect question, there will be some differences in the degrees of the syntactic complexity, and this is compatible with the Minimal Three Approach. Thus, these differences should also be represented on the developmental sequence of the syntactic systems.

To overcome such a limitation, this study proposes a revised syntactic developmental sequence called the Syntactic Developmental Sequence (SynDS) as seen in (7), by drawing on Locality Condition (LC) [2] and Split-CP hypothesis[3]

(7) Syntactic Developmental Sequence (SynDS): V→VP→IP→FocP→CP*
('*' indicates that 'CP' is recursive.)

Schematically, the SynDS in (7) can be represented in terms of X-bar theory as in Figure 2, on each stage of which each relevant syntactic mechanism operates successively from the lowest local or minimal domain up to the highest local or minimal domain of the X-bar formats according to the logic of the LC. That is, the lexical-inserting mechanism is operating on the [V] domain, the theta-assigning mechanism (theta-criterion) is operating on the [VP] domain, the case-marking mechanism (Case-filter) on the [IP] domain, the force-realizing mechanism on the [FocP] domain, and the force-matching mechanism on the [CP*] domain. Thus, each syntactic mechanism operating on each local or minimal domain constitutes an implicational scale. It follows that the LC intertwined with X-bar theory has an important role in the construction of the SynDS in (7) above.

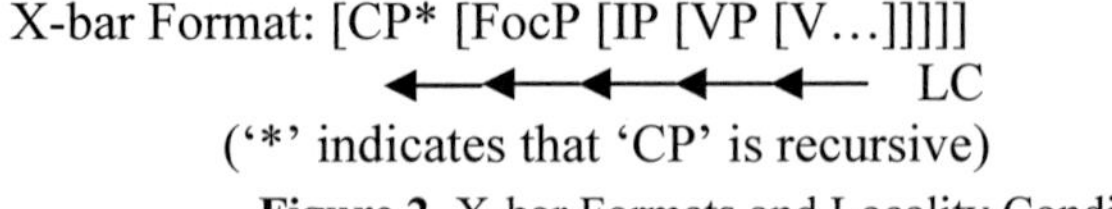

Figure 2. X-bar Formats and Locality Condition

Now, let us examine each stage of the SynDS in brief. First, the V Stage involves the operation of the lexical-inserting mechanism, resulting in the flat [SVO] structures with one-to-one correspondence of IL learners' conceptual structures to argument structures of predicates. The VP Stage involves the theta-assigning mechanism which assigns each relevant semantic role to each constituent of the VP including the subject based on the VP-internal subject hypothesis[4]. This is how the lexical projections are completed, resulting in the '[$_{VP}$ [$_{V}$'[V NP]]]' structures. The IP Stage is concerned with the case-marking mechanism which marks each relevant case to each constituent of IP by virtue of the A(rgument)/H(ead)-to-H(ead) movement (case-driven), and hence functional projections begin to develop, resulting in the '[$_{IP}$ [$_{I}$'[I] [$_{VP}$...]]]' structures. The FocP Stage hinges on the operation of the force-realizing mechanism by which sentential forces (e.g., interrogatives) are realized via the A-bar/H-to-H movement (force-driven) in accordance with the Split-CP hypothesis. Hence functional projections are extended, resulting in the '[$_{FocP}$ [$_{Foc}$'[Foc] [$_{IP}$...]]]' structures. Finally, the Double (Multiple) CP Stages are related to the operation of the force-matching mechanism by which (more than) two forces are combined via the A-bar/H-to-H movement (force matching-driven), and hence functional projections are completed, resulting in the '[$_{CP*}$[$_{FocP}$[$_{IP}$...]]]' structures. Based on the discussion so far, let us assign a developmental stage to each of the above examples in (6) in terms of the SynDS in (7). Of the examples in (6), only (6a) belongs to the FocP Stage, but the others belong to the CP* Stage on the SynDS because they are all structures which have at least two CPs, and on which the force-matching mechanisms operate. Therefore, the SynDS in (7) comes up against the same problems as Vainikka and Young-Scholten's Sequence in (5) in that all the structures except (6a) in (6) belong to the same CP* Stage on the SynDS, just as all the structures of (6) belong to the CP Stages on Vainikka and Young-Scholten's.

To solve this problem, this study devises Markedness on Operation, which quantifies the degrees of syntactic operations resulting from the operation of the force-realizing mechanism for the realization of sentential forces. Examine sentential forces in (8).

(8) a. Mary will invite Tom.
b. What a strange dress you are wearing!
c. Tom, Jane will invite.
d. Whom will Mary invite? /Never will Mary invite Tom.

In (8), a declarative force is realized in (8a), an exclamative force in (8b), a topical force in (8c), and a focal force in (8d), respectively. The degrees of syntactic operation (movements) resulting from the operation of the force-realizing mechanism in (8) can be represented on the continuum as in Figure 3.

As shown in Figure 3, weak forces such as the declarative force are located on the one side of the continuum. These forces are less marked in that fewer syntactic changes occur in a sentence as a result of the operation of the force-realizing mechanism. The feature [-SAI]/[-WH] can be assigned to these forces.

On the other side, there are strong forces such as the focal force, which are more marked in that more syntactic movements take place in a sentence as the results of its operation. The feature [+SAI]/[+WH] can be assigned to these forces.

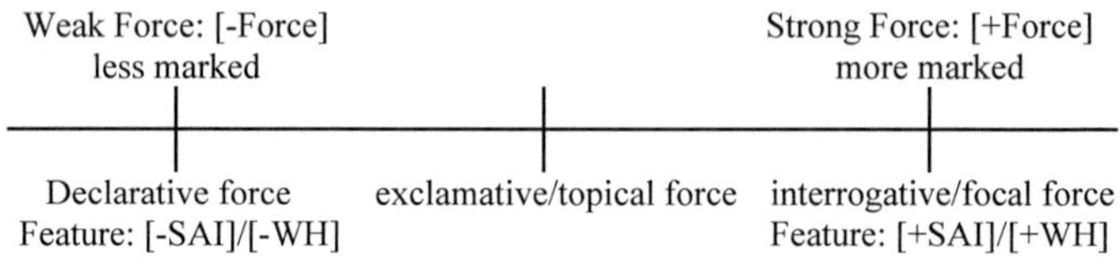

Figure 3. Markedness on Operation: Strong/Weak Force

Therefore, this study postulates that the degrees of Markedness will correspond to degrees of syntactic complexity, and that the degrees of Markedness which result from the operation of the force-realizing mechanism to realize sentential forces will be still related to those which result from the operation of the force-matching mechanism to combine more than two forces. In other words, the less marked the forces related to force-matching are, the less complex the force-matching process will be; the more marked they are, the more complex the process will be. For example, when the most marked forces such as focal forces are combined with each other, the force-matching process will be more complex than when the least marked forces such as declarative forces are combined. Thus, according to Markedness, the Double CP Stages governed by the force-matching mechanism can be decomposed into a number of discrete stages, i.e., the Base/Bare CP, the Non-cancel FocP, the TopP, the Cancel FocP, and the Re-FocP Stage. Now, based on Markedness explained so far, let's assign a developmental stage to each sentence of the above examples (6). (6a) belongs to Base CP Stage, (6b) to Non-cancel FocP Stage, (6c) to TopP Stage, (6d) to Cancel FocP Stage, and (6e) to Re-FocP Stage, respectively.

In sum, the SynDS not only explains the syntactic IL development process of Double or Multiple CP Stages (i.e., embedded clauses) as well as those of Single ones (i.e., simple sentences), but also predict the critical structures and the error patterns manifested at each stage of the SynDS as in Table 5. Thus, the SynDS extends beyond Vainikka and Young-Scholten's Sequence to sequentialising the syntactic IL developmental sequence for Double or even Multiple CP Stages. Therefore, the SynDS and its mechanisms provide a clear definition, or at least an operational one for what Anderson calls declarative knowledge as well as theoretical frameworks for UG-based SLA research.

<table>
<tr><th colspan="2" rowspan="2">Stages</th><th colspan="3">Syntactic Developmental Sequence</th><th rowspan="2">Critical Structures</th></tr>
<tr><th>Sequence</th><th>Mechanism</th><th>Movement</th></tr>
<tr><td rowspan="4">Single CP</td><td>V</td><td>[N]-[V]-[N]</td><td>Lexical-inserting.</td><td>-</td><td>Canonical SVO,</td></tr>
<tr><td>VP</td><td>[VP[V'[V]NP]]</td><td>Theta-marking.</td><td>Pragmatic mov.</td><td>Adv/Do/Wh-fronting</td></tr>
<tr><td>IP</td><td>[IP[I'[I][VP]]]</td><td>Case-marking.</td><td>A-/H-to-H mov (case driven).</td><td>Aux-en/-ing, Y/N-inv.</td></tr>
<tr><td>FocP</td><td>[FocP[Foc'[Foc][IP]]]</td><td>Force-realizing.</td><td>A'-/H-to-H mov (Force driven).</td><td>Wh-inv. Neg-inv.</td></tr>
<tr><td rowspan="5">Double CP</td><td>Base/Bare CP</td><td rowspan="5">[CP₁[CP₂[IP]]]</td><td rowspan="5">Force-matching. (Markedness)</td><td rowspan="5">A'-/H-to-H mov. (Force-matching driven).</td><td>that-clause, for-clause</td></tr>
<tr><td>Non-cancel FocP</td><td>Indirect-question (subject)</td></tr>
<tr><td>TopP</td><td>Relatives (object, oblique)</td></tr>
<tr><td>Cancel FocP</td><td>Indirect-question (object)</td></tr>
<tr><td>Re-FocP</td><td>Long distance-question</td></tr>
<tr><td colspan="2">Multiple CP</td><td>[CP* [IP]]</td><td>Force-matching. (Markedness)</td><td>A'-/H-to-H mov. (Force-matching driven).</td><td>⋮</td></tr>
</table>

Table 5. Syntactic Developmental Sequence on the Syntactic Mechanisms

With all such theoretical contributions, the SynDS and its mechanisms are unable to explain the IL developmental processes of what Anderson calls the procedural knowledge. Take an example, '3SG-s'. From the perspective of declarative knowledge, this rule can be explained as follows: In simple present third person singular statement, '-s/-es' must be added to the end of the verbs as in he speak-s English fluently. However, this apparent simple rule is notoriously difficult for IL learners to process in terms of procedural knowledge. Perceiving the subject of a sentence as a third person singular, they have to hold the person, the number, and the -s in their short-term memory until the verb to which it is attached is produced, and then have to move the -s to the end of the finite verb in real time. This is a psycholinguistic explanation on the rule. In short, what is processed or automatised in language production is procedural knowledge rather than declarative knowledge. Thus, the SynDS and its mechanisms can explain grammaticality in abstract time (without time constraints in the processing of language), but they cannot explain processability in real time. Therefore, it can be argued that the SynDS needs to be complemented by the ProDS on the SPM and its functions.

3.Morphological Developmental Sequence (MorDS)

Based on the hierarchy of language processing procedures[5] intertwined with the Uniqueness Condition (UC), Pienemann (1998) proposed the Morpheme Processability Hierarchy as seen in (9). The UC, one of the Well-formedness conditions in LFG, states that the values attributed to a constituent must be compatible, and hence governs the process of feature unifications in a sentence[6]. Feature unifications, in turn, involve the grammatical encoding of semantic features or relations. Thus, the UC is a prerequisite for the grammatical encoding. From the acquisition perspective, the degrees of the application of the UC into different linguistic contexts determine the development of grammatical encoding.

(9) Morpheme Processability Hierarchy: Lexical→Phrasal→Interphrasal Morphemes

According to Pienemann (1998), the Hierarchy in (9) forms an implicational scale in which Lexical Morphemes are acquired prior to Phrasal Morphemes, and Phrasal Morphemes prior to Interphrasal Morphemes. In this respect, Pienemann first determines a morphological developmental sequence according to the UC. Therefore, the Hierarchy can provide a reasonable explanation as to which grammatical morphemes or features IL learners can process or encode at what stage on morphological IL developmental sequence.

However, in spite of such contributions for SLA, Pienemann's Hierarchy is constructed so sparsely that it seems to have difficulty in explaining the IL developmental processes of Interphrasal Morphemes in (10).

(10) a. *These boys are a good detective.
b. *I demanded that John invited Mary last Sunday.

According to Pienemann's explanation, since, in the two NPs in (10a), these boys and a good detective, each value of the feature [Number] is unified within each phrase, they belong to the Phrasal Morphemes. However, for the sentence to be acceptable, in addition to this phrasal affixation, feature unification has to take place again across the phrasal boundaries, and hence this is considered to be interphrasal affixation rather than phrasal. In the embedded of (10b), the occurrence of feature unification between Past-*ed* and last Sunday would result in a grammatical sentence, but this leads to ungrammaticality as seen in (10b) because of a mismatch between the feature [Subjunctive], the matrix and the embedded clause. Thus, by Pienemann's definition, both examples of (10) belong to the Interphrasal Morphemes on the Hierarchy in (9) since feature unification takes place between phrases. This implies that both examples are at the same developmental stage, thereby assuming that their morphological complexity will also be same. However, there will be some differences in the morphological complexity of these morphemes, depending on what linguistic context the UC is applied to, for example, VP, or IP, or CP adopting Minimalist terminology. Thus, these differences should also be represented on the IL developmental sequence of the morphological systems[7].

To cope with the limitation, this study proposes Unificational Mechanism (UM), which is derived from intertwining the UC with the X-bar formats of the Minimalist program (Chomsky, 1992) as shown in Figure 4.

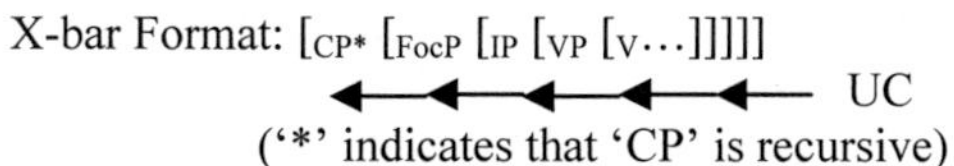

Figure 4. The Unificational Mechanism

Figure 4 illustrates that the X-bar formats consist of V, VP, IP, FocP, and CP* in terms of X-bar theory, and thus the developmental sequence of the syntactic systems constitutes an implicational scale according to the logic of the Minimal Three Approach. In addition, on each stage of the syntactic sequence, each relevant syntactic mechanism operates successively from the lowest local or minimal domain up to the highest local or minimal domain of the X-bar formats, and thus this also constitutes an implicational scale according to the logic of Locality Condition. Therefore, by extrapolating from the syntactic developmental sequence to the UC, the syntactic domains or scopes of the operation of the UC also constitute an implicational scale. From this, the implicational sequence of the application of the UC can be formalized as V-VP-IP-FocP-CP*. This is called the Unificational Mechanisms (UM).

Thus, the UM is on the assumptions that morphology interacts with syntax, and hence that morphological IL development is implicationally contingent on syntactic IL development. It is consistent with epidemiological logic that only when IL learners are able to produce or process a certain syntactic structure, are they able to unify or match grammatical features or morphemes within the structure. Consequently, the UM not only governs the unification processes of grammatical features or morphemes in real time (plays the role of the UC), but also determines the implicational syntactic domains or scopes on which the UC can operate, or in which feature unifications can take place. Therefore, this study proposes a revised morphological developmental sequence called the

Morphological (Unificational) Developmental Sequence (MorDS) on the UM as seen in (11).

(11) Morphological Developmental Sequence on the UM:
Lexical$[_{V}$...→Phrasal$[_{VP}$...]→Clausal$[_{IP}$...]→Sentential $[_{FocP}$...]→Intersentential $[_{CP^*}$...] Stage

Now, explain each stage of the MorDS in (11) according to the UM. The Lexical Stage involves the insertion of grammatical morphemes or features directly from the lexical entry without the operation of the UC or any exchange of grammatical information between constituents in a sentence (corresponding to Pienemann's lexical morphemes). The Phrasal Stage involves the operation of UC within the domain of the $[_{VP}$...] in which feature unifications or exchanges of grammatical information take place (corresponding to Pienemann's phrasal morphemes). The Clausal Stage relates to the operation of the UC within the domain of the $[_{IP}$...], where each grammatical morpheme or feature is unified compatibly (corresponding to Pienemann's interphrasal morphemes). The Sentential Stage involves the application of the UC within the domain of the $[_{FocP}$...], in which feature unifications or exchanges of grammatical information take place. Finally, at the Intersentential Stage, the UC operates across the domains of $[_{CP^*}$...], and hence feature unifications or exchanges of grammatical information take place between the matrix and the embedded clauses. It follows that morphological IL developments goes hand in hand with syntactic IL developments. Now, let's assign a developmental stage to each of the interphrasal morphemes in (10) based on the UM discussed so far. (10a) belongs to the Clausal Stage, (10b) to the Intersentential Stage, respectively.

In conclusion, the UM derived from the extrapolation of the UC to the syntactic developmental sequence, captures the relative morphological complexity involved in unifying or encoding grammatical morphemes or features. In this respect, the UM functions as a sorting mechanism for sequentialising the MorDS as well as predicting the scopes of unifications and critical unifications on each stage of the MorDS as illustrated in Table 6.

Stages	**Morphological Developmental Sequence**		
	Scopes of the UC	**Feature Unifications**	**Critical Unifications**
Lexical	[N],[V],[N]	No unification	-
Phrasal	$[_{VP}$ $[_{V}$...]]	Unification within a VP	Plural agreements
Clausal	$[_{IP}$ $[_{VP}$ ...]]	Unification within an IP	Tense/SV-agreements
Sentential	$[_{FocP(=CP)}$ $[_{IP}$...]]	Unification within a CP	Force-agreements
Intersentential	$[_{CP^*}[_{CP}$...]]	Unification across CPs	Tense-agreements Force/Modality-agreements

Table 6. Morphological Developmental Sequence on the UM

Thus, the MorDS can go beyond the limitations of Pienemann's Morpheme Processability Hierarchy to explaining the interactional processes of morphological development with syntactic development more systematically by incorporating cognitive mechanisms (i.e., the UC) and linguistic mechanisms (i.e., X-bar theory and the LC). However, the MorDS and the UM have trouble in explaining the IL developmental processes of structural systems (i.e., word-order rules), and thus it can be said that the MorDS should be complemented by the ProDS and the SynDS.

Parallel Developmental Sequence (PDS) Model

The three sub-developmental modules discussed so for, i.e., Procedural Developmental Sequence, Syntactic Developmental Sequence, and Morphological Developmental Sequence can be represented as seen in (12).

(12) The Three Sub-developmental Sequence Modules

(a) Procedural Developmental Sequence Module (ProDS)
SPM $f(\alpha, \beta)$=[αIFM]/[βCOM], $f(\alpha, \beta, \gamma)$=[γSCM([αIFM]/[βCOM])*]]
(b) Syntactic Developmental Sequence Module (SynDS)
V→VP→IP→FocP (CP) →CP* Stage
(c) Morphological Developmental Sequence Module (MorDS)
Lexical→Phrasal→Clausal→Sentential→Intersentential Stage

In (12), the three sub-developmental modules (i.e., the ProDS, the SynDS, and the MorDS) are able to provide valid explanations for each of their own domains, but they have the "complementary limitations" of not being able to offer explanations for each of the other domain related to IL development. In order words, the ProDS (12a) explains processability, but can't explain grammaticality. Conversely, the SynDS (12b) explains grammaticality, but can't explain processability. On the other hand, the MorDS (12c) explains the morphological development, but can't explain the structural development (i.e., word-order rules).

A possible alternative to such complementary limitations might be what is called the Modular Approach (Ellis, 1994; Gregg, 1996; Pienemann, 1998; White, 1989), which suggests that each module is in a complementary relation with each other module[8]. According to the Modular Approach, these three sub-developmental modules are integrated into a single modular model called the Parallel Developmental Sequence (PDS) Model as illustrated in Figure 5.

The PDS constitutes the Parallel Developmental Stages sequentially (i.e., 1X, 2X, ..., $1X^2$, $2X^2$, ..., $1X^3$, ..., kX^n). And each Parallel Stage of the PDS incorporates three sub-developmental sequences: the ProDS, the SynDS, and the MorDS. Therefore, the PDS allows the complementary limitations to have "complementary explanations" for each other, and thus, provides an interface between the three sub-developmental sequences.

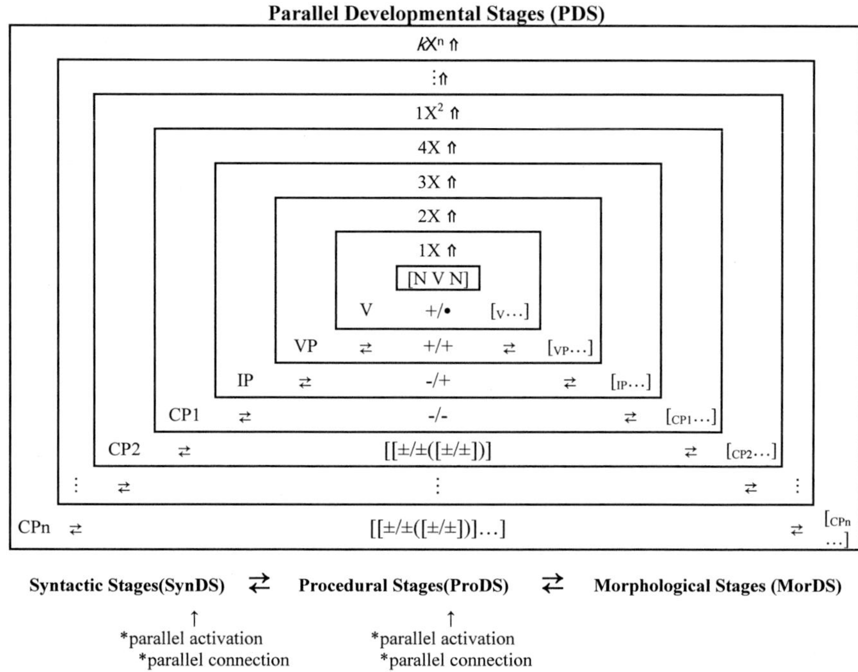

Figure 5. Parallel Development Sequence Model

However, a problem has not yet been settled as to how the three modules interact or interconnect with each of the other modules of each Parallel Stage. On the logic of the parallel connections of the Parallel Distributed Processing Model (Rumelhart, McClelland & PDP Research Group, 1986), one of the three sub-stages of a Parallel Stage on the PDS is activated first, and then interconnected, and finally synchronized with each of the other sub-stages through the synchronization process consisting of parallel activation, parallel connection, and synchronization as seen in Figure 5. Therefore, the PDS assumes that IL learners at any Parallel Stage will first activate one of the three parallel mechanisms (i.e., the procedural, the syntactic, and the unificational mechanisms), and then interconnect them, and finally synchronize them with each other before moving on to the next stage on the PDS, and by repeating these processes recursively, finally, to pass through all the stages of the PDS up to the last Parallel Stage kX^n.

Yet, there has still remained another open question on what leads IL development from one stage to the next on the PDS. By adopting the concepts of gaps and driving force proposed by Faerch and Kasper (1986) and White (1987)[9], this study will suggest parallel developmental gaps as parallel developmental force in order to explain how IL learners pass through each Parallel Stage on the PDS. IL structures (i.e., the output IL learners produce) will be called the triggering force, and TL (target language) structures (i.e., the L2 input the learners receive in the linguistic environment) will be called the triggering cue. And the gaps between the triggering force and the triggering cue will be called the parallel developmental gaps. Thus, this study assumes that IL learners develop from one parallel system to the subsequent one in a stepwise fashion on the PDS, by inducing a clue to bridge the parallel developmental gaps through the interaction between the triggering forces and the triggering cues.

Let us examine more specifically how IL learners proceed from one Parallel Stage to the next relying on the logic of synchronization and the parallel developmental gaps as discussed above. Suppose an IL learner who has already been at Procedural Stage $3X^2$, but hasn't arrived yet at Procedural Stage $4X^2$. At Procedural Stage $4X^2$, the learner can produce structures like (13a) and (13b) below by operating the core parallel systems available up to this point, whereas he or she may produce "interim" indirect questions like (13c) without cancelling wh-inversion due to the absence of the associated cancel mechanisms. As Pienemann (1998) pointed out, these phenomena are almost universal in IL development. However, the learner can be exposed to grammatical sentences like (14a) as positive evidence to (13c) in the L2 input.

(13) a. Whom does John like in the class?
b. Do you know who likes John in the class?
c. *Do you know whom John does like in the class?

(14) a. Do you know whom John likes in the class?
b. $[_{\text{FocP}}$ do$_m$ $[_{\text{IP}}$ you$_n$ [I t_m $[_{\text{VP}}$ t_n known-t_m $[_{\text{CP}}$ whom$_i$ $[_{\text{FocP}}$ t_i $[_{\text{Foc}}$ does$_k$ $[_{\text{IP}}$ John$_l$ $[_{\text{I}}$ t_k $[_{\text{VP}}$ t$_l$ $[_{\text{V}}$ like-t_k t_i]]]]]]]]]]].

At the Procedural Stage, as the learner perceives the procedural gaps through the interactions between triggering forces like (13), and triggering cues like (14a), the learner comes to realize that combing the root wh-question in (13a) with the matrix question *Do you know* results in ungrammatical sentence as seen in (13c). Thus, the learner can infer that when a root question becomes an embedded clause, SAI (Subject/Aux Inversion) has to be cancelled, that is, *does* should be moved back to the original position, and this movement brings about word order changes. Substitute these for the embedded SPM function $f(\alpha, \beta, \gamma) = [\gamma SCM([\alpha IFM]/[\beta COM])]]$. Since what Pienemann (1998) calls cancel inversion takes place, in which wh-movement (what) induces cancel inversion to SAI (since there is a double movement), the value of the variable α is '-'. Since the double movement, in turn, invite word order changes, the value of the variable β is '-'. And since the final landing site of the movements is within the embedded clause, the value of the variable γ is '+'. Finally, the learner can build up the SPM mechanism '[+SCM([-IFM]/[-COM])]', and hence process and produce cancel inversion structures like (14a).

At the Syntactic Stage, perceiving the syntactic gaps, the learner can infer that when a root *wh*-question becomes an embedded clause, the *wh*-phrase *whom* moves from the [Spec, Fop] into the [Spec, CP] position, and at the same time, the Fop, which has already been realized at the Fop Stage, has to be reinverted, that is, the auxiliary *does* is lowered out of the head Foc through the head I onto the head V, as seen in analysis (14b). This process can be called the reverse to H-to-H movement. Consequently, the learner can parse the Cancel-FocP structures '$[_{CP}\ [_{CP}\ wh\ [_{IP}...]]]$' like (14a).

At the Morphological Stage, perceiving the unificational gaps, the learner can infer that when a root wh-question becomes an embedded clause, the [+SAI] feature has to be changed into [-SAI], and hence the operator does has to be substituted by the appropriate morphological form (i.e., -s) to affix the lexical verb *like*. This process can be called reaffixation. As the result, this learner can apply the UC across CPs (i.e., $[_{CP*}...\ [_{FocP}...]])$, and hence unify morphemes or features such as [Tense], [Force], [Subjunctive] between a matrix and embedded clauses (i.e., Tense/Force/Subjective-agreements).

As explained so far, only when IL learners first activate one of the three parallel mechanisms of a Parallel Stage through interaction between triggering forces and triggering cues, and then interconnect them, and finally synchronize with each other through the synchronization processes, will they proceed to the next Parallel Stage.

From the above discussion, the Parallel Developmental Stages can be summarized as shown in Table 7. A closer examination of the table shows that inherent in the PDS is an implicational relation in which the higher stage can include the parallel mechanisms and the critical structures of the lower stages, but not *vice versa*. What this implicational relation means is that no Parallel Stage on the PDS can be skipped or beaten, and hence, in a sense, the PDS constitutes the predetermined shedding processes of the parallel mechanisms. Therefore, L2 learners cannot proceed from one stage to the subsequent until they can process, parse and unify the parallel mechanisms imposed on a given stage in the PDS, just as a caterpillar goes through the ordained shedding process step by step and finally becomes a butterfly. From this, a motivating principle of language pedagogy, which Pienemann (1984, 1998) calls the Teachability Principle, can be derived, which implies that any instruction will be beneficial if it focuses on structures or rules of the next or subsequent stage of L2 learners' current stage on the PDS.

Parallel Stages	**Parallel Developmental Sequence**				
	Parallel Mechanisms				**Error**
	Syntactic M.	**Procedural M.**	**Unificational M.**	**Critical structures**	**Patterns**
1X	Lexical-nserting	[· IFM][+COM]	No unification	Canonical SVO	…
2X	Theta-marking	[+IFM][+COM]	Phrasal $[_{VP}\ldots]$	Adv/Wh/Do-fronting	…
3X	Case-marking	[+IFM][-COM]	Clausal $[_{IP}\ldots]$	Aux-en/-ing, Y/N-questions	…
4X	Force-realizing	[-IFM][-COM]	Sentential $[_{CP}\ldots]$	Wh-questions, Neg-Inv.	…
$1X^2$	Force-matching, Markedness on Operation	[· SCM([· IFM][+COM])]	Intersentential $[_{CP}[_{CP}\ldots]]$	2-sub comp, that-clause	…
$2X^2$		[+SCM([+IFM][+COM])]		Indirect-questions/Relatives(sub.)	…
$3X^2$		[+SCM([+IFM][-COM])]		Relatives(obj., oblique)	…
$4X^2$		[+SCM([-IFM][-COM])]		Indirect-questions(obj.)	…
$5X^2$		[-SCM([-IFM][-COM])]		Long distance-questions	…
kX^3	…	[±SCM([±SCM])]	…	Double complex sentences	…
⋮	⋮	⋮	⋮	⋮	…
kX^n	…	…	…	…	…

Table 7. Parallel Developmental Stages

Methods and Results

This section will present research hypothesis, participants, methods for data elicitation and analysis, and criteria for pass stages, and then discuss the results drawn from the research.

1. Methods

1.1. Research Hypothesis

Since the PDS built by this study might be only "theoretical", there should be an empirical test on whether there is any "error" on the PDS. This came down to the following research hypothesis.

> Research Hypothesis: The performance PDS produced by L2 learners in an empirical test will correspond to the theoretical PDS built by this study.

In order to verify the theoretical PDS, two types of Sentence Construction Tests (SCTs) were composed and carried out on a real-time technique called the Flash Window Method devised by this study.

1.2. Participants

Participants for this research were 136 Korean college students, whose ages ranged from 20 to 30, and whose academic majors were linguistics (80%: Korean, English, French, Japanese, etc.) and humanities and social science (20%: history, law, and economics).

1.3. The Critical Sentence Set as Stimuli

Since there was not much similar research done previously to adapt stimulus sentences from, the present study had to construct the stimuli based on both the longitudinal data from the sequence-based SLA research (Pienemann, 1998; Pienemann & Johnston, 1987; Pienemann, Johnston & Brindley, 1988) and the experimental data from research of relatives and wh-extractions (Doughty, 1991; Juffs & Harrington, 1995). From each Parallel Stage on the PDS (see Table 7.) were first chosen Critical Structures, on which five critical sentences best reflecting the parallel mechanisms of each stage were composed. And in order to minimize the effects of the length of the sentences and words on the experiment, each critical sentence was made up of "7±2" thought groups according to Miller's magic number (1956), using basic words and familiar proper nouns. Finally, these five critical structures consisted of a stimuli called the "critical sentence set" of forty-five items (five items per each Parallel Stage in a total of nine stages from 2X to X^3 Stage (5x9)) (see Appendix A).

1.4. Sectence Construction Tests onto the Flash-window Method

The critical sentences were converted into two kinds of Sentence Construction Tests (SCT): the Sentence Conversion and the Sentence Combination Test. The SCTs are a kind of IL-sensitive tests in that the test items are geared to each stage of the PDS along which IL learners pass through. These tests were played in real time onto the *Flash-window Method.* The Method, as its name suggests, consists of a series of windows, in which one window appears and then disappears in a given time on a computer screen, and then another window appears and so on, in a pre-programmed order by using the *flash* function of a computer.

As seen in Figure 6 and 7, the SCTs consist of four phases (i.e., the Preparation, the Performance, the Completion, and the Relaxation Phase) in the Flash-Window Method. In the Preparation Phase, the participants were asked to read a given sentence or two or more sentences on the screen within a given time (160 wpm). At the Performance Phase, in the case of the Sentence Conversion Tests as seen in Figure 6, they were required to convert the sentence into another pattern (e.g., Y/N or wh-questions) in their mind within a given time (120 wpm). On the other hand, in the Sentence Combination Tests as in Figure 7, they were required to combine two or more sentences to form one complex sentence (e.g., indirect questions, relatives) in their mind within a given time. In the Completion Phase, they were asked to write down the converted or combined sentence they had just processed in their mind (60 wpm). Finally, in the Relaxation Phase, music was played for about 10 seconds to help them to obliterate the previous item in their memories, to relieve their tension, and to prepare for the next item. The SCTs were programmed by the Macromedia Flash MX (Ver. 6).

Window 1: [Preparation] [Preparing Instruction]: **Please read the following sentence carefully.** (A cursor will blink for 3 seconds, and then the following sentence will appear.) **John kissed Mary last night.** (This window will disappear in 2 seconds.)
Window 2: [Performance] [Performing Instruction]: **Change '*last night*' into 'w*hen*' in the following sentence, and make a *wh*-question in your mind.** (This window will disappear in 5 seconds, and then the following sentence will appear.) **John kissed Mary *last night*?** ⇑ **When**

(This window will disappear in 3 seconds.)
Window 3: [Completion] [Completing Instruction]: **Write down the question you thought of on the answer sheet.** (This window will disappear in 15 seconds.)
Window 4: [Relaxation] Along with a buzzer signaling the end of writing, music is played for about 10 seconds, and then another buzzer signals the start of the next item.

Figure 6. Sentence Conversion Tests on the Flash-Window Method

Window 1: [Preparation] [Preparing Instruction]: **Please read the following two sentences carefully.** (A cursor will blink for 3 seconds, and then the following sentences will appear.) **Do you know ...?** **Who kissed Mary last night?** (This window will disappear in 2 seconds.)
Window 2: [Performance] [Performing Instructions]: **Combine the next two sentences to make an indirect-question in your mind.** (This window will disappear in 5 seconds, and then the following will appear.) **Do you know + Who kissed Mary last night?** (This window will disappear in 4 seconds.)
Window 3: [Completion] [Completing Instruction]: **Write down the question you thought of on the answer sheet.** (This window will disappear in 15 seconds.)
Window 4: [Relaxation] Along with a buzzer signalling the end of writing, music is played for about 10 seconds, and then another buzzer signals the start of the next item.

Figure 7. Sentence Combination Tests on the Flash-Window Method

As shown from the explanation of the SCTs onto the Flash Method, the participants have to process such appropriate grammatical changes in parallel under time constraints as constituent movements, word-order changes, and unifications of some grammatical features or morphemes so as to convert or combine sentences in real time. In this respect, the method can elicit more spontaneous, natural responses from L2 learners than simple recall tests since it makes them rely less on their recall and more on actual processes in real time. Thus, the on-line Flash-Window Method can provide a more sensitive measure for research on processability of IL development.

1.5. Data Analysis Procedures

Of all the data elicited from the participants through the SCTs, the followings were excluded in order to minimize the effects of faulty data on the result of the analysis: (a) unintelligible or irrelevant cases, (b) cases unanswered to more than three items in a row, (c) cases filled out the excuse blank (see Experimental Procedures below). The other data were analysed by the following procedures. For the convenience of the analysis, to each response of each participant to each test item, a plus (+), a minus (-) or an equal (=) was given according to the degrees of matching a participant's response with the answer. A '+' was given to a response when it was matched to the answer. A '-' was given when it was either not matched to the answer or incomplete. If a response was not completely matched to the answer, and interim or transitional critical structures were reconstructed from it by the IL analysis, then a '=' was given to the corresponding Parallel Stage which the reconstructed structures belong to on the PDS. Also, only trivial or insignificant lexical errors with no relations to the parallel mechanisms were also overlooked.

1.6. Criterion for Pass of Each Stage on the PDS

If more than four responses of five items in each stage match the answers, a positive (+) was marked on the implicational scale, which means that the learner was considered "passing the stage" in question (called the pass stage). If less than four match the answers, a negative (-) was marked on the scale, which means that the learner was considered "not passing the stage" (called the non-pass stage).

1.7. Experimental Procedures

Participants were given some explanations of two types of the SCTs, and then presented a set of practice items with a beam projector to familiarize themselves with the tests. After the practice items had been run, they were presented the randomized sentence set. The tests took about 60 minutes. After the tests were completed, the participants were asked to fill out a biodata questionnaire and an 'excuse blank': "I couldn't do my best in the test because of '_______' (such as having a cold, being in menstruation, mental distraction, or reluctance)". The excuse blank was intended to give an opportunity to make any excuse for a participant who did not bias for best and hence to exclude his or her data from the corpus.

2. Results (Implicational Scaling)

Of the responses elicited from total 136 participants through SCTs, eight cases falling into the unanalysable categories (see Data Analysis Procedures above) were excluded from the analysis. The others (128 cases) were analysed by implicational scaling according to the Guttman Procedures (Hatch & Lazaraton, 1991).

2.1. Implicational Scalability of the Performance PDS

Table 8 (See Appendix B) displays the implicational scaling of those 128 cases. On the top of the Table, the Parallel Stages of the PDS is listed from the right to the left in the order of hierarchy. For each subject and Stage a positive mark (+) indicates that the participant has passed the stage in question, and a negative mark (-) indicates that the participant has not passed the stage in question. In the table the vertical bold line in a reverse-stair shape represents the marginal line of an idealized implicational scaling (See Table 8 in the Appendix).

The outline of the scalogram displays that there are significant degrees of implicational scaling on the actual PDS. The degrees of the correspondence of the performance PDS to the theoretical PDS were calculated by the Guttman Procedures. The result showed that the scalability of the implicational scale was .83, far greater than the minimum requirement of .60 for an acceptable scale (Hatch & Lazaraton, 1991, p. 212). The high scalability means that the performance PDS produced in real time by the L2 learners through SCTs significantly corresponds to the theoretical PDS built by this study.

2.2. Errors of the Performance PDS

The errors produced by the participants through the real-time SCTs were almost identical to the ones predicted by the theoretical PDS as in the IL sentences (15). These examples can be regarded as additional evidence for the correspondence of the actual PDS to the theoretical PDS.

(15) *Do you watched that news on TV last night? (s54)
*When you saw her on campus? (y24)
*Do you want to know who does my mother wants me to meet? (s43)
*Do you think who does want to invite to reception? (s14)

2.3. Transitional Stages (On-or-Off Stages)

A majority of participants' performances revealed transitional stages on the actual PDS. Table 9 displays the typical examples of this tendency selected from the data.

Subjects	Parallel Developmental Stages								
	kX^3	$5X^2$	$4X^2$	$3X^2$	$2X^2$	$1X^2$	4X	3X	2X
y7	-----	-----	-----	-----	-----	-----	-----	-+++-	+++++
y21	-----	-----	-----	-----	-----	+---+	++--+	+++++	+++++
s14	-----	-----	-----	-----	---+-	+--++	+++++	+++++	+++++
e22	-----	-----	-----	-+--+	-+-++	+++++	+++++	+++++	+++++
s24	-----	-----	-+---	+--++	+++++	+++++	+++++	+++++	+++++
e15	-----	-----	+--++	++-++	++++-	+-+++	+++++	+++++	+++++
e11	-----	++---	+++++	+++++	+++++	+++++	+++++	+++++	+++++
s16	--++-	+++++	+++++	+++++	+++++	+++++	+++++	+++++	+++++

Table 9. The Transitional Stages
(Legend: '+' matched to the answer, '-' not matched to it)

As seen in the Table, the pass stages with 4 or more '+' can be called the acquired stages. The non-pass stages with 4 or more '-' can be called the unacquired stages. Between these acquired and unacquired stages, there exist the transitional stages with more than 2 but less than 4 '+' and '-'. This stage can be called the acquiring stages or the On-or-Off Stages in that the parallel mechanisms of the Parallel Stage in question are 'on or off' operating occasionally. In this respect, it can be argued that the optimal time for teaching, learning and error treatments on the Teachability Hypothesis is on the very On-or-Off Stages. This is another proof for supporting the PDS.

2.4. Non-Parallel Developmental Stages

A closer examination over the implicational scaling scalogram in Table 8 showed that there are 17 cases of the non-parallel developmental stage which imply that the performance PDS produced by the IL learner deviates from the theoretical PDS, thereby distorting the ideal PDS. It is not possible from only the results of the SCTs to find out the sources of the deviations, but participants' reluctance or insincerity to the tests may be one of the causes. In the case of subjects 's17' and 's52' in Table 8 above, careful probes of their responses revealed that their insincerity or reluctance was a cause for deviating from the ideal PDS. Another reason may be found in IL learner's socio-affective factors. According to the Multidimensional Model (Clahsen et al., 1983; Meisel et al., 1981), as Larsen-Freeman and Long (1991) pointed out, standard-oriented learners, preferring accuracy, tend to elaborate IL rules. Supposedly, they will have a tendency to pass one stage to the next on the PDS in a stepwise fashion through the synchronization of three sub-developmental modules. On the contrary, simplifying learners, favouring communicative effectiveness, tend to simplify the rules and hence will have a tendency to skip or beat the stages on the PDS. However, future research needs to be done in order to explain the relationships between the non-parallel stages and the socio-affective factors of IL learner.

Conclusions

The present study was inspired by three L2 developmental modules in procedural development, syntactic development, and morphological development. By integrating three separate modules into one module according to the Modular Approach, the present study proposes a modular model called the Parallel Developmental Sequence (PDS) Model. In essence, the PDS Model proposes that L2 development follows a series of parallel developmental stages sequentially. The PDS Model calls these stages 1X, 2X, 3X, ..., $1X^2$, $2X^2$, ..., $1X^3$, ..., kX^n. Each of these stages incorporates three different dimensions of sequential development: the procedural sequence, the syntactic sequence, and the morphological (unificational) sequence. Therefore, the PDS is on the assumption that an IL learner at a stage will activate and synchronize with the parallel mechanisms (i.e., the procedural, the syntactic, and the unificational mechanism) to process rules in order to understand and produce language in that stage through the synchronization process on the logic of parallel connections of the Parallel Distributed Processing Model. The question then is whether or not the theoretically built sequence of Parallel Developmental Stages does reflect the actual developmental stages of the L2 learner. The PDS Model thus was put to test with empirical research. This study devised Sentence Construction Tests in order to elicit sentences from L2 learners that would accurately reveal the levels of the learners' developmental stages. The test was put on the real-time Flash Window Method, and it was administered to 136 Korean college students to elicit their responses. The responses were analysed to identify their developmental stages in terms of the PDS. An implicational scale was adopted to see the overall developmental stages. The results showed that the scalability of the implicational scale was .83, far greater than the minimum requirement of .60 for an acceptable scale (Hatch & Lazaraton, 1991, p. 212). The high scalability means that the developmental sequence predicted by the PDS Model was strongly supported by empirical evidence.

Based on this finding, this study proposes that the PDS can be adopted to develop a common metric scale (Bachman, 1990) on the Developmental Approach (Ingram, 1985) to assess IL learners' developmental stage in grammar in order to diagnose and remedy their linguistic ability, and hence provide an alternative to the principal questions of recent research on Form-focused Instruction: What rules, when and how to provide for IL learners? (Doughty, 1991; Doughty & Williams, 1998; Robinson, 1996). Specifically, an answer to what rules to teach will be the critical structures or rules of the subsequent stage governed by the associated parallel mechanisms. An answer to when to teach them will be the subsequent stage of IL learners' current stage. And an answer to how to teach them can be obtained by utilizing the real-time Flash Window Method. In addition, this common metric system combined with the on-line Method can be an objective and practical device for research into SLA in sorting out experimental and control groups, evaluating the achievement of the subjects after an experimental treatment, comparing the results of different studies, and so on. Therefore, the common metric system on the PDS with the real time Method can provide not only "timely leaning and tailored teaching" for IL learners but also a practical, reliable measure for SLA research.

In conclusion, the PDS and its Parallel Mechanisms will provide a possible explanation for interacting procedural knowledge with declarative knowledge, and pave a possibility for interfacing developmental problems with logical problems to SLA.

A: The Critical Sentence Set

1. Parallel Developmental Stage 1X

2. Parallel Developmental Stage 2X
    1. Do you wash the dishes everyday?
    2. Who opened the windows on this cold day?
    3. What happened at the party last night?
    4. Who appeared on the concert last night?
    5. Do you play tennis with your friends every weekend?

3. Parallel Developmental Stage 3X
    1. Did you watch that news on TV last night?
    2. Can you go camping with us this weekend?
    3. Have you read an English novel recently?
    4. Do you want to go there this weekend?
    5. Would you like to have a snack after study?

4. Parallel Developmental Stage 4X
    1. When did you see her on the campus?
    2. Where would you like to have a drink after the show?
    3. What have you been writing since last week?
    4. Who do you want to meet at the concert this Friday?
    5. What did you give to Mary at the party last night?

5. Parallel Developmental Stage X^2
   5.1. Parallel Developmental Stage $1X^2$
   1. Did you ask her to go for a drive last night?
   2. What does he want you to do this summer vacation?
   3. Who does she expect to hold a party next time?
   4. Who does he want her to meet this Sunday?
   5. I think that John is going with his sweetheart to the concert today.

   5.2. Parallel Developmental Stage $2X^2$
   1. Did you ask your daughter who liked her in her class?
   2. The man who studies mechanics at college will investigate the car accident.
   3. Do you know who taught English to this class last year?
   4. Have you ever met the lady who was talking with John in the park last night?
   5. Do you know who helped him to fix the broken TV?

   5.3. Parallel Developmental Stage $3X^2$
   1. John has proposed to the girl whom you longed to meet at college.
   2. The girl whom you taught in college is going to marry my son next month.
   3. The man whom Mary spoke to in the theatre studies history at the college.
   4. Have you ever met the man whom my father expects me to marry?
   5. John employed a woman whom he thought to be honest at the job interview.

   5.4. Parallel Developmental Stage $4X^2$
   1. Does she know whom John came with to the party last night?
   2. Do you want to know why Jane decided to divorce her husband last year?
   3. Would you like to know who my mother wants me to meet this Sunday?
   4. Did you ask Tom who he ordered to fire her after the audit?
   5. Did you ask Mary what she handed John during history class?

   5.5. Parallel Developmental Stage $5X^2$
   1. Why do you think John parted from his sweetheart last week?
   2. Where do you think they went to have drinks after the show?
   3. Who does she think John handed the note to during the English test?
   4. Who do you think Mary expects him to invite to the reception?
   5. Who do you suppose John wants to introduce her to the mayor?

6. Parallel Developmental Stage X^3
   1. Do you want to know who John thinks Mary gave the nice gift to at the party?
   2. Who do you guess Mary thinks John loves at the college?
   3. Do you know who Mary thinks John asked Alice to invite to the reception?
   4. Who do you believe John thinks Mary wants to introduce Alice to the president?
   5. Who do you think John believes Mary told Alice to fire after the audit?

Appendix

A: Table 8. The Implicational Scaling Scalogram
(Legend: '+' pass stage, '-' non-pass stage,)

Subjects	Parallel Developmental Stages									
	kX^3	$5X^2$	$4X^2$	$3X^2$	$2X^2$	$1X^2$	4X	3X	2X	1X
s62	+	+	+	+	+	+	+	+	+	+
s49	+	+	+	+	+	+	+	+	+	+
s1	+	+	+	+	+	+	+	+	+	+
s2	-	+	+	+	+	+	+	+	+	+
s7	-	+	+	+	+	+	+	+	+	+
s16	-	+	+	+	+	+	+	+	+	+
s18	-	+	+	+	+	+	+	+	+	+
s22	-	+	+	+	+	+	+	+	+	+
s26	-	+	+	+	+	+	+	+	+	+
s28	-	+	+	+	+	+	+	+	+	+
e21	-	+	+	+	+	+	+	+	+	+
e10	-	+	+	+	+	+	+	+	+	+
e7	-	+	+	+	+	+	+	+	+	+
e2	-	+	+	+	+	+	+	+	+	+
s58	-	+	+	+	+	+	+	+	+	+
s50	-	+	+	+	+	+	+	+	+	+
s42	-	+	+	+	+	+	+	+	+	+
y27	-	-	+	+	+	+	+	+	+	+
y8	-	-	+	+	+	+	+	+	+	+
e28	-	-	+	+	+	+	+	+	+	+
e27	-	-	+	+	+	+	+	+	+	+
e24	-	-	+	+	+	+	+	+	+	+
e23	-	-	+	+	+	+	+	+	+	+
s9	-	-	+	+	+	+	+	+	+	+
s10	-	-	+	+	+	+	+	+	+	+
s12	-	-	+	+	+	+	+	+	+	+
s19	-	-	+	+	+	+	+	+	+	+
s21	-	-	+	+	+	+	+	+	+	+
s45	-	-	+	+	+	+	+	+	+	+
s55	-	-	+	+	+	+	+	+	+	+
s64	-	-	+	+	+	+	+	+	+	+
e1	-	-	+	+	+	+	+	+	+	+
e3	-	-	+	+	+	+	+	+	+	+
e5	-	-	+	+	+	+	+	+	+	+
e11	-	-	+	+	+	+	+	+	+	+
s65	-	-	+	+	+	+	+	+	+	+
e13	-	-	+	+	+	+	+	+	+	+
s34	-	-	-	+	+	+	+	+	+	+
s8	-	-	-	+	+	+	+	+	+	+
s30	-	-	-	+	+	+	+	+	+	+
s31	-	-	-	+	+	+	+	+	+	+
s39	-	-	-	+	+	+	+	+	+	+
s37	-	-	-	+	+	+	+	+	+	+
s43	-	-	-	+	+	+	+	+	+	+
y31	-	-	-	+	+	+	+	+	+	+

e15	-	-	-	+	+	+	+	+	+	+
s60	-	-	(+)	(-)	+	+	+	+	+	+
y1	-	-	(+)	(-)	+	+	+	+	+	+
y22	-	-	(+)	(-)	+	+	+	+	+	+
y25	-	-	(+)	(-)	+	+	+	+	+	+
s15	-	-	(+)	(-)	+	+	+	+	+	+
y32	-	-	(+)	(-)	+	+	+	+	+	+
s27	-	-	(+)	(-)	+	+	+	+	+	+
e20	-	-	(+)	(-)	+	+	+	+	+	+
y19	-	-	-	-	+	+	+	+	+	+
y17	-	-	-	-	+	+	+	+	+	+
y16	-	-	-	-	+	+	+	+	+	+
y15	-	-	-	-	+	+	+	+	+	+
y14	-	-	-	-	+	+	+	+	+	+
y3	-	-	-	-	+	+	+	+	+	+
e25	-	-	-	-	+	+	+	+	+	+
e18	-	-	-	-	+	+	+	+	+	+
e17	-	-	-	-	+	+	+	+	+	+
e8	-	-	-	-	+	+	+	+	+	+
s53	-	-	-	-	+	+	+	+	+	+
s3	-	-	-	-	+	+	+	+	+	+
s6	-	-	-	-	+	+	+	+	+	+
s24	-	-	-	-	+	+	+	+	+	+
s41	-	-	-	-	+	+	+	+	+	+
s48	-	-	-	-	+	+	+	+	+	+
s32	-	-	(+)	-	(-)	+	+	+	+	+
y5	-	-	(+)	-	(-)	+	+	+	+	+
y2	-	-	-	-	-	+	+	+	+	+
y6	-	-	-	-	-	+	+	+	+	+
y12	-	-	-	-	-	+	+	+	+	+
y13	-	-	-	-	-	+	+	+	+	+
e6	-	-	-	-	-	+	+	+	+	+
e12	-	-	-	-	-	+	+	+	+	+
e16	-	-	-	-	-	+	+	+	+	+
e22	-	-	-	-	-	+	+	+	+	+
e29	-	-	-	-	-	+	+	+	+	+
s44	-	-	-	-	-	+	+	+	+	+
s59	-	-	-	-	-	+	+	+	+	+
s61	-	-	-	-	-	+	+	+	+	+
e30	-	-	-	-	-	+	+	+	+	+
e31	-	-	-	-	-	+	+	+	+	+
s11	-	-	-	-	(+)	(-)	+	+	+	+
y23	-	-	-	-	(+)	(-)	+	+	+	+
s63	-	-	-	-	(+)	(-)	+	+	+	+
s25	-	-	-	-	(+)	(-)	+	+	+	+
s36	-	-	-	-	(+)	(-)	+	+	+	+
s17	-	-	-	(+)	(+)	(-)	(-)	+	+	+
s52	-	-	(+)	-	(+)	(-)	(-)	+	+	+
y9	-	-	-	-	-	-	+	+	+	+
y18	-	-	-	-	-	-	+	+	+	+
e9	-	-	-	-	-	-	+	+	+	+
y20	-	-	-	-	-	-	+	+	+	+
s40	-	-	-	-	-	-	+	+	+	+

y28	-	-	-	-	-	-	+	+	+	+
y30	-	-	-	-	-	-	+	+	+	+
e19	-	-	-	-	-	-	+	+	+	+
s13	-	-	-	-	-	-	+	+	+	+
s57	-	-	-	-	-	-	+	+	+	+
e4	-	-	-	-	-	-	+	+	+	+
y26	-	-	-	-	-	-	+	+	+	+
s14	-	-	-	-	-	-	+	+	+	+
s20	-	-	-	-	-	-	+	+	+	+
s23	-	-	-	-	-	-	+	+	+	+
s34	-	-	-	-	-	-	+	+	+	+
e26	-	-	-	-	-	-	+	+	+	+
s46	-	-	-	-	-	-	+	+	+	+
s51	-	-	-	-	-	-	+	+	+	+
s38	-	-	-	-	-	-	-	+	+	+
e14	-	-	-	-	-	-	-	+	+	+
s29	-	-	-	-	-	-	-	+	+	+
y29	-	-	-	-	-	-	-	+	+	+
y24	-	-	-	-	-	-	-	+	+	+
y10	-	-	-	-	-	-	-	+	+	+
y21	-	-	-	-	-	-	-	+	+	+
y7	-	-	-	-	-	-	-	-	+	+
s56	-	-	-	-	-	-	-	-	+	+
s54	-	-	-	-	-	-	-	-	+	+
s5	-	-	-	-	-	-	-	-	+	+
s35	-	-	-	-	-	-	-	-	+	+
y11	-	-	-	-	-	-	-	-	+	+
s47	-	-	-	-	-	-	-	-	+	+
y4	-	-	-	-	-	-	-	-	-	+
s33	-	-	-	-	-	-	-	-	-	+
Tot	**125 3**	**111 17**	**80 48**	**81 47**	**51 77**	**42 86**	**18 110**	**9 119**	**2 126**	**0 128**

Notes

[1] Based on the studies of Gregg (1996) and Pienemann (1998), this study states these two problems as follows: (a) The logical problems: What enables the learner to attain linguistic knowledge or competence, given the limited input (i.e., How is acquisition possible?)? (b) The developmental problems: What causes language developments to change from stage X to stage X+n (i.e., how does acquisition proceed?)?

[2] The locality constraint [condition] on grammatical relations restricts possible syntactic relations: it allows a constituent A to enter into a grammatical relation with a constituent B provided A bears a local relation to B. Thus, locality has impact on selection, on theta-role assignment, on case-assignment, and on movement (Haegeman and Guéron, 1999).

[3] According to the Split-CP hypothesis, the functional projection CP is decomposed into a number of discrete functional projections. In addition to the topmost level, labelled CP, the functional layer dominating IP may contain a projection whose specifier hosts focalized material (FocP), and one or more functional projections whose specifier hosts topicalised material (TopP). For example, a root wh-question which is a typical FocP structure is analysed as follows (Haegeman & Guéron, 1999):

$[_{CP}$ $[_{FocP}$ Whom$_i$ do+ed$_j$ $[_{AGRP}$ you [AGR t_j] $[_{TP}$ [T t_j] $[_{VP}$ invite-t_j t_i]]]]?

or [$_{CP}$ [$_{FocP}$ Whom$_i$ did$_j$ [$_{AGRP}$ you [AGR t_j] [$_{TP}$ [T t_j] [VP invite-t_j t_i]]]?

[4] The VP-internal subject hypothesis postulates that the base-subject position is not [Spec, IP] but [Spec, VP] where the subject can received a semantic role from the verb. Sportiche (1988) suggested the VP-internal subject hypothesis, and this study is based on the analysis of Haegeman and Guéron (1999, pp. 227-235).

[5] A set of processing procedures, a core of the Processability Theory, constitutes an implicational hierarchy of Lemma-Category-Phrasal-Sentential-Subordinate Clause Procedure, in which the processing procedure of each lower level is a necessary prerequisite for the functioning of the higher level (Pienemann, 1998).

[6] Feature unification is one that for each constituent of a sentence to be grammatically acceptable, each value of the grammatical features both within a constituent and between constituents has to be matched. Take the example of "John has a toy". In the NP (noun phrase) a toy, lexical entries *a* and *toy* are both annotated with the feature NUMBER, and in both cases this feature has the value singular. For the NP to be grammatical, the values of two constituents of the NP have to be matched. This matching process is called "feature unification" (Pienemann, 1998, p. 97).

[7] It must be born in mind that Pienemann's Processability Theory has also its full capacities to assign the processability level to each example of (10). According to the feature unifications and the hierarchy of the processing procedures, (10a) calls the S-procedure, and hence belongs to Level 4, whereas (10b) calls the Subordinate Clause-procedure, and hence to Level 6. Thus, this study's analysis of the examples does not mean to falsify the Processability Theory, but just to present another way to explain the morphological development.

[8] It can be said that such "complementary limitations" to each other module meets the two requirements of becoming modular proposed by Ellis (1994, p. 680), who states "For a theory to be truly modular, it is necessary to specify (1) the domain covered by the theory, as narrowly as possible, and (2) the domains that are not covered by the theory, in broad outline".

[9] Faerch and Kasper (1986) suggested that only when there is a gap between L2 learner's output (i.e., the learners' current IL) and L2 input, and then L2 learners perceive the gap as a gap in knowledge, acquisition will take place. Similarly, White (1987) claimed that only when the input is incomprehensible rather than comprehensible, IL learners are able to pay a closer attention to its syntactic features of a sentence, and thus the incomprehensible input is the driving force that causes the grammatical changes.

References

Anderson, J. 1976. Language, memory, and thought. Hillsdale, NJ: Lawrence Erlbaum.

—. 1980. Cognitive psychology and its implications. San Francisco: Freeman.

—. 1983. The architecture of cognition. Cambridge, MA: Harvard University Press.

Bachman, L. 1990. Fundamental considerations in language testing. Oxford: Oxford University Press.

Chomsky, N. 1986. Knowledge of language: Its nature, origin and use. New York: Praeger.

Clahsen, H. 1984. The acquisition of German word order: A test case of cognitive approaches to L2 development. In Second language: A cross-linguistic perspective, edited by R. Anderson, 219-242. Rowley, MA: Newbury House.

Clahsen, H., Meisel, J. and M. Pienemann. 1983. Deutsch als Zweitsprache: Der Spracherwerb ausländischer Arbeiter. Tübingen: Narr.

Doughty, C. 1991. Second language instruction does make a difference: Evidence from an empirical study on SL relativization. Studies in Second Language acquisition 13(4): 431-469.

Doughty, C. and J. Williams. 1998. Focus on form in classroom second language acquisition. New York: Cambridge University Press.

Ellis, R. 1994. The study of second language acquisition. Oxford: Oxford University press.

Faerch, C. and G. Kasper. 1986. The role of comprehension in second language acquisition. Applied Linguistics 7: 257-74.

Flex, S. 1984. Maturational aspects of Universal Grammar. In Interlanguage, edited by A. Davies, C. Criper and A. Howatt, 133-161. Edinburgh: Edinburgh University Press.

Gregg, K. 1996. The logical and developmental problems of second language acquisition. In Handbook of second language acquisition, edited by W. Ritchie and T. Bhatia, 49-81. San Diego: Academic Press.

Haegeman, L and J. Guéron. 1999. English Grammar. Oxford: Blackwell.

Hatch, E. and A. Lazaraton. 1991. The research manual: Design and statics for Applied linguistics. New York: Newbury House.

Hornstein, N. and D. Lightfoot. 1981. Explanation in linguistics: The logical Problem language acquisitions 269-293. London: Longman.

Ingram, D. 1985. Assessing proficiency: An overview on some aspects of testing.
In Modeling and assessing second language acquisition, edited by K. Hyltenstam and M. Pienemann, 215-276. Clevedon: Multilingual Matters.

Juffs, A. and M. Harrington. 1995. Parsing effects in second language sentence processing: Subject and object asymmetries in wh-extraction. Studies in second language Acquisition 17: 483-516.

Kaplan, R. and J. Bresnan. 1982. Lexical-functional grammar: A formal system for grammatical representation. In The mental representation of grammatical relations, edited by J. Bresnan, 173-281. Cambridge, MA: MIT Press.

Larsen-Freeman, D., and M. Long. 1991. An introduction to second language acquisition research. London and New York: Longman.

Meisel, J., Clahsen, H., and M. Pienemann. 1981. On determining developmental stages in natural second language acquisition. Studies in Second Language Acquisition 3(2): 109-135.

Miller, G. 1956. The magical number seven, plus or minus two: Some limits on our capacity of processing information. Psychological Review 63: 81-97.

Paradis, M. 1994. Neurolinguistic aspects of implicit and explicit memory: Implications for bilingualism and SLA. In Implicit and explicit learning of languages, edited by N, Ellis, 393-419. London: Academic Press.

Pienemann, M. 1984. Psychological constraints on the teachability of languages. Studies in Second Language Acquisition 6(2): 186-214.

—. 1998. Language processing and second language development processability theory. Amsterdam: John Benjamins.

Pienemann, M. and M. Johnston. 1987. Factors influencing the developmental of language proficiency. In Applying second language acquisition research, edited by D. Nunan, 45-141. Adelaide, Australia: National Curriculum Resource Center.

Pienemann, M., Johnston, M. and G. Brindley. 1988. Constructing an acquisition-based procedure for second language assessment. Studies in Second Language Acquisition 10(2): 217-243.

Robinson, P. 1996. Consciousness, rules and instructed second language acquisition. New York: Peter Long.

Rumelhart, D., McClelland, J., and the PDP Research Group. 1986. Parallel distributed Processing. Cambridge, MA: MIT press.

Sportiche, D. 1988. A theory of floating quantifiers and its corollaries for constituent structure. Linguistic Inquiry 19: 425-449.

Squire, L. 1992. Declarative and nondeclarative memory: Multiple brain systems supporting learning and memory. Journal of Cognitive Neuroscience 4: 232-243.

Vainikka, A. and M. Young-Scholten. 1994. Direct access to X'-theory: Evidence from Korean and Turkish adults learning German. In Language acquisition studies in generative grammar, edited by T. Hoekstra and B. Schwartz, 265-316. Amsterdam: John Benjamins.

—. 1996. The early stages in adult L2 syntax: Additional evidence form Romance speaker. Second Language Research, 12, 140-76.

—. 1998. The initial state in the L2 acquisition of phrase structure. In The generative study of second language acquisition, edited by S. Flynn, G. Martohardjono and W. O'Neil, 17-34. Hillsdale, NJ: Lawrence Erlbaum.

White, L. 1987. Against comprehensible input: The input hypothesis and the development of L2 competence. Applied Linguistics 8(2): 95-110.

—. 1989. Universal Grammar and second language acquisition. Amsterdam: John Benjamins.

CONTRIBUTORS

Peggy Bosch

Peggy Bosch, M.A. is a psychologist at the University of Bergen, Norway. Her research interests are in schizophrenia, second language research, and consciousness.

Winston D. Goh

Winston D. Goh obtained his PhD in Cognitive Science and Psychology from Indiana University at Bloomington and is presently an Assistant Professor in the Department of Psychology at the National University of Singapore. His current research interests are memory processes, psycholinguistics, speech perception and spoken word recognition.

Gisela Håkansson

Gisela Håkansson is Professor of General Linguistics at Lund University, Sweden. Her research interests encompass first and second language acquisition, language teaching and bilingualism. Her doctoral dissertation, Teacher Talk (Lund University Press, 1987) discusses how teachers modify their speech in the second language classroom. Some relevant publications are *Språkinlärning hos barn* [Language acquisition in children], published by Studentlitteratur, Lund 1998, *Tvåspråkighet hos barn i Sverige* [Bilingualism in children in Sweden] published by Studentlitteratur, Lund 2003 and *The acquisition of Swedish grammar* (editors Josefsson, Platzack and Håkansson) published by Benjamins, Amsterdam 2003. She has also published some teaching materials in Swedish as a second language.

Kenneth Hugdahl,

Kenneth Hugdahl, PhD is professor of biological psychology at the University of Bergen, Norway. His research interests are in hemispheric asymmetry and speech perception.

Yuki Itani-Adams

Yuki Itani-Adams is currently completing her PhD thesis at the University of Western Sydney. She has previously taught a variety of subjects in the languages and linguistics fields at Australian universities. Her PhD research investigates the lexical and morphosyntactic development of Japanese and English by a bilingual child. Her research interests include bilingual first language acquisition and the language behaviour of bilinguals.

Satomi Kawaguchi

Satomi Kawaguchi is a lecturer in second language acquisition and Japanese as a second language at the University of Western Sydney, Australia. She is a member of MARCS AuditoryResearch Laboratories at the same university. Her research interest is in second language acquisition with particular reference to English and Japanese, and also Japanese linguistics and second language teaching pedagogy. Her most recent publications include: (2005) Argument structure and syntactic development in Japanese as a second language. In M. Pienemann. (ed.). *Cross-linguistic aspects of Processability Theory*. pp. 253-298 Amsterdam and Philadelphia: John Benjamins. (2005) Processability Theory and Japanese as a second language. *Acquisition of Japanese as a Second Language*. Vol. 8 pp 83-114

Jörg-U. Keßler

Jörg-U. Keßler worked as a secondary school teacher and is currently seconded to the University Paderborn (Germany). He worked on the evaluation and calibration of *Rapid Profile* for his PhD and is a member of the State Committee for the evaluation of English in Primary Schools in the State of North-Rhine Westfalia. His main research areas are (early) instructed EFL development, language assessment and theory driven applied linguistics. His publications include an edition (with Manfred Pienemann and Eckhard Roos) and various papers on the application of Processability Theory to the EFL classroom.

Yong Myeong Kim

Yong Myeong Kim is a lecturer in the Department of English Education, Hankook University of Foreign Studies, where he has taught courses in English education and applied linguistics since 1995. He received his PhD degree in English language education from the Department of English Education, Seoul National University in 2005. His research interests include the psycholinguistic mechanisms of SLA, language developmental sequence in SLA, the interface between language developmental sequence and language testing and syllabus construction, and computer-adapted testing based on language developmental sequence.

Oryang Kwon

Oryang Kwon received his PhD degree in Teaching English as a Second Language (TESL) from the University of Texas at Austin. His teaching career includes two years in a middle school and about 30 years in universities. He developed English textbooks for Korean primary and secondary schools and participated in developing the 6th and 7th national curricula of English. He was the president of Korea TESOL in 1995-1996, and was on the Advisory

Committee for the Improvement of English Education for the Minister of Education from 2000 to 2002. From 2002 to 2004, he served as the president of the Korea Association of Teachers of English (KATE). He is currently the president of the Korea English Language Testing Association (KELTA). He is also on several advisory committees for the governmental institutes and projects, including the Advisory Committee for the Korean College Scholastic Ability Test in the Korea Institute of Curriculum and Evaluation (KICE), and the Advisory Committee for the Innovation of English Language Education in the Ministry of Education and Human Resources.Dr. Kwon teaches undergraduate and graduate courses in English education and applied linguistics at the Department of English Education, Seoul National University. His interest areas are language acquisition and testing.

Fethi Mansouri

Fethi Mansouri is Associate Professor in Middle Eastern Studies at Deakin University's School of International and Political Studies. His research activities cut across applied linguistics and cultural studies. He has published extensively on various aspects of second language acquisition, Arabic linguistics and multicultural education. His recent publications include 'Grammatical Markedness and Information Processing in the Acquisition of Arabic as a Second Language'. (Munchen, Germany: LINCOM EUROPA Academic Publishers: 2000); Lives in Limbo (with MP Leach; Sydney: UNSW Press 2004); and Australia and the Middle East: a Front-line Relationship (London/New York: Tauris Academic Studies, 2006,)

Catrin Norrby

Catrin Norrby is Senior Lecturer in Swedish at the University of Melbourne, Australia and Associate Professor in Scandinavian Languages at Göteborg University, Sweden. Her research interests include sociolinguistics, conversation and discourse analysis and second language acquisition. Her 1998 dissertation focused on the forms and functions of everyday storytelling and her book *Samtalsanalys* [Conversation/Discourse Analysis], published by Studentlitteratur, Lund, appeared in 1996 with a second edition in 2004. She has also co-authored a series of books intended for the teaching of Swedish and of English as a second language in the Swedish senior secondary school.

Manfred Pienemann

Manfred Pienemann is Professor of Applied Linguistics at the University of Newcastle, UK and the University of Paderborn, Germany. He was previously Professor of Applied Linguistics at the Australian National University. He is on the Editorial Boards of Bilingualism Language and Cognition (CUP) Second

Language Acquisition (Arnolds) and Language Teaching Research (Arnolds). He is author/editor of several books, including *Modelling and Assessing Second Language Development*, 1985; *Language Processing and Second Language Development*, 1998, *Cross-Linguistics Aspects of L2 Processing*, 2004 and *Cross-Linguistic Aspects of Processability Theory* 2005.

Lidia Suárez

Lidia Suárez graduated in Psychology from Universitat Autònoma de Barcelona (Spain) and also has a MBA from Universitat Politècnica de Catalunya (Spain). Currently, she is pursuing her PhD in Psychology at the National University of Singapore under the supervision of Dr. Winston D. Goh. Her topics of interest are memory and language, bilingualism, and second language acquisition.

Maurits van den Noort

Maurits van den Noort, M.A. is a psychologist who is currently finishing his PhD project on the role of working memory in foreign language acquisition at the University of Bergen, Norway. His research interests are in foreign language acquisition and consciousness.

Yanyin Zhang

Yanyin Zhang is a senior lecturer of TESOL and Applied Linguistics at the School of Languages, International Studies and Tourism, University of Canberra, Australia. Her research interests cover such areas as second language acquisition and cross-cultural pragmatics. In recent years, she has been working on the acquisition of Chinese (Mandarin) as a second language from the perspective of Processability Theory, exploring and establishing the processability hierarchy of Chinese grammatical morphology and syntax. She has also worked on the *ABC Chinese-English Comprehensive Dictionary* (2003) and is now editor of the *ABC English-Chinese Chinese-English Dictionary* (in preparation).

INDEX

A

B

C

D

E

F

G

H

I

J

R

S

T

U

V

W

X